THEATRE AUDIENCES

Theatre Audiences explores the spectator's role in the theatrical event, bringing together recent work on audiences and focusing on the interactive relationship between theatre production and reception. It is the first full-length study of the audience as cultural phenomenon to look at both *theories* of spectatorial action and *practice* of different theatres and their audiences.

Susan Bennett concentrates on the non-traditional theatres which have emerged over the last 30 years and which expect their audiences to play an active and creative role in the performance. She examines specific theatres – including their advertising, architecture, staging – as well as the audiences they attract, and analyses the processes of audience inter-pretation in both traditional and non-traditional theatre. She challenges the usual approaches to teaching drama and, es-pecially, the reliance upon dramatic texts which so often ignores the material conditions of production. Her theory of the audience's role brings spectators to the foreground, em-phasizing their creative involvement and showing how they contribute to theatre productions.

With its broad view of the theatre and its innovative explora-tion of the audience's role, *Theatre Audiences* will be of great interest to teachers and students of drama and cultural studies, and to practitioners and others involved in the theatre.

THEATRE AUDIENCES

A Theory of Production and Reception

Susan Bennett

ROUTLEDGE
London and New York

First published 1990
by Routledge
11 New Fetter Lane, London EC4P 4EE

Simultaneously published in the USA and Canada
by Routledge
a division of Routledge, Chapman and Hall, Inc.
29 West 35th Street, New York, NY 10001

Printed in Great Britain by
Richard Clay Ltd, Bungay, Suffolk

British Library Cataloguing in Publication Data
Bennett, Susan
  Theatre audiences : a theory of production and
  reception.
  1. Theatre. Audiences. Effects of theatre
  performances
  I. Title
  792

ISBN 0-415-04495-2   ISBN 0-415-04496-0 (pbk)

Library of Congress Cataloging in Publication Data
Bennett, Susan.
  Theater audiences : a theory of production and
  reception / by Susan Bennett.
      p.   cm.
  Includes bibliographical references.
  ISBN 0-415-04495-2. – ISBN 0-415-04496-0 (pbk.)
    1. Theater audiences.   2. Criticism.   I. Title.
  PN1590.A9B48   1990   89-10955
  792'.01–dc20

To Andrew, Barnaby, and Toby

CONTENTS

ACKNOWLEDGEMENTS

This book is the product not only of my own experiences with the theatrical event, but also of many people's provocative questions and rigorous criticism. Above all my thanks go to Linda Hutcheon who, at every stage of this project, has provided invaluable support and welcome enthusiasm. A number of others have played important roles in the development of this text; I thank Tony Brennan, Douglas Duncan, Maria Di Cenzo, Alison Lee, and Michael Sidnell for all they have contributed. I am also grateful to Helena Reckitt at Routledge for her help and encouragement. Finally I owe much to my family. They have been remarkably patient.

ACKNOWLEDGEMENTS

1
INTRODUCTION

Can theatre exist without an audience? At least one spectator is needed to make it a performance.

(Grotowski 1968: 32).

While this book is a study of the role of theatre audiences, it is not simply a work of reception theory. Indeed, I hope that the dialectic set up here between recent critical theory and modern theatrical practice constantly assures us of the productive role of *any* theatre audience. What this text does seek to be, however, is a study of theatre audiences as cultural phenomenon. Moreover, it is particularly concerned with the diversity of theatres which operate in contemporary culture and the different audiences they attract. Conventional notions of theatre and of theatre audiences too often rely on the model of the commercial mainstream. Perhaps too readily theatre-going is thought of as a middle-class occupation by definition. Over the last thirty years many theatres have emerged which speak for dominated and generally marginalized peoples, and the proliferation of these groups demands new definitions of theatre and recognition of new non-traditional audiences. Many of these emergent theatres have self-consciously sought the centrality of the spectator as subject of the drama, but as a subject who can think and act. That productive and emancipated spectator is my subject.

The approach to theatre audiences in this text is by way of those theories and practices which have suggested this centrality of the spectator's role. It is from these areas that my analysis – and much of my terminology – is drawn. In Chapter three, the site of my own theorizing, I put forward a model of the audience's experience of theatre and this model relies on two frames. The outer frame is concerned with theatre as a cultural construct through the idea of the theatrical event, the selection of material for production, and the audience's definitions and expectations of a performance. The inner frame contains the event itself and, in particular, the spectator's experience of a fictional stage world. This frame encompasses production strategies, ideological overcoding, and the material conditions of performance. It is the intersection of these two frames which forms the spectator's cultural understanding and experience of theatre. Beyond this, the relationship between the frames is always seen as interactive. Cultural assumptions affect performances, and performances rewrite cultural assumptions. The role of those productive and emancipated audiences occupies centre-stage throughout these investigations.

But before such investigations, it is necessary to look at the audience's past roles. Thus I start with historical approaches and contemporary concerns.

HISTORICAL APPROACHES

To return to the quotation which opened this introduction, we see that the participation of the audience in the theatrical event has been foregrounded by recent theorists such as Jerzy Grotowski, but examples of an awareness by the playwright of the spectator's central role can be located in the earliest drama. David Bain's *Actors and Audience* looks to asides and related conventions in Greek drama and demonstrates a 'compact between playwright and audience' (1977: 1). Moreover, the advent of drama as part of the main Athenian religious festivals established an inextricable link to the religious experience of the involved spectator:

> [T]he chorus in the orchestra shows that no physical barrier separated performer from audience; the presence among the spectators of the cult statue of a god [Dionysus] who might also be active on the stage further reveals that the absence of a physical barrier was matched by the absence of any 'spiritual' barrier. Stage, orchestra and auditorium formed a single unit and so too did actors, chorus and spectators, all of whom were sharing in a common act of devotion.
>
> (Walcot 1976: 4–5)

Greek theatre was also clearly inseparable from the social, economic, and political structures of Athens. Its social importance is apparent simply from the size of an auditorium.

2

With an estimated 14,000 people attending the City Dionysia, theatre audiences represented the majority, rather than the 'educated' (and other) minorities of more recent years. This, of course, was obviously appropriate for a social art form which represented Athenian democracy. Not only its sheer size, but its architectural form illustrates the theatre's centrality in Athens. The building is what Richard Schechner terms a sociometric design: 'The Greek amphitheatre is open, beyond and around it the city can be seen during performances which take place in daylight. It is the city, the *polis*, that is tightly boundaried geographically and ideologically' (1977: 115). The importance accorded to theatre is further substantiated by the economic support it received, with production costs largely met by state funds.

Greek theatre, then, clearly illustrates a direct relationship to the society it addresses and, at every level, includes the audience as active participant. A history of audiences in the theatre demonstrates, of course, a changing status. Medieval and sixteenth-century audiences did not enjoy the power of the Greek audiences, but nevertheless still functioned in an active role. There was a flexibility in the relationship between stage and audience worlds which afforded, in different ways, the participation of those audiences as actors in the drama. With the establishment of private theatres in the seventeenth century, however, there is the beginning of a separation of fictional stage world and audience. Higher admission prices probably limited the social composition of the audience, and with the beginning of passivity and more elitist audiences came codes and conventions of behaviour. In terms of English theatre, audiences became increasingly passive and increasingly bourgeois. With the exception of the first forty years of the nineteenth century – when the working-class audience created noisy disturbances and occasional riots in the pits – this is a steady progression to a peak in the second half of the nineteenth century. After 1850, with the pits replaced by stalls, theatre design ensured the more sedate behaviour of audiences, and the footlights first installed in the seventeenth-century private playhouses had become a literal barrier which separated the audience and the stage. As Michael Booth puts it, 'After 1850 behaviour improved, and complaints were eventually made, not of uproar in the pit and gallery, but of

3

stolid indifference in the stalls' (1975: 21). In the last hundred years, of course, there have been many challenges and disruptions of the codes and conventions which demand passivity. These have led to the productive and emancipated spectator who is at the centre of this text.

If the nature of the audience changed, then so did the cultural status of the theatrical event. While theatre never returned to the status it enjoyed in early Greece, its existence has remained dependent on those same economic, political and social structures. The survival of theatre is economically tied to a willing audience – not only those people paying to sit and watch a performance but increasingly those who approve a government, corporate, or other subsidy. Any new directions in the shape of both new playwrighting and new performance objectives/techniques depend precisely on that audience. As Alan Sinfield points out: 'Any artistic form depends upon some readiness in the receiver to cooperate with its aims and conventions' (1983b: 185). Even in his Poor Theatre, 'scientifically' stripped to its essentials, Grotowski recognizes the audience as a crucial part of the theatrical process. Yet dramatic *theory* has often neglected the role of the addressee, the process of an audience's interpretation.

While the community nature of Greek theatre might be expected to have fostered an interest in the spectator's contribution, the earliest (and most influential) theorists paid scant attention to this central aspect of their theatre. In Aristotle's *Poetics* the audience is chiefly of interest in so far as they prove the power of good tragic texts/performances. In Horace's *Ars Poetica* the audience is marked as the recipient of the poets' work: 'Poets intend to give either pleasure or instruction/or to combine the pleasing and instructive in one poem' (1977: 333–4). It is not the intention of this study, however, to offer an historical survey of the drama theorists' attention to audience. I feel that this approach to the audience is readily available elsewhere, either in anthologies of primary material or in critical surveys.[1] The background to my theorizing comes, instead, from other approaches to production and reception and this, I hope, will provide different points of entry. I propose, however, to start with the emergence in the nineteenth century of the stage director when performance takes up concerns which have dominated theatre in this century: in other words, I start with naturalist theatre and reactions to it.

In almost all reactions to naturalist theatre, the audience has been acknowledged as a creative aspect of the dramatic process, and the spectator generally confronted, often co-opted, into a more direct role in the theatrical event. The new attention paid to the audience can be well demonstrated in the ideas of Futurist Filippo Marinetti. He sought amazement and surprise as the effects of his new art and in his Variety Theatre manifesto he proposes that the audience constantly be taken off guard by such devices as 'the use of itching and sneezing powders, coating some of the auditorium seats with glue, provoking fights and disturbances by selling the same seat to two or more people' (Kirby 1971: 23). Marinetti sought to replace the sought-after passivity of fourth-wall-removed naturalism with a theatre which resembled smoke-filled night-clubs in the creation of 'a single undivided ambience for performers and spectators' (Kirby 1971: 22). The title of the 1913 manifesto came from Marinetti's admiration for variety theatre 'because its spectators actively responded during the performance with indications of approval or disdain, rather than waiting passively until the curtain went down to applaud' (Kirby 1971: 23).[2]

Less extreme, but more important for its immediate influence on theatre practice and theory, is the work of Meyerhold. His earliest writings challenge the conventions and underlying assumptions of naturalist theatre and pay direct attention to the creativity of audiences: 'How did medieval drama succeed without any stage equipment? Thanks to the lively imagination of the spectator' (Meyerhold 1969: 27). He continues: 'The naturalistic theatre denies not only the spectator's ability to imagine for himself, but even his ability to understand clever conversation. Hence, the painstaking *analysis* of Ibsen's dialogue which makes every production of the Norwegian dramatist tedious, drawn-out and doctrinaire' (1969: 27).

Meyerhold's 1917 production of Lermontov's *Masquerade* showed two important things. It demonstrated how the creation of a *mise en scène* had replaced the author's text as the crucial aspect in the signifying process: the play 'has been in preparation and intermittently rehearsed for five years'! (Braun in Meyerhold 1969: 79). It also attested to Meyerhold's

5

determination in exaggerating the trappings of naturalist theatre in order to take the theatrical experience into the audience: 'everything of significance was made slightly over life-size in order to produce the required impact on the spectator.... [T]he auditorium lighting was left on throughout the performance. Tall mirrors flanked the proscenium opening, in order to break down... the barrier between stage and audience' (Braun in Meyerhold 1969: 79–80). Meyerhold also showed an awareness of the shifts in the ideological base of Russian society and wrote in 1920 concerning his production of Verhaeren's *The Dawn*: 'We have a new public which will stand no nonsense – each spectator represents, as it were, Soviet Russia in microcosm.... Now we have to protect the interests not of the author but of the spectator. The interests of the audience have assumed a vital significance' (1969: 170–1). Once again, naturalism is blamed for suppressing the (rightful) participation of the audience: 'More than anyone, the Moscow Art Theatre is to blame for the passivity of the spectator whom it held in thrall for so long' (Meyerhold 1969: 174).

Meyerhold demystified the technical apparatus of theatre. All the trappings of commerical theatre were eschewed in favour of non-illusionistic staging and politically relevant scenic components (placards, leaflets, actors concealed in the audience to guide reactions). The breaking of the traditional barrier of the proscenium provided, as Edward Braun points out, 'an additional advantage... that this implied a polemic against the bourgeois theatre of escapism and illusion' (1977: 39). In the closing act of *Mystery-Bouffe*, 'the action spilled into the boxes adjacent to the stage, and at the conclusion the audience was invited to mingle with the actors onstage' (Braun in Meyerhold 1969: 166). This production achieved the political contract between script, actor, and audience that Meyerhold had been seeking for his theatre. *Mystery-Bouffe* and its companion in repertory, *The Dawn*, were seen by 120,000 spectators in five months (Braun in Meyerhold 1969: 166). This provided tangible evidence that his theatre *without* illusion, but *with* the co-operation of the audience (albeit manipulated at a certain level), had achieved its aims. Beyond this, however, Meyerhold is a rare example, as Stourac and McCreery point out, of a practitioner who tried seriously to analyse the effects of his works on audiences. A code was developed for notation of response:

> a silence; b noise; c loud noise; d collective reading; e singing; f coughing; g knocks or bangs; h scuffling; i exclamation; j weeping; k laughter; l sighs; m action and animation; n applause; o whistling; p catcalls, hisses; q people leaving; r people getting out of their seats; s throwing of objects; t people getting onto stage.
>
> (Stourac and McCreery: 20).

The work of Meyerhold is described here at some length as, both in theory and practice, he attacked the hegemony of text-centred criticism as well as denarrativizing productions and drawing the audience from being passive addressees to co-creators. In 1930 he wrote:

> Nowadays, every production is designed to induce audience participation: modern dramatists and directors rely not only on the efforts of the actors and the facilities afforded by the stage machinery but on the efforts of the audience as well. We produce every play on the assumption that it will be still unfinished when it appears on the stage. We do this consciously because we realize that the crucial revision of a production is that which is made by the spectator.
>
> (Meyerhold 1969: 256)

Surely today many theatre groups formed and operating in opposition to dominant cultural and political practice would willingly endorse that description of theatre practice. The intensity of interest in audience sparked by the rejection of naturalist practice has, in the latter half of the twentieth century, become an obsession. Both texts and performances have shown a growing absorption with the relationship of their art to those who view it *actively* in the theatre. As marginalized social groups have found theatrical forms to address their interests and their constituencies, the productive role of those constituencies has always played a part. Yet this has still not inspired much theoretical attention. Criticism has remained, by and large, text-oriented and, as a brief survey of some of the central analyses of the theatrical event published in Britain and North America in the last thirty years makes all too obvious, discussions of audience reception have remained simple and cursory.

In recent years many analyses of what constitutes drama have been published and, as their titles often suggest (for example, J. L. Styan's *Elements of Drama* (1960) and Martin Esslin's *An Anatomy of Drama* (1976)), these books attempt to account for all the components of the dramatic experience, from the author's creation of a play to the critical reception of text-in-performance. However, Eric Bentley's *The Life of the Drama* all but ignores the presence of audience except to note that its 'involvement is not an innocent one' (1964: 156) and that 'if one took from theatre the element of voyeurism, the occasion would lose much of its appeal' (1964: 56). Generally, in fact, the audience constitutes one chapter of these investigations and is identified as an important contributor to the social act. Styan emphasizes: 'it is clearly as important to know what is being returned by the spectator to the actor, and by the actor to the script, as to know the intentions of the script in the first place. Arguably, intentions are of no consequence whatsoever' (1960: 7). Even with an obviously tentative devaluing of the author's contribution, attention to the reception process is signalled. On the other hand, Bernard Beckermann identifies 'a three-way communication: between the play, the individual and collective audience. The play projects doubly, to each member of the audience as an individual... and to the audience as a whole, in that distinctive configuration that it has assumed for a particular occasion' (1970: 133). Most common has been discussion of the feelings and perceptual processes that take place within a theatre audience. As the collective nature of theatre is stressed, so its links in ritual are traced; for Esslin 'in ritual as in drama the aim is an enhanced level of consciousness, a memorable insight into the nature of existence' (1976: 28). Theodore Shank makes a similar claim: '[the dramatic work] articulates for the audience something vital about their own emotive lives that previously they had not been able to grasp' (1969: 172).

The expansion of performance art and theory (which has devalued language/texts in favour of the event), as well as contemporary opppositional drama, has, however, changed the emphasis of dramatic theories in the last twenty years. Esslin's anatomy shows this well: '[theatre] in very practical terms teaches them [the audience], or reminds them of, its codes of conduct, its rules of social coexistence. All drama is therefore a political event' (1976: 29).[3] Beckermann more generally observes: 'The random audience, nourished by the mass media and universal education, may be evolving into a new communal type. If so, the theater artist will have to learn what its predispositions are and how to deal with them' (1970: 136). As in other areas, the implications of the relationship between theatre as cultural institution, sharing or challenging the dominant ideology, and the audience's collaboration in the maintenance or attempt to overthrow that ideology are not explored in any detail. We get only a sense of *a* theatre audience, not of theatre audiences; similarly the theatre equates almost always with the mainstream, and fails to acknowledge a diversity of theatres with quite different practices and objectives. Yet the relationship of ideology, theatre, and audience, as later discussion of Brecht and other political theatre will show, has become increasingly important. The more generalized theories of dramatic components which dominated to the mid-1970s nevertheless avoided any overt political statements. In their conservative humanism, they echo the earlier literary criticism of Arnold, Eliot, and Richards in directing the dramatic transmission to those in the right stage of receptiveness (in other words to those with beliefs, levels of education, and literary 'sensitivity' which more or less match those of the writer and/or director) with the purpose of some general cultural and intellectual benefit. Part of the polemic in this book is to foreground the assumptions of those theatre studies which maintain a limited (mainstream theatre) focus and to assert those theatres which speak from fragmented and marginalized positions.

CONTEMPORARY CONCERNS

In the last ten years, two areas of dramatic theory have, however, given emphasis to the need for a more developed theory of audiences. The first of these to emerge was performance theory. Performance theorists responded to mainstream North American theatre theorists who berated the devaluation, or even total rejection, of the text by performance artists. Traditional theory generally saw this as the final straw

9

in the alienation of audiences, sending them to the (culturally-inferior) entertainments of cinema and television.

Richard Schechner and Mady Schuman's collection of essays, *Ritual, Play and Performance* (1976), reveals in its subtitle, *Readings in the Social Sciences/Theater*, the methodological base of performance theory. Theory from non-literary studies – as diverse as Huizinga's writings on the significance of play, Victor Turner's work on social dramas and ritual, and Jane Goodall's research on the behavioural patterns of chimpanzees – is investigated in an attempt to replace paradigms for dramatic theory that are seen as outmoded. It is easy to see how such an interdisciplinary approach would open up interest in the field of audience response and, indeed, from the importation of the social sciences, new paradigms are constructed. Among these, the audience emerges as a tangibly active creator of the theatrical event:

> Along with the artist, the audience enters the performance arena as participant – or, ideally, the audience disappears as the distinction between doer and viewer... begins to blur. For this the tribal/oral is a particularly clear model, often referred to by the creators of 1960's [*sic*] happenings and the theatrical pieces that invited, even coerced, audience participation toward an ultimate democratizing of the arts.
>
> (Rothenberg 1977: 14)

It is, of course, not only performance art which moves audience from viewer to doer. Many groups working with specific community (or other) issues look to such a process as essential in a theatre of empowerment. *In the Neighbourhood of My Heart*, a production by Toronto's Ground Zero, presents a drama not simply constructed to inform and encourage the homeless to take action. It goes beyond this as members of the housing co-operatives which fostered the production act, recount their histories, and bear witness to the possibility of empowerment. Boundaries between the subjects, the creators, and the receivers are no longer distinct and such a move signals a democratizing of the arts. This goal is characteristic of the emergent interests of the 1970s and 1980s. Theatre no longer remains the sole domain of the educated and economically-able few. Moreover, democratization is not only seen as a desirable, but as a crucial, aspect of new developments in performance and theory.

The sociological/psychological/anthropological studies of Victor Turner and Erving Goffman using theatrical paradigms to describe universal patterns suggest to Schechner 'a universal dramatic structure parallel to social process: drama is that art whose subject, structure and action is social process' (1977: 121). This is evident too in Elizabeth Burns's *Theatricality*, a full-length study of the social processes which both inform and constitute drama. It is indicative of the hermetical nature of dramatic theory in English that her opening chapter includes some exposition of her use of theory from the sociology of theatre which she remarks is 'even less known in Britain and America than the rather tenuous thread of sociological writings on literature which are connected with the names of Georg Lukács, Ernst Auerbach, Lucien Goldmann, Robert Escarpit, Umberto Eco, and Eduardo Sanguineti' (Burns 1972: 5). From Burns's study published in 1972 to the present, not much seems to have changed. In a recent article, Maria Shevtsova accounts for slow progress towards the establishment of a dialogue with sociology: 'the discipline we know as theatre studies has considered sociology to be alien to it, a perception that goes hand-in-glove with the idea that theatre art and sociology are so different from each other as to warrant mutual exclusion' (1989: 23).[4]

In Schechner's analysis, however, any everyday process or any community ritual can be staged as theatrical event 'because context, not fundamental structure, distinguishes ritual, entertainment, and ordinary life, from each other. The differences among them arise from the agreement (conscious or unexpressed) between performers and spectators' (in Schechner and Shuman 1976: 217–18). Schechner's own group TPG (The Performance Group) has carried out many experiments which show the interplay of the sociological and theatrical. This has often included new ways of incorporating the audience in the creative process. One attempt involved the establishment of real time and regular time audiences. The real time audiences were invited to the theatre at the same time as the performers arrived and thus were included in all that constituted the theatrical event: from the unlocking of the theatre through costuming and make-up to the arrival of the regular time audience, and on to the clearing-up process and the final shutting of the theatre. This, Schechner states, was 'an attempt to make both performers and audiences aware of the overlapping but conceptually distinct realities of drama, script, theatre and performance' (1977: 44). He continues:

> Too little study has been made of the liminal approaches and leavings of performance – how the audience gets to, and into, the performance place, and how they go from that place; and in what ways this gathering/dispersing is related to the preparations/cooling-off aspects of the performers' work. The coming and going of both audience and performers guarantees (in Goffman's usage) the existence of the 'theatrical frame' so that events can be experienced as *actual realizations*: in other words, the reality of performance is in the performing; a spectator need not intervene in the theatre to prevent murder as he might feel compelled to in ordinary life – this is because the violence on stage is actually a performance. That doesn't make it 'less real' but 'different' real.
>
> (Schechner 1977: 122)

Thus performance theory brings into play aspects of the audience's contribution hitherto ignored. The introduction of such liminal aspects to the process of theatre attendance complicates the more traditional concerns about the audience's perception of the play performance. My own theorizing looks to the implications of liminalities in terms of effects upon perception, but also, as liminalities are always ideologically encoded, considers how the audience's expectations of the theatrical event as a whole are accordingly shaped.

While performance theorists have broadened the scope of what we might consider theatre, a second area of dramatic theory has, in recent years, paid a new attention to the multivalent components of theatre. Semiology has considered these components (not simply what takes place on the stage, or even in the auditorium) and their interaction in the signifying process. The Prague School, working from both Russian Formalist and Saussurian linguistic theory, marked in the 1930s and 1940s the first semiotic examination of theatre. Mukǎrovský's essay 'On the Current State of the Theory of the Theatre' (1941) is indicative of the questions examined and the problems identified. Concerning theatre audiences he writes:

> [T]he roles of the actor and the spectator are much less distinguished than it might seem at first glance. Even the actor to a certain extent is a spectator for his partner at the moment when the partner is playing; in particular, extras who do not intervene actively in the play are distinctly perceived as spectators. The inclusion of actors among the audience becomes quite apparent, for example, when a comedian makes a co-actor laugh by his performance. Even if we are aware that such laughter can be intentional (in order to establish active contact between the stage and auditorium), we cannot but realize that at such a moment the boundary between the stage and the auditorium runs across the stage itself: the laughing actors are on the audience's side.
>
> (Mukařovský 1941: 218–19)

Mukařovský's essay provides a useful survey of the contradictions and tensions that inform what appear to be quite individual components in a theatrical event and, as might be expected in a Prague School analysis, he finds that the organization of these theatrical components takes on the appearance of 'a structure which freely hovers before the spectator's eyes and consciousness without being bound unequivocally to existential reality by any of its components but thereby figuratively signifying all of the reality which surrounds and creates man of a given period and society' (1941: 219).

Despite this conclusion, which certainly foregrounds the research potential for theatre semioticians, it was only in the late 1960s that semiotics emerged as an important theoretical base for theatre studies. Since that time, however, work in this field has covered almost every aspect of the theatrical event. Some studies have concerned themselves with specific components of theatre – such as Anne Ubersfeld's *Lire Le Théâtre* (1977) (a semiotic analysis of the written dramatic text) and Mihai Dinu's mathematical breakdown of character configurations in 'The Algebra of Scenic Situations' (1984) – while others have attempted a more complete semiotic analysis of theatrical communication – such as the work of Girard, Ouellet and Rigault in *L'univers du théâtre* (1978) and Elam in

The Semiotics of Theatre and Drama (1980). Elam (and others including Ross Chambers and Marco De Marinis) has also been concerned with the development of speech-act or action-theory as a pragmatic model of theatrical response. The actual result of these diverse semiotic readings of theatre has not been the original target of their investigations: that is, they have not produced a model by which a complete analysis of performance can be constructed; they have instead recognized that this initial target was not necessarily desirable. The work, by virtue of its own plurality, has nevertheless provided a more thorough understanding of the plurality of signifying processes that take place in the theatre. Patrice Pavis writes:

> Semiology in no way resembles a machine or a technique meant to *produce* ready-made discourses about a text or the stage. It is necessary in fact to *construct* this analytical machine which is not preconceived and which has to be built up according to the theatrical subject studied. To analyze the codes and signifying systems of a performance is not to rediscover what the author and director had previously established secretly, once and for all. It is to organize the performance and the text as a possible circuit of meaning whose productivity and coherence are more or less great according to the theatre event in question, but also according to the analyst.
>
> (Pavis 1982: 195)

Despite this breadth of semiotic interest, the audience has been as neglected almost as much as elsewhere. As Marvin Carlson points out (1984: 508), Keir Elam's book devotes only 9 of 210 pages to an examination of the audience. We might add that the more 'traditional' study of J. L. Styan, *Drama, Stage and Audience* (1975), devotes a similar percentage, 18 of 247 pages. Elam, for his part, discusses the primary condition of audience as 'the ability to recognize the performance *as such*' (1980: 87) and thus it signals, or permits, the performance itself. He asserts: 'It is with the spectator, in brief, that theatrical communication begins and ends' (1980: 96–7).

Semioticians have undoubtedly subjected drama and per-formance to a more rigorous examination of all constitutive elements (and without the controlling bias towards performance aspects of the Schechner programme) and I will return to their work at other points in this book. Alongside these fields of performance and semiotic theory, there has, however, been other recent research which has taken account of the theatre audience. Particularly interesting – although rather outside the concerns of this study – is the reading of dramatic texts for implicit strategies of reception. Shakespeare studies, in particular, has attracted a number of reader-response approaches, such as Ann Pasternak Slater's *Shakespeare the Director* (1982) and Jean E. Howard's *Shakespeare's Art of Orchestration* (1984). Howard, for example, explains: 'I assume that in writing plays for performance Shakespeare was partly writing with an eye to the potential responses of the audience; that is, as he orchestrated the play, he was indirectly orchestrating the theatrical experience of the viewer' (1984: 6). Also of interest is Una Chaudhuri's 'The Spectator in Drama/ Drama in the Spectator' (1984), a discussion of Peter Shaffer's *Equus* in terms of a 'schizophrenic' contemporary response (hated by critics, loved by audiences). She looks to 'an archetypal paradigm at work in *Equus*, not merely as a theme or an explanatory mechanism, but as something directing the spectator's *experience*' (Chaudhuri 1984: 292). Her analysis does perhaps account for the gap between the box-office and critical reception of this play, but more importantly the reading promotes 'a spectator-oriented criticism. The description of how a play works on a spectator – rather than of what it means – can supply the terms our criticism needs in order to erase the gap between theory and its object' (1984: 296). The pedagogical implications of this are, I think, both exciting and challenging for those of us who teach in the field of dramatic literature and theory. Indeed, the refusal in much contemporary drama to take up either the issues or forms that are familiar to audiences 'trained' in the traditional experience of theatre (or, perhaps more significantly, theatre studies) begs that dramatic criticism adopts new discourses in questioning how plays engage audiences. Richard Webb, looking at approaches of contemporary French companies, concludes:

> Experiments which involve the spectator in the performance or which extend to him a creative role in the dramatic process must call into question our conventional understanding of theatre and artistic creation. They

15

require that the dramatic critic should look again at his
assumptions and vocabulary.... The creative acts of the
experimentalists invite equally creative responses from
the critics.

(Webb 1979–80: 215–16)

Two recent full-length studies of the audience should be dealt
with here. The first of these is Daphna Ben Chaim's *Distance
in the Theatre: The Aesthetics of Audience Response* (1984). This
approach is, by her own admission, necessarily limited, but
covers what the author sees as a growing twentieth-century
interest in the concept of distance both in aesthetic and dramatic theory. The watershed, in Ben Chaim's view, has been the
work of Edward Bullough, and his 1912 essay on the concept
of psychical distance is a central intertext in this consideration
of the theatrical situation. Ben Chaim also looks to the theories
of Sartre, Brecht, Artaud, and Grotowski. Her arguments concerning Grotowski's experiments are important in terms of
my own study. She suggests that his attempts to abolish
distance illustrate the limits of theatre. When distance dis-
appears then art does too. While theoretically this vanishing
point seems possible, it is questionable whether it can in fact
be reached. Even the abandonment of traditional auditoria,
traditional stage–audience relationships, and other visible
theatrical conventions does not mean that the concept of
theatre will necessarily disappear as well. With the name of
Grotowski attached to any project, the audience is provided
with a particular set of *theatrical* expectations. One of my
concerns here is to look at how limits are in flux, how they are
shifted and reinterpreted by different forms of theatre practice.
It should also be noted that Grotowski has since discontinued
the paratheatrics Ben Chaim describes and has looked instead
to a Theatre of Sources and Objective Drama.[5] Now a professor
at the University of California (Irvine), Grotowski appears to
have returned to experimentation which exploits precisely
that flexibility of theatre to test an audience's balancing of
stage and other worlds.

In the absence of drama theorists who discuss the audience's
involvement with fictional worlds, Ben Chaim looks to the
film theorists, Christian Metz and André Bazin. Both contend
that the real signifiers of theatre performance restrict the

imaginative involvement of the audience with the stage world (Ben Chaim 1984: 55). Film, in Bazin's opinion, is much closer to reality and the lessening of distance leads to fuller engagement with the spectator. Distance, of course, remains a necessary element in the screen–auditorium relationship so that the spectator is placed precisely in the role of voyeur. From this, Ben Chaim establishes the parameters for distance:

> The combination...of unreality with recognizable human characteristics seems to be the minimum requirement for identification, and both of these conditions are variable and provide the borders within which distance operates. Those qualities that make the object seem like ourselves (humanization) pull the object toward us; those aspects which distinguish the object from ourselves and our real world (an awareness of fictionality) push the object away from us. The aesthetic tension between these two opposing tendencies constitutes distance and provides the conditions for the variability of distance....
>
> The most intense personal relationship with a minimum awareness of fictionality is 'low' distance and the combination that the realist film and realistic play aspire to. An increased awareness of fiction combined with the lowest humanization is largely the province of farce in the theatre, of Punch and Judy, and stylized theatre of extreme abstraction. The combination of a high (but varying) perception of unreality and a high (but varying) humanization is the corner occupied by Brecht in such plays as *Mother Courage*.
>
> (Ben Chaim 1984: 67)

Distance, then, is instrinsic to art and the question this poses, Ben Chaim suggests, is how it 'affects the perception of theatrical art' (1984: 71). As 'the deliberate manipulation of distance is, to a great extent, the underlying factor that determines theatrical style in this century' (1984: 79), the various levels of engagement with the audience are, in this way, central to any analysis of the audience's experience.

Ben Chaim's discussions are important in establishing distance as so crucial in aesthetic experience. It is nevertheless, as Ben Chaim readily points out, only a partial study and the real importance of distance can only be measured in relation to all other aspects (social, cultural, political, aesthetic) which constitute the experience of theatre. A more recent study of the audience, Jill Dolan's *The Feminist Spectator as Critic* (1988), looks at the process of being a feminist spectator and helpfully reminds us of 'the varied responses of spectators mixed across ideologies of gender, sexuality, race, and class' (1988: 121).

Moving through particular discourses of feminism and through plays of and/or about women, Dolan's self-conscious exploration of what constitutes feminist spectatorship serves to deconstruct the notion of intended audience for mainstream productions (white, middle class, heterosexual, male). As she puts it:

> the feminist spectator might find that her gender – and/ or her race, class, or sexual preference – as well as her ideology and politics make the representation alien and even offensive. It seems that as a spectator she is far from ideal. Determined to draw larger conclusions from this experience, she leaves the theatre while the audience applauds at the curtain call and goes off to develop a theory of feminist performance criticism.
>
> (Dolan 1988: 3–4)

Perhaps most useful is Dolan's examination of theatres (and their audiences) which work outside dominant modes of representation and which 'break the heterosexual contract that informs representation and the enculturation of gender' (1988: 101). Her book concludes with the lesbian subject in support of her belief that 'personally, artistically, and spectatorially, hers is closest to the view from elsewhere, and offers the most radical position from which to subvert representation' (Dolan 1988: 119). Dolan raises issues which extend, as she suggests, beyond gender specificity.

In general, the considerations of theatre audiences examined here testify to that difficulty in moving from 'the stage of proclamations' Pavis identified. Audiences clearly play a role in the theatre, but what kind of role? And what kind of audience? What constitutes the theatrical event in which they play that part? In what way do the liminalities of performance bear upon the communication model of the performance itself? In a self-conscious communication-oriented theatre (such as Schechner's TPG or the Living Theater of Beck and Malina), the audience's role (although not their social construction) is, at least in some ways, visible. But in theatre demanding the (theoretically) more or less total passivity of the audience, how can their relationship to the self-contained dramatic world be described? Many of the problems stem from the ephemeral nature of performance. But these problems suggest that what a theory of theatre audiences needs is not the neglect it has historically received, but a systematic, if cautious, approach that would make clearer the relationship between the art form we acknowledge as drama and the audience, both locally and at large, that supports it. Elizabeth Burns writes:

> During the course of the history of the theatre first dramatists, then actors, and at the present time [1972], producers have been in ascendance. But the position of the audience, however much its social structure may have altered, has remained constant. Although at different periods it has been less or more articulate, either vocally or in writing, it has always held the power of making or breaking a play by attendance or abstention, and has always been ultimately responsible for sustaining the performance.
>
> (Burns 1972: 184–5)

In short, drama depends on its audience. Bernard Dort has written of the rise to power of the director as an historical phenomenon which brought about a shift in interest from text to production plan, but which also subordinated all other theatre workers. He suggests, however, that:

> the rise of the director and the acceptance of the performance as the actual site of meaning (not as the translation or decoration of a text) represent only the initial phase.... I shall call it the progressive emancipation of the elements of the theatrical performance: it implies a change of structure in the performance – the abandonment of an organic unity laid down in advance, and the choice of a meaningful polyphony open to the spectator.
>
> (Dort 1982: 63–4)

The liberated performance which Dort identifies places yet another demand on an expanding dramatic theory to ask questions and to make proclamations about the audience. The need to take account of the many disparate statements and investigations has become more acute. It is the intention here

19

to offer such an assembly of statements from theory and performance, and to look to a more comprehensive understanding of audience contribution to, and involvement in, the theatrical event.

Dramatic practice, unlike theory, has always been concerned, for the reasons Burns suggested, with the involvement of the audience. The playwright invariably shapes a text and the director invariably shapes a production to provoke particular expectations and responses within an audience. The interactive nature of theatre is particularly evident from the rewriting a playwright often chooses (or is called) to do while a play is in rehearsal and from the cuts or changes a director makes after previews, try-outs, or, indeed, during a run. Clearly, then, the audience affects not only the performance but the dramatic text too. Here, however, it is intended to concentrate on the audience's relationship with performance (or, at least, text-in-performance) rather than with specific dramatic texts. Much contemporary theatre occurs without a text available for academic study and deliberately so. In the explosion of new venues, companies, and performance methods, there is a non-traditional theatre which has recreated a flexible actor–audience relationship and a participatory spectator/actor. The practices of these theatres are as valid as those of any mainstream operation in designating theatrical art.

2

THEORIES OF READING
AND VIEWING

Two somewhat different spheres of cultural activity form the
starting points for my own theorizing. Both have influenced
this study a great deal. The first is the work of Bertolt Brecht.
His dramatic theory and practice today occupies an important
place not only for his significant role in the canon (as it were)
of drama studies. It also seems as if Brecht's name – and ideas
– appear everywhere: in renaissance studies, in theories of
postmodernism, in contemporary theatre practice and research,
in cultural studies, in film theory, in Marxist studies and
elsewhere. Certainly Brecht's work foregrounds the audience
and it is in post-Brechtian oppositional theatre that the audience
has taken an increasingly productive role.

The second starting point is reader-response theory. Notwithstanding the often performative metaphors used by these
theorists, very little attention is given to the phenomenon of
theatre. I found their work at once liberating and frustrating.
The usefulness of a discourse which took account of receptive
processes was undercut by its neglect of the dramatic text and
performance. Nevertheless I have started with the work of
these and other reception-oriented theorists as many of their
ideas applied in some way to the particular structures of
theatre, and as their vocabulary has been helpful in finding
my own model for the audience. My account of the theories of
Holland, Fish, Iser, Jauss and others is skeletal. I hope to
familiarize non-specialists with this work and to give a background to the terms I have borrowed, recontextualized, and,
most importantly, politicized. It is perhaps worth noting at
this juncture the obvious difference between the projects of
those theorizing the printed or the filmic text and my own

concern with performance. The literary, as well as the filmic, text is a fixed and finished product which cannot be directly affected by its audiences. Even the serial form or the revised novel only allows limited input from readers. In the theatre every reader is involved in the making of the play. Indeed, the audience of even the most 'culinary' theatre is involved in a reciprocal relationship which can change the quality and success of a performance. No two theatrical performances can ever be the same precisely because of this audience involvement. In much contemporary theatre the audience becomes a self-conscious co-creator of performance and enjoys a productive role which exceeds anything demanded of the reader or the cinema audience. The theatre audience is, like its cinematic counterpart, also a social gathering. Reading is, by and large, a private experience. Beyond this, the many components of theatre – director, actor, theatre building, lighting, seating, and so on – intercede between text and reader. Their involvement necessarily complicates the theoretical model. These differences I will account for in Chapter three.

STARTING WITH BRECHT

The work of Brecht, both as playwright and theoretician, is clearly important for any study of audience/play relations. His ideas for a theatre with the power to provoke social change, along with his attempts to reactivate stage-audience exchange, have had a widespread and profound effect not only on theatre practice, but also on critical responses to plays and performance.

Brecht's epic theatre looked, above all, to change the conventional modes of production and reception. All the technical developments to promote what Brecht terms in *The Messingkauf Dialogues* 'a theatre of the scientific age' (1977: 105) were devised to provoke a critical, yet entertained, audience. Walter Benjamin describes the process:

A double object is provided for the audience's interest. First, the events shown on stage; these must be of such a kind that they may, at certain decisive points, be checked by the audience against its own experience. Second, the production; this must be transparent as to its artistic armature.... Epic theatre addresses itself to interested

22

parties 'who do not think unless they have a reason to.'
Brecht is constantly aware of the masses, whose conditioned use of the faculty of thought is surely covered by
this formula. His effort to make the audience interested in
the theatre as experts – not at all for cultural reasons – is
an expression of his political purpose.

(Benjamin 1973: 15–16)

The idea of a theatre engaging an audience for other than
'cultural reasons' was one which not only made clear theatre's
diminishing importance and failure to connect with the issues
of the time, but further revealed theatre as a social institution
supported by and reflecting the dominant ideology. In this
way, epic theatre reactivated stage-audience relations in an
overtly political context. Benjamin talks of it shaking 'the
social validity of theatre-as-entertainment by robbing it of its
function within the capitalist system' (1973: 9), and certainly
Brecht's theory and practice raise the issue of the ideological
status of theatre and of the political undertaking, either implicit
or explicit, of an audience.

A concern with the audience for epic theatre is an intrinsic
part of all Brecht's theoretical writings. In *A Short Organum for
the Theatre*, Brecht points out how contemporary practice frus-
trated a direct relationship between stage and audience: '[t]he
theatre as we know it shows the structure of society (represented on the stage) as incapable of being influenced by
society (in the auditorium)' (Willett 1964: 189). To counteract
this, Brecht proposes a more immediate and interactive theatre:

> The bare wish, if nothing else, to evolve an art fit for the
> times must drive our theatre of the scientific age straight
> out into the suburbs, where it can stand as it were wide
> open, at the disposal of those who live hard and produce
> much, so that they can be fruitfully entertained there with
> their great problems. They may find it hard to pay for our
> art, and immediately to grasp the new method of enter-
> tainment, and we shall have to learn in many respects
> what they need and how they need it; but we can be sure
> of their interest. For these men who seem so far apart
> from natural science are only apart from it because they
> are being forcibly kept apart; and before they can get
> their hands on it they have first to develop and put into

23

effect a new science of society; so that these are the true
children of the scientific age, who alone can get the theatre
moving if it is to move at all.

(Willett 1964: 186)

Brecht is always aware of the theatre's need to be 'geared into
reality' (Willett 1964: 186) in order to make contact with the
widest audience. Moreover he makes it clear that this demand
is not met by simple representations of reality on the stage.
Ibsen's *Ghosts* and Hauptmann's *The Weavers* (both of which
evoked strong critical reaction to their first performances) are
cited by Brecht as plays which provide no more than a setting.
For this reason, an audience can only learn/ask questions
about that particular situation, and does not explore any
relationship between this slice of life and their own social
reality. The characters of these plays, Brecht suggests, do not
interact with the audience; their 'feelings, insights and impulses... are forced on us' (Willett 1964: 190). Identification
with the psychological experience of the characters is fostered,
and the audience is concerned with issues of individual moral-
ity rather than with larger social structures. Furthermore, the
acting style of naturalist theatre excludes audience intervention. As the Philosopher of *The Messingkauf Dialogues*
remarks with typical cynicism:

'Ah yes, then the audience is tacitly assuming that it's not
in a theatre at all, since nobody seems to take any notice
of it. It has an illusion of sitting in front of a keyhole. That
being so it ought not to applaud till it starts queuing for
its hats and coats'.

(Brecht 1977: 51)

Yet Brecht's comments constitute more than a critique of the
aesthetic form of naturalism. They question the ideology underlying the accepted codes of cultural production and reception.

In a published letter written more than twenty years before
A Short Organum, Brecht declared his intention to counteract
current theatre practice which privileged the beliefs of an
elite. He writes:

This generation doesn't want to capture the theatre, audience and all, and perform good or merely contemporary
plays in the same theatre and to the same audience; nor

24

has it any chance of doing so; it has a duty and a chance to capture the theatre for a *different* audience. The works now being written are coming more and more to lead towards that great epic theatre which corresponds to the sociological situation; neither their content nor their form can be understood except by the minority that understands this. They are not going to satisfy the old aesthetics; they are going to destroy it.

(Willett 1964: 21–2)

'The old aesthetics' may not have been destroyed, but Brecht's attack laid bare a previously covert relationship between theatre and the dominant ideology which supported it. As a Marxist, Brecht clearly sought to establish an oppositional cultural practice, and the search for a new audience was a crucial part of Brecht's theatre practice. His political convictions influenced every aspect of his dramaturgy, as Iring Fetscher notes: 'even as a Marxist theoretician Brecht was a practical writer, whose reflections on theories and relationships were never divorced from the possibilities of the theater (as his basic reality).... He was interested only in the kind of thinking that converts into action (1980: 15–16). The chronological arrangement of John Willett's *Brecht on Theatre* shows well how Brecht's ideas and assumptions were always in process rather than constituting a fixed theory against which performance might be judged. Indeed, Brecht argued against Lukács's preference for the model of nineteenth-century realism precisely on the grounds that an historically fixed system could not continue to make contact with its audience in the changing conditions of social reality.

Brecht's revolutionary theatre was not, of course, the first to oppose the codes and assumptions of cultural institutions. The declaration of the Philosopher in *The Messingkauf Dialogues* – 'We want to demolish the fourth wall' (Brecht 1977: 52) – clearly identifies Brecht's work as part of an on-going challenge to naturalism. Meyerhold's theatre, as we saw, marked the establishment of a new self-reflexive practice, structured specifically to disrupt the spectators' usual interpretive process. Other challenges came from Eisenstein and Piscator, both of whom provided important models for Brecht's own work.

Piscator's theatre rejected not only naturalist practice but also what he saw as 'the pathetic emotionalism of the Expressionists' (Innes 1972: 192). Like Meyerhold, he sought to reconstitute the production–reception contract as a bi-directional discussion and, to provoke this exchange, he too had recourse to the strategy of positioning actors among the audience. Piscator's theatre was, however, predominantly a political instrument. With §218 (the production title refers to a civil law on abortion), he achieved performance dialogue and political change. The audience interposed comments, offered other views, and finally voted to reject the law; there were subsequent riots in the streets and Piscator spent a month in prison... for tax evasion! (Braun 1977: 42; Innes 1972: 137–8).

Piscator, like Brecht, sought out a working-class audience for his plays, forming the *Proletarisches Theater* in 1920 which performed in venues in industrial districts. Influential in Piscator's development of a performance theory was Walter Gropius's design for 'Total Theatre'. Gropius's ideas concerned only the architectural component of theatre but were radical in creating the option of a stage area to encircle the audience. Piscator expanded this concept to involve all available media with the aim of 'the absolute integration of the onlooker in the play' (Innes 1972: 150). While the anticipated presence of an audience is, by virtue of the genre, always inscribed in a play, for Piscator this was more than usually concrete. He could locate precisely the social and political background of a significant proportion of his audience and in this way incorporate their presence directly into his *mise en scène*:

In the 1920s Piscator was able to use at least the proletarian part of his audiences as a positive element in his productions because they were already politically committed, and therefore, although they were unrehearsed, he could allow accurately for their actions. A slogan, a symbolic gesture or a familiar tune was enough to provoke a known and invariable reaction from the seats allotted to the Subscribers' Club, which was composed of members of the General Workers' Union, the Syndicalists and the Communist Youth – at least at a simple level, as when the *International* was sung 'spontaneously' at performances of *Hoppla!* or *Rasputin*.

(Innes 1972: 145)

With audience reaction so particularly inscribed in the production text, both through the predictability of response from an identifiable social group and through actors as prompts to audience reaction, Piscator (and, indeed, Meyerhold) did not, it seems, liberate their audiences. Instead audience input was carefully controlled, not to say manipulated, and the locus of authority left strictly within the text/*mise en scène*.

The theatre of both Meyerhold and Piscator is important, however, in a number of ways. The effect of their experiments, beyond any immediate political impact, was to demystify theatre practice and to make available new components which might more readily address a popular audience. For the purposes of this study, the effect on receptiveness of the virtually complete correlation of cultural codes between Piscator's theatre and audience is of particular interest. More recently, the oppositional practice of some theatre companies (particularly feminist, gay, or minority ethnic groups) has relied on a similar correlation of codes. In much of this later theatre, authority has been self-consciously relinquished and traditional models unhesitatingly challenged. An an influence upon Brecht's work,[1] however, Piscator's practice supplied some useful tools for low-budget, portable, working-class theatre. While Brecht would have argued against the political specificity of Piscator's theatre, the technical apparatus was clearly identified as potentially effective in a more rigorous examination of social structures.

The film work of Sergei Eisenstein also influenced the development of Brecht's epic theatre. Eisenstein, who had once been Meyerhold's assistant, eschewed theatre for cinema, a form he felt more 'appropriate for the materialist process argued for in a dialectical aesthetics; images had a direct connection to actuality, and their manipulation through montage could reproduce the manipulation of objects by the logic of history' (Polan 1985: 45). The montage structuring of Eisenstein's work broke through the surface reality of naturalism to demonstrate the political circumstances behind general patterns of social relations. This clearly influenced Brecht's theatre. The single frame Eisenstein saw as a multiple-meaning ideogram to be read only in juxtaposition (Eisenstein 1949: 65–6). Thus cinema could address the emotions through its descriptive powers and the intellect by the abstract relations between frames

27

(Eisenstein 1949: 62). Paradoxically Eisenstein's work exploits the production–reception contract of naturalist practice to promote a politically appropriate decoding of the montage structure. As Dana Polan indicates 'the very appeal of film as a "natural" medium is an appeal that can be utilized by the dialectical artist to trick audiences virtually into believing that they are seeing the same old naturalistic art' (1985: 43). In the process of naturalizing montage and by using what Polan describes as 'the mathematically calculated affective pull of the montage pattern, the filmmaker presents his or her audience with a film that has, or seems to have, the same perceptual attributes as the most "unbiased" documentary' (1985: 43). Eisenstein acknowledged this potential for conveying what he calls 'ideologically pointed theses' (1949: 62) and saw film primarily as a structure demonstrating the relationship of the author to the content 'compelling the spectator to relate himself to the content in the same way' (1949: 168). While Eisenstein is concerned more with the aesthetics of film than with the relationship between art form and audience, Brecht took the ideogrammatic form of the frame as model for his own development of the social *gest*. Their montage assembly left for the audience a plurality of possible meanings. As Roland Barthes suggests, 'nothing separates the scene in epic theatre from the Eisenstein shot (except that in Brecht the tableau is offered to the spectator for criticism, not for adherence)' (1977: 71).

Barthes's distinction is an important one. The work of Meyerhold, Piscator, and Eisenstein was a necessary prolusion to Brecht's epic theatre in breaking with technical conventions and establishing new audiences, but it did not ultimately change stage–audience relations. The performance was, as Barthes indicates, offered for 'adherence'. The shock value of their theatre practice, literally surrounding the audience with innovation, had the effect of inducing the desired mass response. While Brecht's theatre employs many of the same techniques, it does so in a more interrogatory manner. As his critique of the American entertainment industry indicates, Brecht felt that innovation in itself did not necessarily challenge existing modes of production and reception:

Hollywood's and Broadway's methods of manufacturing certain excitements and emotions may possibly be artistic, but their only use is to offset the fearful boredom induced in any audience by the endless repetition of falsehoods and stupidities. This technique was developed and is used in order to stimulate interest in things and ideas that are not in the interest of the audience.

(Willett 1964: 160)

Not unlike the Hollywood/Broadway practitioners, Meyer-hold and Piscator relied on the complete emotional involvement of the audience, albeit with the intention of political action rather than the economic motivations of the former. The virtual mass hysteria sought by Meyerhold and Piscator (somewhat the opposite extreme to the passivity sought by naturalist theatre) was, however, rejected by Brecht. His theatre looked to an audience which was participatory, but thoughtful; to reiterate Barthes, it was 'for criticism, not for adherence'. This crucial difference between Brecht's theatre and that of the earlier 'revolutionaries', Meyerhold, Eisenstein, and Piscator, is marked by Brecht's concept of *Verfremdung*.

Of all the critical commentary on Brecht, it is this central term of the *Verfremdungseffekt* which has attracted the most attention and the most controversy.[2] As other components of Brechtian dramaturgy can be linked to an emerging oppositional culture which broke with conventional practice, the *Verfremdungseffekt* can also be linked to earlier work. Its theoretical precursor is found in the work of Russian formalist Victor Shklovsky and, in particular, in his explanations of defamiliarization (*ostranenie*). Shklovsky discusses defamiliarization as the device by which literature is recognized as literature. It is a means by which the perceptive processes of the reader (audience) are challenged; it makes objects 'unfamiliar' (Shklovsky 1965: 12). But Brecht's *Verfremdung* is not simply a translation into dramaturgical practice of Shklovsky's *ostranenie*.[3] In Brecht's usage, the term is not merely part of an aesthetic code, but positioned politically. Fredric Jameson points out:

The purpose of the Brechtian estrangement-effect is... a political one in the most thoroughgoing sense of the word; it is, as Brecht insisted over and over, to make you aware that the objects and institutions you thought to be natural were really only historical: the result of change, they themselves henceforth become in their turn changeable.

(Jameson 1972: 58)

Thus, through the *Verfremdungseffekt*, the stage–audience relationship is politicized in a way quite unlike that in the theatre of Meyerhold and Piscator, or in the cinema of Eisenstein. The self-reflexive nature of text/performance is not simply a means of foregrounding a specific political issue (as in the case of Piscator's *§218*) or eliciting a specific political response (as in Eisenstein's *Strike*). Neither is it, as Sylvia Harvey reminds us, simply an appeal to audiences jaded by stale naturalism through 'that particular sort of aesthetic pleasure which is offered to highly educated audiences on the basis of a recognition of the transgression of certain aesthetic codes and taboos' (1982: 52). Brecht's foregrounding of the theatrical process and establishment of *Verfremdung* in stage–audience communication operates in a context that questions not specific concerns, aesthetic or political, but instead questions those social relations which are generally accepted as universal or natural. Again it is evident how Brecht calls the audience's attention to theatre as cultural institution, an apparatus of the society in which it exists:

We are free to discuss any innovation which doesn't threaten its [the theatre's] social function – that of providing an evening's entertainment. We are not free to discuss those which threaten to change its function, possibly by fusing it with the education system or with the organs of mass communication. Society absorbs via the apparatus whatever it needs in order to reproduce itself. This means that an innovation will pass if it is calculated to rejuvenate existing society, but not if it is going to change it – irrespective whether the form of the society in question is good or bad.

(Willett 1964: 34)

Understanding of Brecht's *Verfremdungseffekt* (or perhaps more accurately the lack of understanding) has not, however, illuminated strategies of audience reception. The confusion arises in what seems to be a paradox. On the one hand, *Verfremdung*, as distance, seems virtually to exclude the audience and, on the other, it is part of a process where the 'episodes must not succeed one another indistinguishably but must give us a chance to interpose our judgment' (Willett 1964: 201). Stephen Heath's consideration of *Verfremdung* as process is helpful:

[It] is not that the spectator is held separate to the action of the play and, from there, effectively placed in a relation of identification to the hero as totalising consciousness, but rather that the spectator is himself included in the movement from ideology to real, from illusion to objective truth (the political analysis of forms of representation in their determinations, the activity of the play).

(Heath 1974: 116)

Verfremdung, then, displaces the audience's perception of stage events and looks for an interactive relationship. Brecht, in a dialogue with playwright Fredrich Wolf, emphasizes this refusal of separation. While empathy for a character (either by audience or actor) is to be avoided in performance, emotion is not denied by the *Verfremdungseffekt*:

It is not true, though it is sometimes suggested, that epic theatre (which is not simply undramatic theatre, as is also sometimes suggested) proclaims the slogan: 'Reason this side, Emotion (feeling) that.' It by no means renounces emotion, least of all the sense of justice, the urge to freedom, and righteous anger; it is so far from renouncing these that it does not even assume their presence, but tries to arouse or to reinforce them. The 'attitude of criticism' which it tries to awaken in its audience cannot be passionate enough for it.

(Willett 1964: 227)

Despite the misunderstandings surrounding the *Verfremdungseffekt*, Brecht's work sets up a number of starting points for the study of audiences in theatres. It consolidated a developing theatre practice self-consciously concerned with production and reception. Performance, hitherto almost hermetically sealed, demanding of the audience only the role of receiver, became essentially a co-operative venture. Thus a role of activity was established for audiences and their centrality to the dramatic process acknowledged. This not only encouraged what Althusser calls 'the production of a new spectator, an actor who starts where the performance ends' (1969: 151), but questioned the dominant ('natural') model of stage–audience communication. Citing the parallel between Brecht's stress on audience involvement and radical models of the communication process, Carl Gardner explains:

> The 'receiver' of any 'message' is never passive – here we see the false analogy with the radio-receiver – but is an active *producer* of meanings. It is precisely one of the ideological functions of the bourgeois media to obscure this – the relations of consumption of the cinema, for example, attempt to reduce the process of *creation* of meanings on the part of the audience to an absolute minimum.
>
> (Gardner 1979: 5–6)

Brecht's theatre resisted the idea of an obvious and fixed perceptive process. Instead it identified this process as one bound in the conventions and codes that form the discourse of a particular ideology. The ideological basis of the play will not necessarily coincide with that of the audience (or indeed of the performers or of the producing company) but it is this interaction which will constitute performance. Because of his stress on the theatrical experience as contract, ideologically situated, Brecht has, not surprisingly, become an important reference point for politically-committed cultural theorists. His ideas lie behind, and support, the parameters of their research. Janet Wolff, for example, challenges the concept of aesthetic autonomy precisely through the relationships Brecht has identified:

> [T]he nature of the audience is determined, amongst other things, by the nature and practice of culture in general in that society . . . by the general ideology of that society and of its sub-divisions, and by the general mode of production and relations of production of that society. In other words, the possibility for the reception of radical or 'negative' culture is itself determined by the economic base, and by the extent and type of autonomy accorded to general and aesthetic ideology by the stage of development of that society.
>
> (Wolff 1981: 93–4)

As a complement to the influence of his theory, Brecht's plays have been central in the creation and development of recent oppositional theatre. In the United States, there were landmark productions of *In the Jungle of the Cities* and *Man is Man* by Beck and Malina's Living Theater. In Britain, by way of Joan Littlewood and Ewan McColl's work as well as the Berliner Ensemble's 1956 London performances, the plays have provided the primary model. Certainly the reception history of Brecht in Britain substantiates Wolff's system of cultural relations. Immediately following the 1956 visit of Brecht's troupe, there was a general rush 'to be Brechtian'. First attempts (such as John Osborne's *Luther*) did little more than replicate the surface characteristics of epic theatre. Where writers more consciously tried to translate the political impetus of epic theatre into a British format (as in John Arden's *Armstrong's Last Goodnight*), their plays were generally poorly received and almost always misunderstood. Edward Bond bore the title of the British Brecht as criticism rather than praise. Only with the emergence over a longer period of time of an oppositional theatre practice was Brecht's theory understood and successful productions of his plays undertaken. Nevertheless, as Steve Gooch's description of the transfer of a successful production of *The Mother* from the East End of London to the Roundhouse at Chalk Farm (Hampstead) makes evident, this possibility was still precarious: 'Although the production and personnel were identical, the particular experience the show offered was vastly altered by the move to a bigger building, with a different producing management and an NW3 audience rather than the usual pilgrims to E1' (1984: 50). Gooch makes the point that in the 1970s concerns over content and style were joined by concerns about audience and theatre. As he puts it, 'the struggles to "get it right" were considerable' (1984: 50).

By the late 1970s in Britain, Brecht's plays were recuperated as classic texts. In 1976, the National Theatre staged an exhibition of Brecht in Britain; in 1980, *The Life of Galileo* was produced for the Olivier. More recently (1986), the Berliner Ensemble made its North American debut in Toronto. David Burgess comments that the Ensemble's production of *The Threepenny Opera* 'would have done the D'Oyley Carte Company proud' (1987: 76) and that performances of *The Caucasian Chalk Circle*

33

reinforced 'accepted values and confirmed prejudices just as surely as a Sylvester Stallone movie or a Noel Coward play' (1987: 77). Burgess continues:

> Ironically, it [the production of *The Caucasian Chalk Circle*] taught that official culture can co-opt a play of any political stripe, and make it serve its own static ends; it taught, as Brecht pointed out in his Short Organum and elsewhere, that a production which is only an aesthetic success, can be a disaster when considered in other ways.
>
> (Burgess 1987: 77)

The academic debate of Brecht's *Verfremdung* has placed even more emphasis upon audience participation in theatre. Dana Polan suggests that distance can function as an indicator that usual modes of reception are ideologically determined and that Brecht's theatre 'break[s] down the socially unquestioning way that people watch spectacle' (1985: 96). Polan's example of Bruce Conner's film, *Report*, is well chosen. Conner, refused footage of the Kennedy assassination by the CBS, made a film of all the events surrounding the shooting without that central incident. The screen images disappear at the point of the assassination, leaving only the soundtrack (composed of radio news coverage). *Report* demonstrates, as Polan notes, that we never 'know' an event but only its media coverage:

> *Report* takes a typical moviegoing desire and quotes it through a critical stance. In one loop-printing, the car moves toward its destination but is bounced back by the editing. The next shots are from the synchronic presentation; this, *Report* shows us, is the real event, not the documentary payoff our habits of viewing have led us to want from films promising to be 'about' the Kennedy assassination.
>
> (Polan 1985: 97)

Howard Brenton and David Hare's play *Pravda* tackles the medium of newspaper reporting. They show that 'truth' (played upon in the title) is always mediated by social, economic, and political considerations and that it is inevitable that ideals of 'truth' (represented in the character Andrew May) are compromised to the exigencies of a controlling ideology. Like Conner's film, *Pravda* refuses the audience their customary explanations. Hare, in an interview (significantly given to a mainstream newspaper), makes clear the propagandist element of so-called news-reporting: 'You could say all news is a matter of opinion. Which is plainly Fleet Street's line of defence. But the spin that's put on almost all the stories you read? Are we supposed to believe it's all one way by coincidence?' (1984: 37).

Brecht's work then has been central in two ways: he has shown that the media institutions are always contingent, and has foregrounded the audience as already-always interpellated by ideology.[4] What he has laid bare becomes the core of radical theatre and film theory. Claire Johnston's polemic for a Marxist film culture emphatically inscribes the relationship between film and audience, specified both historically and institutionally, as crucial to 'the possibility of working through strategies in relation to the ideological struggle' (1979: 86). Chris Rawlence looks to the practice of theatre companies such as Red Ladder (with which he is involved) to 'act as a catalyst in reminding this audience from the working class of its own cultural and political potential' (1979: 64). In any production-reception contract, therefore, the audience's response will be shaped by the general system of cultural relations as identified by Wolff. Within that system, their receptive process will be immediately directed by the material conditions of production and the positioning of the world on stage vis-à-vis its extratheatrical referents.[5]

Above all, Brecht's work makes manifest the productive role of theatre audiences and positions that role ideologically. Any research in reception then must also look to production and deal with issues which are cultural as well as individual. Sylvia Harvey emphasizes this necessity:

[T]he ability to decipher certain codes or certain code-breaking operations is culturally and socially determined; and as there are institutions of cultural production and consumption so also there are institutions of reading; a reader approaches a text from within a particular 'apparatus of reading.' Any cultural producer who fails to investigate the relationship between social class and reading competence produces in a vacuum.

(Harvey 1982: 55)

It is this question that reader-response theory might be expected to address.

READER-RESPONSE THEORY

The term reader-response has been coined retroactively to cover developments in theory concerned with the relationship between text and reader. The explosion of interest in the reading process started in the late 1960s and continued through the 1970s, and this umbrella term of reader-response now incorporates a diversity of approaches to textual reception. While reader-centred studies continue to be published,[6] reader-response no longer occupies a central place in critical theory. It can now be considered an historically-situated movement with events of the late 1960s, both in academia and more generally, shaping its development. More recent post-structuralist theory has made evident the limitations of the reader-response approach, but the diversity of investigations undertaken does, however, offer some useful models for this particular study. There is, at least in part, a response to Harvey's concern with the 'apparatus of reading'. Indeed, without the existing corpus of reader-response theory, it is unlikely that there would be the current concern of drama theorists for the role of the audience.

In her introduction to *The Reader in the Text*, a 1980 anthology sub-titled *Essays on Audience and Interpretation*, Susan Suleiman describes the general trend in the humanities 'toward self-reflexiveness – questioning and making explicit the assumptions that ground the methods of the discipline, and concurrently the investigator's role in delimiting or even in constituting the object of study' (Suleiman and Crosman 1980: 4). This 'self-reflexiveness', she argues, 'has its analogue in the principles of relativity and uncertainty as they emerged in physics early in this century' (Suleiman and Crosman 1980: 4). Furthermore, self-reflexivity had, of course, surfaced as a particular interest in texts. John Fowles's novel *The French Lieutenant's Woman* (1969) and Peter Handke's play *Offending the Audience* (1966) are well-known examples of works which address the assumptions of their art and the role of their audiences, and which anticipate a theory with the same concerns.

More specifically, the political milieu of the late 1960s

shaped emergent reader-response theory. Challenges to dominant social and political practices had widespread repercussions for academic institutions. Pressures for change came in many forms and areas; the events of 1968 in Paris are an obvious example. In a period when the ideology and practices of academia were under attack, it is not difficult to understand the appeal of theory which devolved power from the traditional loci of authority in favour of a more egalitarian process.

In North America, reader-response emerged as an assault on the hegemony of New Criticism and particularly, as Jane Tompkins points out in her introduction to *Reader-Response Criticism*, 'in direct opposition to the New Critical dictum issued by Wimsatt and Beardsley in "The Affective Fallacy" (1980: ix). Mary Louise Pratt's assessment of New Criticism and reader-response in the United States makes some valid points about their relationship:

The rise of American New Criticism is often seen as part of a general shift in the academy from a stress on encyclopedic knowledge, to a stress on knowledge as technique or method. New Criticism is both an agent in this shift of values and a pedagogical response to it. With students who have technical knowledge and lack encyclopedic knowledge, what you have left to teach *from* is the text, and what you have left to teach are techniques. In analogous fashion, reader-response criticism and pedagogy clearly capitalize on the culture's intense focus on self-knowledge and self-observation, and on the validity now accorded to personal and intuitive knowledge. Students come to us trained, like ourselves, in observing their own responses, in talking about them, and in considering them important...this is an improvement over formalism, if only because it is true, among other things, that readers make meaning.

(Pratt 1986: 27)

True it may be, but the tentativeness of early reader-response studies such as Walter Slatoff's *With Respect to Readers* (1970) demonstrates the magnitude of the revolution needed to overthrow the supremacy of the text. While Slatoff ultimately remained resolutely anti-theory, his book nevertheless traces the issues which were to dominate theoretical investigations of later reader-response theory.

One omission in Slatoff's text was consideration of the responses of the unconscious mind as part of an individual's experience in the realization of a text. Slatoff acknowledged this gap and directed readers to Norman N. Holland's *The Dynamics of Literary Response* (1968). This work, as well as Holland's later books, made a significant contribution to reader-response theory in establishing a subjective, or psycho-analytic, approach to the act of reading. Psychoanalytic theory, and particularly the work of Freud, has led to the considerable interest of some theatre practitioners in drama which seeks to express the workings of the inner mind.

Freud's interest in audience response is evident from his discussions of *Hamlet* and *Oedipus Rex*. The success of *Oedipus* – and the failure of many modern tragedies – Freud accounts for in the presentation of the protagonist who falls in love with his mother and who is jealous of his father, 'a universal event of early childhood' (Freud 1953–74: vol. V 265). The effect of the play, then, is to evoke an Aristotelean *catharsis* in the audience. Freud writes: 'While the poet, as he unravels the past, brings to light the guilt of Oedipus, he is at the same time compelling us to recognize our own inner minds, in which those same impulses, though suppressed, are still to be found' (1953–74: vol. V 263). Through the double distancing of Sophocles's fiction and the actor's performance, the members of the audience experience wish-fulfilment and a purgation of their own Oedipus complex. *Hamlet*, according to Freud, works in much the same way, although in the case of this play's protagonist, the impulses remain repressed, as in life. Freud suggests that it is necessary to the dramatic form that these impulses, although recognizable, remain unnamed: 'so that in the spectator too the process is carried through with his attention averted, and he is in the grip of his emotions instead of taking stock of what is happening' (1953–74: vol. VII 309). Holland's theories of reading, with their fundamental reliance on Freud's work, are thus helpful in approaching some aspects of the audience's experience of theatre. Discussion in *The Dynamics of Literary Response* is initiated by a question: 'What is the relation between the patterns he finds objectively in the text and a reader's subjective experience of the text?' (Holland 1968: xiii).

The first stage of Holland's psychoanalytic model is to establish that all texts have 'a central core of fantasy' (Holland 1968: 62) and that the fantasies are handled 'by techniques that resemble familiar defensive or adaptive strategies' (1968: 58). Fantasy, however, generally provides anxiety as well as pleasure. But, through the agents of form and meaning, the fantasy will be 'modified to reduce the anxiety' (Holland 1968: 182). With an analysis of Brecht's dramatic technique and of Ionesco's absurdist drama, theatre which denies pre-existent textual *meaning*, Holland demonstrates how readers make, and need, meaning. In Holland's terms, the metatheatrical nature of Brechtian drama foregrounds for the audience their willing suspension of disbelief. Ionesco provides nothing in which to believe and this creates a need in the audience which they endeavour to fulfil through their 'own problem-solving faculties' (Holland 1968: 179). The evidence of this need for meaning suggests to Holland that meaning, like form, acts as 'a defense to permit the partial gratification of fantasy' (Holland 1968: 183). In other words, meaning provides for the reader 'a mastery of the fantasy content' (Holland 1968: 185). The pleasure derived from the reading process equates with 'the feeling of having a fantasy of our own and our own associations to it managed and controlled but at the same time allowed a limited expression and gratification' (Holland 1968: 311–12).

This early study by Holland shares with Slatoff's book the reluctance to dismiss completely the objectivity of the text and again, although for very different reasons, suggests a necessary coexistence. Both texts and readers, Holland argues, hold a central core of fantasy and it is the interaction of the two which produces meaning. As reader-response inquiry became a more familiar approach, the need to measure it against New Criticism lessened, and oppositions of objective and subjective were replaced by other debates. Holland's later work, at least in part for these reasons, shows a departure from his initial model. The fantasy Holland once located in the text he now identifies as a creation of the reader's own drives. Interpretation now is solely a function of the reader through what Holland describes as an identity theme. Different interpretations of a text result from the different identity themes of critics (Holland 1975: 122). Holland's governing principle is that:

[I]dentity re-creates itself.... That is, all of us, as we read, use the literary work to symbolize and finally to replicate ourselves. We work out through the text our own characteristic patterns of desire and adaptation. We interact with the work, making it part of our own psychic economy and making ourselves part of the literary work – as we interpret it.

(Holland 1975: 124)

One problem with Holland's theory is, as Steven Mailloux points out[7], a difficulty in explaining how, if we all possess unique identity themes which we replicate in our readings of literary texts, views are often shared. Jonathan Culler's criticisms are more serious. He points out that Holland has merely 'transferred the concept of unity from text to person' (Culler 1980: 55). While Holland's work may be considered marginal in terms of literary theory, his interests have been shared by some of the most important and influential theatre practitioners in this century. Most obviously we look to Antonin Artaud. In his first manifesto for the Theatre of Cruelty, Artaud states:

Theatre will never be itself again, that is to say will never be able to form truly illusive means, unless it provides the audience with truthful distillations of dreams where its taste for crime, its erotic obsessions, its savageness, its fantasies, its utopian sense of life and objects, even its cannibalism, do not gush out on an illusory, make-believe, but on an inner level.

(Artaud 1981: 70–1)

Artaud also sought to abandon what he saw as a 'foolish adherence to texts' (1981: 59) in order to re-situate theatre as an immediate experience for both performers and audience. To go beyond the simple fascination with a show's 'magic', he looked to a theatre of affect: 'To reforge the links, the chain of a rhythm when audiences saw their own real lives in a show. We must allow audiences to identify with the show breath by breath and beat by beat' (Artaud 1981: 95). While Artaud never quite matched the intensity of his vision in his own theatre practice, his ideas have been pursued by other theatre practitioners and the search for a theatre which spoke on and to 'an inner level' has been continued. The theatre of Jerzy Grotowski is the most notable example, but the earlier work of Tadeusz Kantor, some projects of Malina and Beck, and some productions by Peter Brook have shown a similar foregrounding of, to use Artaud's term, 'an inner level'. Grotowski has written: 'We are concerned with the spectator who has genuine spiritual needs and who really wishes, through confrontation with the performance, to analyse himself' (1968: 40). Allowing an interchangeability of performance and literary text, this aim is very close to Holland's proposition that the reader interacts with a work, incorporating it as part of his psyche, and making himself part of the work (Holland 1975: 124).

The confused reception of those performances which indeed sought the activation of an audience's identity theme(s) suggests that this is a process which audiences have been trained to resist and repress. Peter Brook writes that the audience who attended the first public performance of his experimental programme came 'with the usual mixture of condescension, playfulness and faint disapproval that the notion of the *avant garde* arouses' (1968: 145). His production of Artaud's *The Jet of Blood* received a mixed reception: 'Part of the audience was immediately fascinated, part giggled' (1968: 145). While Holland would, no doubt, explain the laughter as defence, it is nevertheless evident that audiences do resist the immediate relationship sought by Artaudian theatre. A production, it seems, is more likely to reveal its director's identity theme than to call into play the psychic economy of the audience.

Perhaps surprisingly, Holland's theory appears to have been ignored by psychoanalytic critics of theatre texts. Roy Huss's *The Mindscapes of Art*, where Holland's work is acknowledged as a 'milestone' and applauded for its emphasis on 'the integrative function of art' (1986: 15), is typical in confining consideration to text and author. With Holland's work so praised, Huss might well have extended his criticism beyond an examination of fantasy *within* the dramatic texts, beyond psychobiographical analysis, to include the response of

41

reader/audience. A notable addition to the field, however, is Christian Metz's 'The Fiction Film and Its Spectator: A Meta-psychological Study' (1976). Metz bases his investigations on Freud's theory of (day)dreams, and his findings suggest that Holland's pursuit of the reader's private world might well find some application in a model of theatrical communication. Metz poses the question: '[H]ow does the spectator effect the mental leap which alone can lead him from the perceptual donnée, consisting of moving visual and sonic impressions, to the constitution of a fictional universe, from an objectively real but denied signifier to an imaginary but psychologically real signified?' (1976: 85). For the theatre spectator, the signifiers are, of course, present as part of the on-stage fictional world, but otherwise the relationship Metz suggests holds. Metz provides answers in the analysis of the 'waking sleep' under-taken by the filmic spectator and it does indeed seem that psychoanalytic theory might well fill some of the otherwise unchartable gaps of the perceptive process.

While Holland's theory rests on the existence of an indi-vidual's identity theme, the theory of Stanley Fish has come to rely on a concept of 'interpretive communities'. Fish's early work, like that of Slatoff and Holland, made only a cautious break with text-centred criticism. His 'Affective Stylistics' turned attention away 'from the spatial context of a page and its observable regularities to the temporal context of a mind and its experiences' (Fish 1980: 91). At this stage Fish relies on the concept of an informed reader, defined by his/her linguistic competence, mature semantic knowledge, and literary competence (1980: 48). The text, however, remains important as an objective entity which, in particular ways, manipulates the reader, however informed. From this point Fish moved to discussion of language as constituted by the commitments and attitudes of those who produce it; literature is 'ordinary' language around which we have drawn a frame (1980: 107–9).[8]

Fish's conclusions about language took him into his next, and perhaps most influential, theory: the idea of the interpretive community:

Interpretive communities are made up of those who share interpretive strategies not for reading (in the conventional sense) but for writing texts, for constituting their properties and assigning their intentions. In other words, these strategies exist prior to the act of reading and therefore determine the shape of what is read rather than, as is usually assumed, the other way round.

(Fish 1980: 171)

Critical debates occur not because of any intrinsic textual stability, but 'because of a stability in the makeup of interpretive communities and therefore in the opposing positions they make possible' (Fish 1980: 171). Not all interpretations of texts will be accepted. Indeed, some can be ruled out. These are the result of interpretive strategies which, at the time of their making, lie outside those authorized by literary institutions (Fish 1980: 342). These institutions – comprising, of course, interpretive communities – do, however, change. Interpretive communities are not stable, holding privileged points of view, but represent different interpretive strategies held by different literary cultures at different times.

Diachronic analysis of play reception corroborates Fish's concept of the interpretive community. The reception history of Harold Pinter's *The Birthday Party* is exemplary. In 1958 the play premiered in London at the Lyric Hammersmith, and the review on 20 May from the drama critic of *The Times* was less than enthusiastic: 'Mr. Pinter's effects are neither comic nor terrifying: they are never more than puzzling, and after a little while we tend to give up the puzzle in despair' (*The Times* 1958: 3). The critic's confusion and despair clearly extended to the audience at large and the run survived only a few performances. By contrast, pre-London performances of *The Birthday Party* in Oxford and Cambridge had been more enthusiastically received where audiences were likely to be constituted, at least in part, by the local academic community. Thus they would be more aware of, and receptive to, the traditions of the European avant-garde underlying Pinter's play. Furthermore, when *The Birthday Party* was revived at the Aldwych in London some six years later, it was heralded as a success and enjoyed a much longer run. On 18 June 1964 a *Times* review declared: '*The Birthday Party* is the Ur-text of modern British drama: if John Osborne fired new authors into writing, Pinter showed them how to write' (*The Times* 1964:

43

18). In Fish's terms, the experiences of 1958 show the contrasting responses to Pinter's play by different interpretive communities and those of 1964 demonstrate that the interpretive strategies of the London theatre-going public had been redefined and reshaped by an increased exposure to 'new' drama. Indeed, Fish's assertion that texts are accorded value not by any intrinsic properties but by interpretive communities (1980: 338) can be extended to include even the existence of those texts. Historically there has been virtually no academic or theatre company interest in drama by women playwrights of the nineteenth and early twentieth centuries. Yet, recent research clearly demonstrates that women's theatre was not only in existence at this time, but in fact prolific. In Britain, Mrs Worthington's Daughters, a feminist theatre company, has revived hitherto 'lost' plays and these productions have afforded further re-evaluation.

The role of the drama critic is another area which might usefully be explored through Fish's idea of interpretive communities. Patrice Pavis, in his analysis of the collected reviews of Peter Brook's production of *Measure for Measure* at the Bouffes du Nord in 1978, has emphasized the shared strategies within the genre of theatre criticism. Reviews, Pavis found, converged in discussion of the theatre space and type of *mise en scène* in order to distinguish Brook's work from more ordinary productions. What Pavis finds most remarkable is the general inadequacy of critical discourse: 'Saying that the *mise en scène* is "cold", "dense", "self-effacing", "assured", "adroit", "of a refreshing lack of affectation" does not really help the reader to perceive it' (1982: 103). He concludes:

Finally, the critical discourse – probably because Brook has the status of a public monument – does not take the risk of discouraging or encouraging the public to go and see the play.

The unexpressed judgment seems to be: 'obviously it is good because it is Shakespeare, directed by Brook, although it hasn't got that particular twist of the novel and the exceptional'.

(Pavis 1982: 104)

Clearly, as Pavis points out (1982: 104–5), the discourse of the critics reflects shared assumptions of what constitutes theatre.

Pavis sees the theatre critic's role as 'voice for the arts' with at least partial freedom from the political assumptions underlying the newspaper or journal represented, although it all reflects 'what Barthes called the bourgeois sense of the quantitative and the visible' (Pavis 1982: 105). In the 'alternative' press, however, theatre criticism has been overtly linked to the political bias of the publication represented. The arrival in the 1970s of London's *Time Out* was without doubt instrumental in the establishment of emerging feminist and gay theatre. The reviews in *Time Out* were important not only for their radical political alignment, but for their information value, bringing to attention a wealth of theatre which was outside both traditional theatre spaces and traditional publicity mechanisms. It is a role which continues. Alisa Solomon, one of several theatre critics for *Village Voice*, has stressed the interactive relationship between marginalized theatre companies and those reviewers seen as sympathetic to their political and/or performance objectives. She notes, however, that any unfavourable reviews might be instrumental in the loss of financial grants for a company whose objectives she, in general, supports. The interpretive communities of theatre critics are clearly influential but not necessarily helpful, either to the companies reviewed or to the public seeking their opinions. This highlights aspects of the interpretive community which Fish explores only in passing, its inevitably political underpinning and relationship to the dominant ideology. The preceding examples of the repertory of a company such as Mrs Worthington's Daughters and the concerns of critics such as Solomon underscore the link between power and knowledge made explicit in Foucault's work. Fish, on the other hand, ignores politics and, indeed, any notion of the role of class, race, or gender in the constitution of the interpretive community.

A number of critics have noted Fish's reluctance to deal with the political implications of the interpretive community, and they generally concur that this is a deliberate strategy. William Cain writes:

The thrust of Fish's theory is radical and liberating, for he subverts the myth that an authority is a natural fact, and that we are forever bound to the existing shape of our institutions. Yet even as Fish points toward the radical force of his theory, he weakens it, turning his theory's demystifying power into a restatement of authority's necessary dominion over us. As Fish's concern for 'constraints' in his early work testifies, he is strongly committed to order, discipline, and control.

(Cain 1981: 87)

The theory of Wolfgang Iser is a notable counterpart to Fish's work, particularly in light of their publicly expressed disagreements.[9] Developed from the work of phenomenologists Edmund Husserl and Roman Ingarden, Iser sets up a three-way approach to the analysis of reading: consideration of the text, of the reader, and, most importantly, the conditions of interaction between the two. At the centre is the concept of the implied reader which 'offers a means of describing the process whereby textual structures are transmuted through ideational activities into personal experiences' (Iser 1978: 38). Yet Iser's real interest is the text itself. *The Implied Reader* (1974) is largely a study of strategies in the novel genre and the later *The Act of Reading*, while more theoretical, often makes recourse to the same textual examples.

In his phenomenology of reading, Iser explores the interaction between text and reader. The textual repertoires and strategies 'simply offer a frame within which the reader must construct for himself the aesthetic object' (Iser 1978: 107). Wandering viewpoint is Iser's explanation for 'the inter-subjective structure of the process through which a text is transferred and translated' (1978: 108). The reader measures what he or she reads against events of the past and expectations for the future, and Iser suggests that this leads to syntheses which are 'neither manifested in the printed text, nor produced solely by the reader's imagination, and the project of which they consist are themselves of a dual nature: they emerge from the reader, but they are also guided by signals which "project" themselves into him' (1978: 135).

Iser's final stage is concerned with communication. Successful communication results when reading is controlled by the text and this, Iser argues, is achieved through blanks and negations. Blanks represent what is concealed in a text, the drawing-in of the reader where he or she has left to make connections (Iser 1978: 168). Negations 'invoke familiar or determinate elements only to cancel them out. What is cancelled, however, remains in view, and thus brings about modifications in the reader's attitude toward what is familiar or determinate – in other words, he is guided to adopt a position *in relation* to the text' (Iser 1978: 169). Blanks allow the reader to bring a story to life, to assign meaning, and '[b]y making his decision he implicitly acknowledges the inexhaustibility of the test; at the same time it is this very inexhaustibility that forces him to make his decision' (Iser 1974: 280).

In *The Act of Reading*, Iser discusses how 'a controlled proliferation of blanks' (1978: 191) can bring commercial success. His examples are Dickens's serialized novels and the preview 'short' for a movie. Both, he suggests, 'use the technique of strategic interruption in order to activate the basic structure of the ideational process for purely commercial purposes' (1978: 192). The strategic breaks in Dickens's serials and their effect on the reading audience bring to mind similar strategic breaks in the theatrical performance. Curtains or blackouts to denote act breaks or scene changes clearly work in the manner of Iser's blanks. They generally herald a change in perspective and permit the audience some time for the juggling of expectations and memories that Iser defines. The intermission is, of course, the most pronounced form of strategic break and, with the generally traditional rush to the bar, it might well be considered a strategic interruption for commercial purposes! The comments of the theatre reviewers in Stoppard's *The Real Inspector Hound* provide, in parodic form, further evidence of an audience's creative exercising in any intermission. The 'action' breaks with Inspector Hound's dramatic question, 'And now – who killed Simon Gascoyne? And why?' (Stoppard 1968: 34–5). This leads the drama critics Moon and Birdboot first to a naive response (the play as reality – Simon Gascoyne got what he deserved), and then to their own personal preoccupations. Finally, they respond as professional drama critics. Clearly Stoppard agrees with Pavis

47

that newspaper reviews tell prospective spectators little or nothing about a play:

> BIRDBOOT (*clears throat*): It is at this point that the play for me comes alive. The groundwork has been well and truly laid, and the author has taken the trouble to learn from the masters of the genre. He has created a real situation, and few will doubt his ability to resolve it with a startling denouement...

> MOON: If we examine this more closely, and I think close examination is the least tribute that this play deserves, I think we will find that within the austere framework of what is seen to be on one level a country-house weekend, and what a useful symbol that is, the author has given us – yes, I will go so far – he has given us the human condition.

> (Stoppard 1968: 35–6)

Certainly, in the terms of theatre performance, where the reading time is controlled by the performer and not the audience, any opportunities for review (as in scene changes or intermission) have the potential to provoke the process Iser identifies in an exaggerated form. Lack of opportunity can lead to an intensity of activity when these few invitations arise.

While for Fish and Holland the reader was all important, for Iser the necessarily interactive process of reading is predominant. In light of this, Iser's attention to the experience of the theatre audience is particularly interesting. He examines the quality of laughter peculiar to Beckett's drama. With evidence to suggest that laughter tends to be individual, accompanied by an 'unprecedented degree of discomfort' (1981a: 140), and then stifled, he sets up the following thesis:

> The mutual influence [of literary work and human behaviour] is at its most effective when the work releases modes of conduct that are not required or are suppressed by our everyday needs, but which – when they *are* released – clearly bring out the aesthetic function of the work: namely, to make present those elements of life which were lost or buried and to merge them with that which is

already present, thus changing the actual makeup of our present.

(Iser 1981a: 141)

Comedy, Iser argues, derives from situations of opposition which, instead of resolving as winner and loser, generally provoke a domino effect of losses. Instability is thus created, an effect which extends to spectators. Drawing on Helmuth Plessner's *Laughing and Crying*, Iser proposes that laughter results not only from this instability in the on-stage world, but also from the upsetting of the spectator's cognitive and emotive capabilities. In psychoanalytic terms, it is a defence mechanism. But what happens, Iser speculates, if this declaration of non-seriousness 'is also nudged and toppled? Supposing that, at the very moment when we have recognized the non-seriousness as a means of self-liberation, it suddenly turns into seriousness again? In such cases, we can no longer escape from the tension, and instead, our laughter dies on our lips' (1981a: 145). For Iser, this is the effect of Beckett's drama.

Adopting Jurij Lotman's term Iser describes *Waiting for Godot* as a series of minus-functions. In other words, all its components thwart conventional expectations. For instance, Estragon's line opening the play 'Nothing to be done' (Beckett 1956: 9) – indicates an ending rather than a beginning. Frequent laughter arises from audience superiority but it is, Iser suggests, a laughter which is short circuited by the play. Meanings we construct out of the failed actions are inevitably undercut by the play itself. The audience of the Beckett play does not, then, watch a comic situation; 'instead, the comedy *happens* to him, because he experiences his own interpretations as that which is to be excluded' (Iser 1981a: 158). The moment of laughter, Iser decides, depends 'on the disposition of the individual spectator so that laughter as a reaction to and a relief from his entanglement is deprived of a collective confirmation at the very moment which it is most needed' (1981a: 160). Laughter is stifled not only by the recognition of defective interpretation, but by the embarrassing realization that the laughter is not generally shared. *Endgame* takes language as a game, Iser purports, and the play destroys the possibility of making meaning. He writes: 'The constant obliteration of linguistic referents results in structured blanks, which would

49

remain empty if the spectator did not feel the compulsion to fill them in' (1981a: 176). As audiences construct meaning for the actions in *Godot*, so they perform for the words of *Endgame* with the result, for Iser, that they become the actors undertaking the roles which Estragon and Vladimir carried out in the earlier play. The result of this is to place the spectator in a 'position of detachment by giving him the chance to see himself in the role of a comic figure – a role he is compelled to play because of his own basic experiences' (Iser 1981a: 181). Thus, Iser argues, the spectator is both producer and receiver of the drama and this 'makes it possible for a decentered subjectivity to be communicated as an experience of self in the form of projects continually created and rejected by the spectator' (1981a: 181). Iser finds Beckett's plays ultimately dissatisfying and he is undoubtedly right to see Beckett's theatre as an attack on the macrocosmic interpretive community of audiences. Cultural training produces an inescapable desire to make meaning. But Iser's interpretation of the dramatic structures as systems of non-fulfilment (Lotman's minus-functions) seems naive. Perhaps at first audiences were unaccustomed to Beckettian theatre practice and responses were, as we saw in the earlier example of Pinter's *The Birthday Party*, at best confused. But certainly after Martin Esslin's publication of *The Theatre of the Absurd* (1961) and, more importantly, the opportunity to *see* more such plays, this theatre practice became familiar and thus generally expected from playwrights like Beckett and Pinter.

Iser suggests that gaps are a common strategy in the modern text, used to provoke the reader into seeking closure, only to find the task impossible (1974: 280). It might well be argued, however, that gaps in fact merely provoke readers into accepting gaps. In any event, the gap is obviously a strategy in Beckett's work. With Iser's own acknowledgement of this general practice, why then does he expect audiences to be unsettled by this procedure? Audience laughter can, and does, come from the realization of defective interpretation, but it is also stimulated by more obvious theatrical techniques in Beckett's plays: body movements which undercut or replace language, aspects of staging, vaudeville routines, stock comic jokes. In other words, Beckett works with material that we find conventionally comic. It provides another indication of the importance of ritual when everything else is lost. The laughter is stifled not so much by self-recognition, as by the performance framework. In *Endgame*, for example, the meta-criticism of Nagg telling his perennial trouser joke or of Hamm in his closing speech denies the audience its usual responsibility for qualitative analysis, its ability to act as a group and provide a consensus. Nevertheless Beckett's theatre captures audience attention, not the least by the brilliance with which he exploits the mechanics of theatre. While Iser made the point that Beckett's novels appeal to readers as they enable them to understand the nature of the novel (1978: 225), he does not seem to recognize that Beckett's theatrical appeal is similarly generated.

Indeed, a number of possible responses are always available to theatre audiences. They can, as Iser points out, refuse to play the game (1981a: 182). They can take up the challenge Iser presents. Or they can apply their revised cultural training – one which acknowledges Beckett's refusal to make meaning and which shares his worldview. Then laughter becomes a statement of concord with Beckett's despair. Iser, it seems, is guilty of *reading* Beckett and not taking full account of the plays in performance. In *The Act of Reading* Iser notes that reading is different from all other forms of social interaction because there is no *face-to-face situation* (1978: 166). With the face-to-face encounters of performers and spectators, complicated by the presence of real (albeit, in Beckett's theatre, minimal) signifiers, the system of response is necessarily different. If Beckett's plays are dissatisfying to audiences in their refusal to mean, then they are surely satisfying as theatrical art.

Notwithstanding my disagreement with his analysis of Beckett's drama, aspects of Iser's theory of the reading process are suggestive, as my examples demonstrate, for particular aspects of theatrical performance. The work of Hans Robert Jauss classifies other aspects which I intend to develop in my own theorizing. While Iser concentrated upon the individual reader, Jauss has turned to the reader in history. His 1969 essay 'Literary History as a Challenge to Literary Theory' charts the reasons for the then prevalent disregard for literary history. He enumerates the shortcomings of past practices which had described themselves as literary history, as well as the problems inherent in Marxist and Formalist criticism. The problem of literary history remained unresolved in the dispute between Marxist and Formalist critics, Jauss argues, precisely because of the limited attention they pay to reader or audience (Jauss 1982b: 18). His project, then, is for an aesthetics of reception.

In his methodology for this aesthetics of reception, Jauss is first concerned with literary history as based 'on the preceding experience of the literary work by its readers' (1982b: 20). Unlike political events, literary texts do not have inevitable repercussions. Texts have an effect only if readers continue to read and respond to them. In other words, texts are inevitably mediated by the reader's horizon of expectations,[10] and the establishment of literary history depends on an objectification of that horizon of expectations. Beyond this, the initial reception of a text is not arbitrary, subjective or impressionistic. It is instead, Jauss argues, 'the carrying out of specific instructions in a process of directed perception, which can be comprehended according to its constitutive motivations and triggering signals' (1982b: 23). Avant-garde texts are thus never completely 'new' – if they were they would be incomprehensible – but merely contain instructions to the reader which demand revision of the horizon of expectations of earlier texts.

A text's immanent horizon of expectations, according to Jauss, permits the determination of 'artistic character by the kind and the degree of its influence on a pre-supposed audience' (1982b: 25). The aesthetic distance between a given horizon of expectations and a new work 'can be objectified historically along the spectrum of the audience's reactions and criticism judgment (spontaneous success, rejection or shock, scattered approval, gradual or belated understanding)' (Jauss 1982b: 25). At its first publication/performance, a work is measured against the dominant horizon of expectations. The closer it correlates with this horizon, the more likely it is to be low, pulp, or 'culinary' art. Although there can be a marked distance in contemporary reception, later readings may, of course, change this. Works initially successful can in this way either become outmoded (and thus 'culinary') or, in the case of 'classics', require to be read '"against the grain" of the accustomed experience to catch sight of their artistic character once again' (Iser 1982b: 26).

52

By recovering the horizon of expectations of a given period, Jauss suggests, we can understand the hermeneutic difference between the understanding of a work then and now. This brings to light the history of a text's reception and dispels the notion of objective and timeless meaning contained independently within a text. Because of this, we can learn about an unknown work by measuring it against its intertexts (implicitly or explicitly cited). Following from the synchronic/diachronic models of Saussure's linguistic theory, Jauss proposes the development of a synchronic analysis for literary history which has previously only concerned itself with the diachronic perspective. A synchronic analysis could show 'the heterogeneous multiplicity of contemporaneous works in equivalent, opposing, and hierarchical structures, and thereby... discover an overarching system of relationships in the literature of a historical moment' (Jauss 1982b: 36). By a diachronic comparison of synchronic analyses, it would be possible, Jauss argues, to determine whether a work was current or otherwise (and, in this latter case, whether a work was old-fashioned or ahead of its time). As well as synchronic and diachronic analysis, literary history has to be viewed in its relationship to the more general category of history. Jauss writes:

> The social function of literature manifests itself in its genuine possibility only where the literary experience of the reader enters into the horizon of expectations of his lived praxis, preforms his understanding of the world, and thereby also has an effect on his social behaviour.
>
> (Jauss 1982b: 39)

Literary works are measured not only against other works, but against the reader's social experience.

A number of difficulties are evident in Jauss's theory. The 'reading against the grain' required to recognize the special qualities of a classic 'great' text surely raises the possibility of this kind of reading for 'culinary' works. As Holub points out, this is a result of a general inadequacy in marking distance between the horizon of expectations and the work itself as the 'criterion for determining literary value' (1984: 62). Beyond this, Suleiman is right in remarking that Jauss ignores the likelihood of 'different horizons of expectations co-existing among different publics in any one society.... Jauss's notion of the public and its expectations does not allow for enough diversity in the *publics* of literary works at a given time' (Suleiman and Crosman 1980: 37). To answer this, we are back with the interpretive communities of Stanley Fish though in a broader sense than the one in which Fish coins his term. A criticism by Frank Lentricchia that Fish dealt only with 'an isolated contemporary moment' (1980: 148) might, however, be addressed by a melding of the communities with Jauss's diachronic analysis. Readings then would be identifiable as socially and historically mediated and open to investigation in this light. As we saw in the reception history of Pinter's *The Birthday Party*, both the interpretive community and shifts in 'horizon of expectations' determined the nature of response. Jauss has clearly realized the problem. In a later essay, he makes what he describes as an overdue clarification and redefines the reader's role as arising from two horizons. The first recalls Iser's theory; it is the literary horizon of expectations suggested by the text read. The second is the social horizon of expectations of the reader.

Nevertheless, as Holub notes, the horizon of expectations holds an altogether diminished role in Jauss's later work and his new centre of attention is the aesthetic experience. In this case, Jauss posits a dialectical relationship between the production and reception of the aesthetic experience: 'The work does not exist without its effect; its effect presupposes reception, and in turn the audience's judgment conditions the author's production' (Jauss 1979: 138). In *Aesthetic Experience and Literary Hermeneutics*, Jauss explores this dialectic relationship of production/reception as an attack on what he calls the purism of Theodor Adorno's aesthetics of negativity. Instead Jauss proposes:

that attitude of enjoyment which art creates and makes possible is the aesthetic experience par excellence which underlies both preautonomous and autonomous art. It must again become the object of theoretical reflection where renewed meaning is to be given to the aesthetic practice of a productive, receptive, and communicative attitude for our time.

(Jauss 1982a: 21)

Central to this new thesis, and working from Freud's descriptions, is the concept of aesthetic pleasure. Jauss tests his theory in a series of interaction patterns of identification with a hero (1982a: 159) and suggests Holland's work on the management of fantasy in the reception process as a useful co-ordinate to his own model. As Metz's article on the film spectator made clear, and this seems particularly true in relation to a hero figure, the daydream element is active at the primary level of aesthetic experience. Thus, in describing audience perception, merger of understanding and fantasy at a primary level would appear appropriate.

While Jauss's theory of the aesthetic experience is undoubtedly useful in the study of theatre audiences, it nevertheless fails to deal in any depth with the sociological underpinning of that experience. Janet Wolff rightly assesses the theory as only a partial account:

> For the existence of a 'great tradition' is still made to appear relatively unproblematic, as long as we fail to see the specific material and ideological practices in which works are produced in the first place (the sociology of literary production), those conditions and practices which locate certain people or groups *as* audiences and, particularly, those key members of audiences whose task it is to formulate and conserve the literary heritage (the sociology of reception and of criticism).
>
> (Wolff 1983: 35–6)

In part for the reasons Wolff suggests and in part for his reliance on the perceptions of the individual as constitutive of history, East German theorists have found much to criticize in Jauss's work.

The work of Manfred Naumann illustrates well the alternative approach(es) of the East German theorists. Naumann sets up an interactive relationship in his discussion of the realization of texts. Like Iser he identifies 'that readers can realize a work only within the limits of the possibilities which it marks out for this purpose on the basis of its availability. The reader's freedom in dealing with a work has its limits in the objective properties of the work itself' (Naumann 1976: 116). Like Jauss, he sees reception as a bi-directional relationship: 'In making themselves subjects of the receptive relationship, the readers simultaneously make themselves objects of an effect relation, and conversely in that the work exerts a power upon the readers, the latter simultaneously take power over it' (1976: 117). The point of departure from the 'bourgeois' theorists (such as Iser and Jauss) is the importance granted to social mediation. Naumann explains the factors involved: 'Before they reach the reader, the works produced always have forms of social appropriation already behind them; they have been selected for reception through social institutions, made available by the latter, and in most cases also have already been evaluated thereby' (1976: 119). Naumann looks to the interpretive community as mediator, but – unlike Fish – sees this as obviously and always political:

> Examples of this mediating function are to be found in publishing houses, bookstores, and libraries, as well as in literary criticism and propaganda, literary instruction in schools, the study of literature, and all other institutions which mediate, materially or ideally, between the work produced and the reader. It is not therefore literature or works 'in themselves' to which the reader establishes a relation in reading them. It is works, rather, which out of the potential stock of produced works have been selected, propagated, and evaluated by social institutions, according to ideological, aesthetic, economic, or other viewpoints, and whose road to reader has additionally been cleared by measures of the most varied sort (advertising, book production, reviews, commentary, discussions of the work, public readings, literary prizes, popularization of the author, and so on). By his individual decision to choose a particular work from among those selected, the reader at the same time constitutes a social relationship.
>
> (Naumann 1976: 119)

The effects of processes of evaluation are particularly acute in the case of theatre. While publishers of novels survive on a fairly modest success rate, both big and low budget theatres can collapse under the economic burden of a single failed production. Pre-performance evaluation certainly reduces the range of productions available and does this more stringently than other kinds of artistic production.

The illustration of a London production (1974) of Tennessee

Williams's *A Streetcar Named Desire* renders unmistakable the mediating function of production. The programme announced that, by arrangement with Donald Albery, Bernard Delfont, and Richard M. Mills (for Bernard Delfont Organisation Ltd), the Piccadilly Theatre presents Hillard Elkins's production of the play. The coalition of one of London's most influential theatre owners, a powerful media organization, and the husband of the leading lady suggests the complexity of the production process. Between the ideological, aesthetic, and economic choices of the production strata and the availability of *Streetcar* for reception lies, as Naumann suggests in his general model, advertising, popularity of the playwright, Marlon Brando and Vivien Leigh's 'definitive' movie performance, reviews, the presence of a star (Claire Bloom) in the lead role, the recent television work of Bloom and other cast members, and so on. Naumann notes that:

> Through the mediating organs operative in the interval between the produced work and the beginning of the individual reception process, there is always an indication given, along with its availability for reception, of what processes of reception and effect have been going on in and after its realization.
>
> (Naumann 1976: 120)

And, of course, the spectator's choice of this particular production of *Streetcar* among a broad and numerous selection of plays available concurrently within the same geographic area constitutes, as Naumann suggests, another social relationship. Naumann describes it as the 'before' of reception and as determined by a viewer's 'world view and ideology' (1976: 121). This 'before' is also determined:

> by his membership of a class, stratum, or group, by his material situation (income, leisure, living and working conditions, and general way of life); by his education, knowledge, and level of culture, his aesthetic needs; by his age, and even by his sex, and not least by his attitude to the other arts, and especially to the very literature that he has already given a reception to.
>
> (Naumann 1976: 121)

While the audience's experience of text in performance represents the core of interpretive activity, it clearly requires the contextualizing which Naumann suggests and which earlier discussion of Brecht foregrounded. (And it is worth noting that, while Naumann seems almost apologetic for its inclusion, 'his [?] sex' is most certainly part of the 'before' of reception.) The social appropriation of literature, Naumann continues, exists 'in the context of production, transmission, and function of literature, within socially conditioned and class-conditioned *literary relationships*, which are part of the overall social and historical nexus' (1976: 123). It is this nexus, he concludes, which makes possible the concretization of 'the relations entered into by the "active subjects," when by means of their receptive activity they realize and make productive the values contained in literature and its works' (1976: 123).

Holub has pointed out how reception theory has been conducted in isolation from other contemporary theories (notably semiotics and deconstruction) (1984: 163), but the omission of social, economic, and political relations is surely more serious. It is only in the Marxist criticism of Naumann that these factors have been acknowledged. As Mailloux puts it, the reader-response critics simply do not 'examine the status of their own discourse' (1982: 192). Jane Tompkins concludes her survey of the reader in history with the observation that 'virtually nothing has changed as a result of what seems, from close up, the cataclysmic shift in the locus of meaning from the text to the reader' (1980: 225). The reason she suggests for this is the control of North American academia where interpretation is all. Pratt, however, argues that it is more complicated: 'The weakness of this explanation is that it requires us to separate the institution of criticism from the critics who participate in it, thus mystifying the former and atomizing the latter. Clearly, the institution of criticism is a power structure constituted by and through critics' (1986: 29).[11]

OTHER APPROACHES TO THE READER

In her critique of reader-response criticism, Pratt presents a convincing argument which suggests the failure of much of that theory to break with formalism results from the maintenance of the former's ideological commitments. That break, she proposes, will only be achieved after 'exploring the specifics of reception as a socially and ideologically determined process, and coming to grips with the questions of artistic *production*' (Pratt 1986: 30). Certainly the economic strictures that theatre companies almost always face underscore the necessary counterpointing of production and reception. Without an audience willing to attend, a play cannot survive many performances. Indeed, the very public nature of theatre arts stresses the necessity to consider both production and reception as socially and ideologically determined.

Furthermore, Pratt notes: '[d]espite all the cries that readers make meaning, it is still easy to lose sight of the fact that reception of art *is* production – the production of meaning according to socially constitutive signifying practices, which is what, in a different mode, artistic production is as well' (1986: 31). A theory which takes account of the social construction of meaning is, indeed, an objective of this study and, to this end, it is helpful to look at the only positive model Pratt locates. This is Jacques Leenhardt's 'Toward a Sociology of Reading' (1980).

The project of Leenhardt, director of the Ecole des Hautes Etudes en Sciences Sociales in Paris, was to devise a methodology for a sociological study of reading. His research was empirical. In collaboration with the Institute of Popular Culture in Budapest, 500 readers with different social backgrounds (in both France and Hungary) were surveyed about their reading of two novels. A significant discovery was that:

> the reader's attitude toward the events, characters, or any sign of the author's intervention actually formed a system. Value judgments, reading attitudes, and expectations in the sphere of pleasure appeared to be organically interrelated to such an extent that we were able, for each national sample, to ascertain four large systems, four tendencies, that expressed the ideological specificity of the reader's relationship to the text.
>
> (Leenhardt 1980: 214)

The research undermined any concept of a unified reading public. Leenhardt says, 'we only met *readers*, who form *publics* according to their sociodemographical characteristics' (1980: 214). The general patterns of reading in France were, however, different from those for Hungary, although both, interestingly, applied stereotypic responses to the work from the other's country. Levels of education, not surprisingly, emerged as a decisive factor in the patterns utilized. Leenhardt concludes that the sociology of knowledge needs to take account of 'the specific hierarchization of the processes of meaning, at every point of social reality. Such an approach would not overlook the fact that cultural objects are produced and received according to schemes elaborated by collective rather than by individual entities' (1980: 223–4). The obvious result of this is that 'the "code" in no way transcends the text but, on the contrary, is produced by the "message" at the moment when the latter manifests itself in social reality' (Leenhardt 1980: 223–4). Leenhardt's empirical research evidently supports Naumann's theoretical position.

In contrast to work such as Leenhardt's, Pratt argues that reader-response and institutional literary criticism generally suffer from a lack of clearly defined objectives. Apart from the sociological project, Pratt identifies reception-oriented studies in feminist literary criticism as potentially useful. Certainly the explosion of feminist theory and criticism has been instrumental in spotlighting the sociological and ideological processes involved in our choice and evaluation of works. Kate Millet's *Sexual Politics*, published in 1969, was clearly a watershed text and, as Toril Moi reminds us, Millet not only broke with dominant New Critical practice but openly revealed how conflict 'between reader and author/text can expose the underlying premises of a work. Millet's importance as a literary critic lies in her relentless defence of the reader's right to posit her own viewpoint, rejecting the received hierarchy of text and reader (Moi 1985: 24–5). The idea of reading against the ideology of the text is developed in Judith Fetterley's *The Resisting Reader*. Fetterley states in her preface that the book is 'a self-defense survival manual for the woman reader lost in the "masculine wilderness of the American novel." At its best, feminist criticism is a political act whose aim is not simply to interpret the world but to change it' (1978: viii). Her argument is that, in a system where the 'universal' view of reality is in fact the male view of reality, the female reader is without power. To overturn this state of powerlessness, Fetterley proposes that the female reader becomes 'a resisting rather than an assenting reader' (1978: xxii).

Fetterley's feminist (re)reading of the canonical texts of American literature ultimately has, as Annette Kolodny describes it, an 'actively self-protective coloration' (1985: 148) – though probably no more so than Slatoff's early venture into reader-based analysis. Like Millet, however, Fetterley has been concerned with the work of male authors and revising responses to the canon can only represent part of a feminist theory of reading. It can be argued that analyses (recoveries) of women authors provide a more useful model. Kolodny's 'A Map for Rereading' provides a juxtaposition of the politics of production with those of reception. Kolodny argues of her cited texts by women authors that they 'examine the difficulty inherent in deciphering other highly specialized realms of meaning – in this case, women's conceptual and symbolic worlds' (1985b: 58).

What Fetterley and Kolodny's studies show is that gender in its sociological and ideological constitution must be considered in analyses of both production and reception processes. The problems encountered by feminist critics in their description of reading as well as in their relationship to texts in general have been repeated in the creation of a feminist theatre. Feminists working in the theatre have, like their academic counterparts, sought to recover 'lost' women's texts and to reread classic works, particularly Shakespeare (Melissa Murray's *Ophelia*, Elaine Feinstein's *Lear's Daughters*, Avon Touring's version of *Measure for Measure* changing Claudio to Claudia). Beyond this, however, they have challenged the assumptions of theatre as a cultural institution and, in this way, have radically restructured the audience/performance dialogue. Groups such as Le Théâtre Parminou (based in Quebec) and the Women's Theatre Group (touring in England) have involved audiences in the creation of texts for performance. They not only rely on audiences in pre-production stages, but in their *mise en scènes* include the spaces of 'open' scenes or post-production discussion.

As Michelene Wandor's book *Understudies* (1981) (and the revised version, *Carry On, Understudies*(1986)) made all too apparent, women have long been marginalized in theatre practice. In fact, Susan Bassnett-McGuire argues that theatre, as it is generally understood, is a male entity (1984: 462). Not only was the work of women playwrights 'lost', but women have had only the most limited access to directing and technical work. This has even been true of amateur theatre where membership is predominantly female. Roles for actresses in most plays are remarkably limited. This has led to feminist theatre workers seeking out new ways of writing and performing, new theatre spaces, and, above all, new audiences. As Wandor's critique suggests, emerging feminist theatre was treated at best with suspicion by existing theatre institutions and practitioners. Largely for this reason, alternative performance models were sought and initially this strategy meant, as it did for similarly emergent gay theatre, 'constituency' audiences.

In many cases, the opportunity to work directly with the audiences whose interests the companies share has led to a complete rejection of the mainstream. Cynthia Grant made it clear that her decision to leave her post as artistic director of the successful Nightwood Theatre in Toronto was the result of a growing dissatisfaction in working within an established institution. Her present participation in a co-operative venture, The Company of Sirens, permits a more direct and important contact between actors and audience without the constraints of the conventional theatre system. Grant says:

> Part of the move out of Nightwood had to do with making feminist theatre more accessible. Large numbers of people are put off by the idea of coming into a theatre, so we are taking theatre to them. We are very excited about playing venues as diverse as a union hall in Windsor or a cultural community centre here in Toronto.
>
> (cited in Levine 1987: 8)

Elsewhere, feminist writers such as Caryl Churchill and Franca Rame have had their plays produced by mainstream theatres and the incorporation of their works in academic studies of modern drama affirms that the impact of feminist practice extends beyond constituency interest.

Feminist criticism is useful not only for its discussions of *how* we read but for identifying alternative conditions of production and reception. It reminds us of the failure of most reader-response criticism to situate reading explicitly as social and political action.[12] In terms of the psychological complexities of reading, however, we have looked only at the theories of Holland. While Holland too neglected social and political implications, Wendy Deutelbaum suggests that the defects of his theory go beyond this. She refutes Holland's notion of identity theme which implies that the self is a fixed and uniform entity, and suggests instead:

[i]f identity there be, the reader's 'identity' is constituted in the act of imaging other identities through the interactions with social and verbal fictions of that plural self. If these heterogeneous and motive selves frighten us in everyday life because they menace the coherent self conception of the ego, their play gives rise to pleasure in the protected, ecstatic space of reading.

(Deutelbaum 1981: 99)

Deutelbaum's interest in the participation of the plural self in a pleasure of reading is drawn from the work of Roland Barthes. While strategies of reading represent only part of Barthes's interests, his plurality of approaches have been immensely influential. To a less obvious extent, but nevertheless significantly, his work has contributed to challenges made upon traditionally-held perspectives on theatre. Probably, however, Barthes is best known for his proclamation: 'we know that to give writing its future, it is necessary to overthrow the myth: the birth of the reader must be at the cost of the death of the Author' (1977: 148).

The label of reader-response is too narrow for Barthes's theory. His writings have been structuralist, ideological, semiotic, Freudian, and more.[13] When he does turn his attention to the work of the reader, it is an inventive – Barthes would have argued at this early stage scientific – examination. This is S/Z (1974). In this work, he suggests the multiplicity of codes available to readers in their construction of texts. Furthermore, texts are either readerly (closed) or writerly (open), with the latter, of course, preferred by Barthes. In *The Pleasure of the Text* (1975), Barthes approaches reading not from the semiotic perspective of S/Z, but in a hedonistic mode. The readerly/writerly opposition is replaced by bliss (orgasmic *jouissance*) and pleasure. Here he explores the reading relationship Deutelbaum proposed in her criticism of Holland:

Text of pleasure: the text that contents, fills, grants euphoria; the text that comes from culture and does not break with it, is linked to a *comfortable* practice of reading. Text of bliss: the text that imposes a state of loss, the text that discomforts (perhaps to the point of a certain boredom), unsettles the reader's historical, cultural, psychological assumptions, the consistency of his tastes, values, memories, brings to a crisis his relation with language.

(Barthes 1975: 14)

Barthes's descriptions for texts of bliss recall Artaud's desires for a theatre that abolished masterpieces and sought an immediate physicality. The text of pleasure coincides with Peter Brook's concept of 'deadly' theatre, the text of bliss with the envelopment possible in 'immediate' theatre. Both Artaud and Brook put the emphasis on contact with the individual spectator and desire to break through the comfortable, reassuring, complacency of the audience as group. In a medium clearly more social than the private act of reading, they strive for the asocial character Barthes assigns to bliss: 'it is the abrupt loss of sociality, and yet there follows no recurrence to the subject (subjectivity), the person, solitude: *everything* is lost, integrally. Extremity of the clandestine, darkness of the motion-picture theater' (1975: 39).

Barthes's argument in *The Pleasure of the Text*, as so often in his work, is against the orthodoxies of traditional criticism. He writes:

Imagine an aesthetic (if the word has not become too depreciated) based entirely (completely, radically, in every sense of the word) on the *pleasure of the consumer*, whoever he may be, to whatever class, whatever group he may belong, without respect to cultures or languages: the consequences would be huge, perhaps even harrowing (Brecht has sketched such an aesthetic of pleasure; of all his proposals, this is the one most frequently forgotten).

(Barthes 1975: 59)

It is typical to find the work of Brecht cited. Barthes remembers his discovery of Brecht at the Berliner Ensemble's production of *Mother Courage* in Paris 'where I was literally inflamed with enthusiasm for that production, but, let me add right away, inflamed also by the twenty or so lines of Brecht printed in the theater program. I had never read a language like that on theater and art' (Barthes 1985a: 225). Indeed, Brecht's theories repeatedly provide exemplary models in Barthes's writings, and one of the few Barthes articles *directly* concerned with theatre practice concerns 'The Tasks of Brechtian Criticism (1979b).' It is pertinent to this study that Barthes's interest stems not from a knowledge of Brecht's *texts*, but from the impact of the Berliner Ensemble's *performance*.

Barthes's definition of Brechtian criticism conveys directly the central importance he accords to Brecht's work. It is, he argues, 'thorough criticism by spectators, readers, and consumers and not by the learned scholar' (Barthes 1979b: 27). Barthes's discussion of Brechtian criticism opens with the statement: 'we have not yet established adequate modes of questioning for the definition of different theatre audiences' (1979b: 27), and, because of this, looks to contemporary reactions from the press, categorized by their political commitment.

Ideologically Brecht's work is so central for what Barthes describes as its ceaseless invention of Marxism (1979b: 28). Certainly Brecht's intention to provoke audiences to see anew (and ideologically) the commonplaces of everyday life was understood by Barthes. In 'The Photographic Message' (1982), Barthes examines the seeming reality of the photographic image as critically as Brecht uncovered the practices of naturalist theatre. As Barthes points out, in both cases it is the audience's reception which is crucial. Of *Mother Courage* Barthes comments:

> you may be certain of a misunderstanding if you think that its 'subject' is the Thirty Years War, or even the denunciation of war in general; its *gest* is not there, but in the blindness of the tradeswoman who believes herself to live off war only, in fact, to die of it; even more, the gest lies in the *view* that I, spectator, have of this blindness.
>
> (Barthes 1977: 76)

Barthes also looks at critical distance and observes that the gap in Brechtian theatre between signifier and signified draws attention to the complexities of codes activated in theatrical performance. In 'Theatre and Signification', Barthes develops this 'polyphonic system of information':

At every point in a performance you are receiving (*at the same second*) six or seven items of information (from the scenery, the costuming, the lighting, the position of the actors, their gestures, their mode of playing, their language), but some of these items *remain fixed* (this is true of the scenery) while others *change* (speech, gestures).

(Barthes 1979c: 29)

Perhaps the most influential aspect of Barthes's work on theatre, however, was his study of Racine. This research is important not so much for Barthes's discussion of Racine's plays but for his attack on traditional (academic) approaches to literary criticism. Leenhardt, in 1980, still speaks of 'the sacred awe we feel in France toward *the* text – an awe cultivated by our educational system' (1980: 210). Barthes concludes his study with proposals which radically undermine 'standard' approaches to Racine:

The first objective rule here is to declare one's system of reading, it being understood that no neutral one exists. Of all the works I have cited, I contest none; I can even say that in various respects I admire them all. I regret only that so much care should be put in the service of a confused cause: for if one wants to write literary history, one must renounce the individual Racine and deliberately undertake the study of techniques, rule, rites, and collective mentalities; and if one wants to install oneself inside Racine, with whatever qualification – if one wants to speak, even if only a word, about the Racinian *self* – one must expect to see the humblest scholarship suddenly become systematic, and the most prudent critic reveal himself as an utterly subjective, utterly historical being.

(Barthes 1964: 172)

The ire with which Raymond Picard responded to Barthes's study indicates its impact. Picard's *Nouvelle critique ou nouvelle imposture?* (1965) was, however, less a dismantling of those views on Racine than, as Culler suggests, a 'spirited defence of the cultural patrimony against irreverent ideologies and their jargon' (1983: 65).

Barthes's challenge was none the less a relevant one. The emergence of oppositional theoretical positions has been decisive in reshaping dramatic analysis. As we have seen, almost from the time that naturalism appeared on the stage, other theatre practices had been attempting such a counter-action. But, as Carlson points out, it is not until the more widespread theoretical and social shift in the 1960s that traditional methods are seriously questioned:

> Western Europe in the first part of the twentieth century had experienced very little of the sort of radical interpretive freedom represented by Meyerhold, for example. The iconoclasm of the futurists and dadaists made little impact on the text-centered approach of Copeau and his followers in France and did not affect the English-language theatre at all. By 1960, however, the widely held assumption that each play calls for a certain more or less predictable production interpretation began to be seriously challenged, primarily (as in Barthes) in the name of historical relativism.
>
> (Carlson 1984: 444)

Despite a protracted and often hesitant response to his work, Brecht has played a crucial role in the establishment of new areas for theatrical research. Barthes's enthusiasm for Brecht's interest both in the possibilities of pleasure and of critical analysis has shown this. More generally, recent critical practice, particularly in France (not only that of Barthes, but of Derrida, Lacan, and Foucault), has led to radically different ways of reading theatre. This can be seen in the investigations into audience by theorists such as Anne Ubersfeld, Patrice Pavis, and Josette Féral. Before looking to their work, however, it is important to return to the semiotics of reading, an analytic method brought into play by Barthes, but more thoroughly explored in the work of Umberto Eco.

Eco's research has been into a theory of semiotics generally, and his interest in the reading process represents only one aspect of that work. His motivation for *The Role of the Reader* (1979) was Charles Sanders Peirce's 'idea of unlimited semiosis' (Eco 1979: 3) and this becomes a starting point for Eco's examination of the reader's role in *producing* texts. It is Eco's contention that 'the standard communication model proposed by information theorists (Sender, Message, Addressee – in which the message is decoded on the basis of a code shared by the virtual poles of the chain) does not describe the actual functioning of communicative intercourses' (1979: 5). The reading process, Eco proposes, proceeds from activation of basic dictionary (possible meanings for words read) to the establishing of co-textual relations. Ambiguities are effectively put on hold until further textual clues clarify the relationship. This progression will always be mediated by the reader's selection of 'frames'. These frames can be taken from the text (meaning of word established because of the circumstances in which it is uttered), from genre rules (literary conventions), and from intertextual competence (measuring the text against other texts read previously). The text can be overcoded through the use of metaphors and tropes (the effect, for example, of beginning a story 'Once upon a time') and will always be ideologically overcoded. The ideological bias of a reader will come into play and can, as Eco indicates, help to uncover or ignore the ideological structure of the text. It also acts as a code-switcher, 'leading one to read a given text in the light of "aberrant" codes (where "aberrant" means only different from the ones envisaged by the sender)' (1979: 22).

We do not in the course of reading take into account all the properties our encyclopedic frame can offer for a given word: 'Semantic disclosures have a double role: they *blow up* certain properties (making them textually relevant or pertinent) and *narcotize* some others' (Eco 1979: 23). The foregrounding or otherwise of these properties is regulated by the textual topic(s). These act to limit a potentially infinite semantic encyclopedia and to reduce the risk of failure in the reading operation. Topics can be marked by titles or key words, or may be hidden and require the reader's deductive analysis. However managed, they are the means of directing 'the right amalgamations and the organization of a single level of sense, or isotopy' (Eco 1979: 26). The establishment of an isotopy enables the actualization of a text's discursive structure.

Each step in the reading process – even within a single sentence – Eco suggests involves the reader in predicting possible outcomes. These forecasts, constructed from the reader's holding of intertextual frames, are then held or dismantled by later steps in the linear progression. The recourse to these frames Eco describes as '*inferential walks*: they are not mere whimsical initiatives on the part of the reader, but are elicited by discursive structures and foreseen by the whole textual strategy as indispensable components of the construction of the *fabula'* (1979: 32). The reader, through this analysis, can be seen as making numerous and selective decisions, even at the level of a naive reading.

The attraction of Eco's discussion of the reading process – and I sketch only aspects of it here – is the microscopic analysis he makes of the elements involved and their possible hierarchical arrangement. In looking at or staging a dramatic text, Eco acknowledges that the response process is necessarily more complicated. In 'Semiotics of Theatrical Performance' (1977), Eco turns his attention to the implications of one of Pierce's examples for theatrical analysis. Pierce posed the question of what sign was suggested by a drunkard displayed in a public situation by the Salvation Army in order to promote the advantages of temperance (in Eco 1977: 109). Eco attempts to answer this question. A naive attitude represents the best starting point for an analysis, but we cannot, Eco suggests, dismantle our background knowledge:

> We have read not only Aristotle but also Francis Ferguson, Etienne Souriau, Peter Szondi, Umberto Eco and Woody Allen. We know Sophocles, Gilbert and Sullivan, and *King Lear, I Love Lucy* and *En attendant Godot* and *A Chorus Line, Phèdre* and *No, No Nanette, Murder in the Cathedral* and *Let My People Come* and *The Jew of Malta* and *Oh Calcutta!*. Therefore we immediately suspect that in that sudden epiphany of intoxication lies the basic mystery of (theatrical) performance.
>
> (Eco 1977: 109–10)

The act of placing the drunkard on the stage incurs a shift from man to sign. By ostension, he now represents the class to which he belongs. What we see are some of the essential characteristics of drunkards (red nose, frayed clothes, etc.) which have been established by social codes making what Eco calls an 'iconographic convention' (1977: 111). He points out that the choice of this man by the Salvation Army was a semiotic one; they have found the right man as the writer chooses the right word. The difference is only that words are transparently signs, whereas the drunkard *appears* not to be: 'in order to be accepted as a sign, he has to be recognized as a "real" spatio-temporal event, a real human body.... In the *mise-en-scène* an object, first recognized as a real object, is then assumed as a sign in order to refer back to another object (or to a class of objects) whose constitutive stuff is the same as that of the representing object (1977: 111).

Eco also points out that in performance non-essential characteristics of the sign 'also acquire a sort of vicarious representative importance. The very moment the audience accepts the convention of the *mise-en-scène*, every element of that portion of the world that has been framed (put upon the platform) becomes significant' (1977: 112). Within the framework of the *mise en scène*, of course, an audience deals not simply with the linear text manifestation (reading model) but with a multiplicity of sign systems. Eco cites the thirteen isolated by Tadeusz Kowzan in *Littérature et Spectacle*: 'words, voice inflection, facial mimicry, gesture, body movement, makeup, headdress, costume, accessory, stage design, lighting, music, and noise' (1977: 108). The status of words is particularly complicated. They are not simply signifiers; they do not refer to a signified and through it to a referent. Instead, Eco argues, they refer back to other signifiers; when the on-stage drunkard says that he loves liquor, it 'does not mean that the subject of the utterance loves liquor – it means that there is somewhere somebody who loves liquor and who says that. In theatre and cinema, verbal performances refer back to verbal performances *about which* the *mise-en-scène* is speaking' (1977: 115). Furthermore, the drunkard represents, through the act of framing (the background of the Salvation Army), the advantages of abstaining from liquor. In other words, his representation is ironic. Eco describes the ideological level of the performance: 'Our drunken man is no longer a bare presence. He is not even a mere figure of speech. He has become an ideological abstraction: temperance vs. intemperance, virtue vs. vice' (1977: 117). It is, Eco argues, the Salvation Army contextualization which situates the drunkard within a particular value hierarchy. Thus a semiotic analysis of the *mise en scène* will provide a semiotic analysis of the production of ideology (Eco 1977: 117).

Eco has isolated two distinct features of the theatrical performance which affect the nature of audience response. There is primarily the constitution of the on-stage sign, represented not by language as in a written text, but by a real object or person. The audience's awareness of actor as actor works to a greater or lesser extent in marking at all times the fictiveness of the stage world. Furthermore, there is feedback: 'the audience looking at the drunk can laugh, can insult him and he can react to people's reaction. Theatrical messages are shaped also by the feedback produced from their destination point' (Eco 1977: 117).

Semiotics has, as Carlson notes (1984: 512), provided the main thrust of recent dramatic theory. While this field of dramatic study has, like its predecessors, somewhat neglected the presence of the audience, there clearly lies within a model such as Eco's a concern with the multilayering inevitable in any performance. Only when the interrelationship of performance elements is investigated in such detail can the audience's role within that structure be fully understood.

All the varieties of reader-oriented criticism discussed in these two sections have, despite their defects, stimulated a concern with how the theatre audience might engage with a dramatic production. In part, the relationship resembles that between a reader and a printed work, and in these aspects the investigations of reader-response criticism are surely helpful. The detailed examinations of texts and their addressees undoubtedly lend themselves to studies of how playwrights shape their writing to meet, surprise, or thwart the expectations of the intended and/or actual audiences. Barthes's attack on academic approaches to Racine furnishes a fitting conclusion to this discussion as it provides in microcosm the omissions of traditional criticism:

> On Racine's public... there are many incidental remarks, valuable figures, as we might expect... but no recent synthesis; the heart of the matter remains quite mysterious. Who went to the performances? According to Racinian criticism, Corneille (crouching in a loge) and Mme. de Sevigné. But who else? The court, the town – exactly who? And still more than the social configuration of this public, it is the very function of the theatre in the public's eyes that would interest us: diversion? dream? identification? distance? snobbery? What was the proportion of all these elements?
>
> (Barthes 1964: 157)

SEMIOTICS AND POST-STRUCTURALISM IN THEATRE AND FILM STUDIES

Beyond theories of reading, there has in the last twenty years been a development of critical interest in the act and nature of viewing. The process of viewing has, as we saw in Eco's analysis of the theatrical performance, been a concern of semiotic studies and this work has further developed interest in the audience. Two European journals have published special volumes in this area: 'Semiologie du Spectacle: Réception' was the title for the summer 1982 issue of *Degrés* and 'Semiotica della ricezione teatrale' was the subject of an issue of *Versus* in 1985.

The multilayering of scenic components described by Eco and Barthes creates an on-stage 'text' which is far more complicated than its printed equivalent, and the question of how these multivalent components are received by spectators has not been entirely ignored. While reader response criticism, concerned primarily with the novel or poem, can provide a core of receptive concerns, it is self-evident that theatre demands a more complex communication model. Unlike the printed text, a theatrical performance is available for its audience only in a fixed time period. Furthermore, the event is not a finished product in the same way as a novel or poem. It is an interactive process, which relies on the presence of spectators to achieve its effects. A performance is, of course, unlike a printed work, always open to immediate and public acceptance, modification or rejection by those people it addresses. This inevitably complex relationship between performance and audience has indeed been illustrated in the attention of the semiotician to models of theatrical communication.

The interest in a semiotic approach to theatre studies emerged in the 1970s as an attack on the text-centred criticism of traditional dramatic writing, and the predominant concern of early work was the relationship between the dramatic text and the *mise en scène*. Initially, as in more orthodox dramatic criticism, the spectator was neglected. More recently, however, as the objectives of semiotic study have been redefined, the spectator has increasingly become an important focus. The starting points for their investigations repeat concerns of the reader-response theorists. Levels of cultural competence are taken into account (Elam 1980: 55–62; Pavis 1982: 72), as are Jaussian horizons of expectations. Elam, for example, explores the codes/systems of expectations which provide the necessary markers for what is (or is not) included in a production:

> During the performance, not only may various kinds of extra-textual 'noise' arise, having to be ignored or tolerated (late arrivals, malfunctioning of equipment and, within limits, the forgetting of lines by the actors), but certain licensed activities not contributory to the representation proper may take place on stage and will be duly discounted by the spectator (the entry and exit of stagehands, for example, in set changes). It is not that the excluded events – such as audience activity – have no semiotic value (it *does* make a difference if one is allowed to see the stage hands or if the entire audience is noisily eating popcorn), but that they are understood as belonging to a different level of action.
>
> (Elam 1980: 88–9)

The conventions of particular cultural codes determine an audience's ability to tolerate 'disattendance factors'. This, as Elam points out, creates some of the difficulties Westerners encounter in watching performances of Oriental theatre (1980: 89). Within the Western tradition, it is worth noting the clever exploitation of disattendance by John Arden. In *Waters of Babylon*, a play written specifically for the Royal Court Theatre in London where audiences have to 'disattend' the frequent, rather noisy interruptions of subway trains passing directly below, Arden opens his play: 'there is heard a crescendo then diminuendo of noise, as of an Underground train passing' (1964: 19). During the opening address by the central character, Krank, presented directly to the audience, the sound of a train is repeated and direct reference to its nuisance made. Audiences of the time (1957) were baffled by Arden's use of non-naturalistic methods yet Arden exploits this very simple device, an incorporation of the real world into the fictional stage world, both to undermine the conventions of naturalist practice and to illustrate that audiences have been quite capable of certain, *expected*, breaks in illusion. Peripheral noise is utilized to foreground the acceptability of familiar codes and to suggest that the Brechtian style of Arden's play is only confusing through lack of familiarity.

The main thrust of theatre semiotics has, however, been in those areas identified in Eco's theorization of theatrical performance. Primarily, semioticians have explored the density of signs evident in any performance, the interrelationship of those signs, and, in particular, the Western tradition of concentration on the signs that emanate from the actor. In *L'univers du théâtre* Girard, Ouellet, and Rigault stress that signs provided for the spectator are seldom detached, removed from context; words are usually accompanied by facial expressions and so on. In an almost infinite number of possible combinations, signs reinforce, repeat, make more precise, cancel, correct, contradict, and constitute other concurrently present signs (Girard, Ouellet, and Rigault 1978: 21–2). This clustering of signs clearly challenges the centrality of the word. As Pavis suggests,

> [w]hat is fundamental to the stage, much more so than the signifieds of the text, is the *iconization* (*mise en vue*) of the word: the text is revealed in all its fragility, constantly menaced as it is by the gestuality which might at any time interrupt its emission, and which always guides the spectator in the rhythm of his reception.
>
> (Pavis 1982: 80)

Indeed, the word has not the indispensability apparent for the written text: 'After all, mime and silent film are possible, but verbal theater without facial and body expression is unconceivable, and the decoding process at the spectator's end leans heavily on the kinetic-visual channel, at times the only one through which messages are being coded' (Poyatos 1982: 89–90).

Interpretation of the stage sign usually goes beyond its immediate signified, often utilizing several connotative possibilities. Indeed, the flexibility of the theatrical performance allows a rapid switching between denotation and connotation. In, for example, the opening sequence of Max Frisch's *The Fire Raisers*, the first visual picture is of Biedermann lighting a cigar. The cigar is in this first frame denotative. As the lights come up, and the audience becomes aware that Biedermann is surrounded by firemen, it seems as if the cigar might represent a fire hazard. The opening line – Biedermann says 'One can't even light a cigar nowadays without thinking of fire!... It's revolting' (1962: 3) – links verbal sign to stage object correcting the first interpretation. The cigar is not *per se* a fire hazard but a reminder of an apparently ever-present danger of fire. Claude Bruzy has noted the importance of the chronology of signs (1982: 7), and the instability of a sign's meaning is evident under temporal assessment. Following that opening speech, 'Biedermann hides the smoking cigar and withdraws' (Frisch 1962: 3). In this picture, the connotative meaning of the cigar is made more precise. Its hidden, but known, presence both implicates Biedermann and reminds the audience of the truism 'there's no smoke without fire'. In the next sequence (opening scene I), the audience is presented with a picture of Biedermann 'sitting in his room reading the newspaper and smoking a cigar. Anna, the maid, in a white apron, brings a bottle of wine' (Frisch 1962: 4). The previous connotative impact of the cigar is reinforced and, furthermore, the cigar operates as part of a sign-cluster connoting a comfortable, bourgeois lifestyle. Elam points out that this semantic versatility can also take place at a denotative level: 'What appears in one scene as the handle of a sword may be converted, in the next, into a cross by a simple change of position, just as the set which stands in one context for a palisade is immediately transformed, without structural modification, into a wall or garden fence' (1980: 12).

The rapid transformability of objects through shifting denotative and connotative signs is, as the above example suggests, only one level of the complex process open for reception. Signs must also be received in what Erika Fischer-Lichte defines as 'combinatorial possibilities' (1982: 57). In scene I of *The Fire Raisers*, the object 'cigar' combines with others (the leisure of Biedermann, the bottle of wine, the physical presence of a maid) to signify a bourgeois setting, which at once advances the narrative and provides an ideological framework for that narrative. The relationship of sign-cluster to the social composition of the audience (middle class or not, Western or Eastern Europe, and so on) further shapes interpretation.

The audience as a social phenomenon has also received

some attention from semiotic researchers. As in the case of the on-stage sign, it is difficult to consider the individual spectator (an off-stage sign of the theatrical event) in isolation. Anne Ubersfeld notes how an individual is unlikely to swim against the current of his/her neighbours' reception, how difficult it is to adopt the role of sole admirer or critic within an audience (1981: 306). As Elam describes, there is a tendency towards integration, the surrendering of the individual to the group for the duration of the performance (1980: 96). While their research has dealt with the presence/influence of audience as simply one of many elements of theatrical communication, semioticians have always emphasized the centrality of the spectator's role. Pavis argues that production and reception form a hermeneutic circle, each presupposing the other (1985: 93). Marco De Marinis discusses 'two dramaturgies of the spectator' (1987: 101), one where the spectator is passive, the 'mark or target for the actions/operations of the director, the performers, and, if there is one, the writer' (101) and the other where he or she is active, carrying out the operations of reception: 'perception, interpretation, aesthetic appreciation, memorization, emotive and intellectual response, etc.' (101). Elam states that 'the spectator, by virtue of his very patronage of the performance, can be said to *initiate* the communicative circuit' (1980: 34). Within the communicative circuit, there are, as Wilfried Passow describes, different levels of interaction:

> [O]f constitutive importance for theater is the theatrical interaction which divides into (A) scenic interaction within the 'make-believe world' (fictitious scenic interaction) and (B) the interaction of the audience with this 'make-believe' world (audience–stage interaction in the field of fiction). However there exists further (C) the interaction of the members of the theater company amongst each other (real interaction on stage), (D) the interaction of the audience with the actors (real audience–stage interaction) and (E) the interaction within the audience.
>
> (Passow 1981: 240)

For this study categories (B), (D), and (E) represent important fields of interest. The relationship between the actors and the audience (D) has, historically, been the focus of Western interest. The work of semioticians has now emphasized components (B) and (E), and exploration of the meaning-generating operations of on-stage signs has illuminated the audience's relationship with the 'make-believe world.' Spectator–spectator interaction, Ubersfeld asserts, takes in the four other forms, while taking the spectator as subject (1981: 311).

Ubersfeld's research, however, moves beyond models of theatrical communication to consider the pleasure of the spectator. Her interest in pleasure has obviously been stimulated by French post-structuralism (for example, Barthes's *The Pleasure of the Text* (1975)) but may well in part be an attempt to address what is often seen as a weakness of Brecht's theory. Much of his writing is devoted to the production of a critical spectator, but there is an evasively scant attention to the pleasure produced by the entertainment Brecht considered such an important part of any drama. Accounting for pleasure is, Ubersfeld suggests, at once easy and difficult:

> One can say almost anything about the spectator's pleasure, and the most contradictory formulas can appear valid: the pleasure of liking and or disliking; the pleasure of understanding and of not understanding; the pleasure of maintaining an intellectual distance and of being carried away by one's emotions; the pleasure of following a story... and of looking at a tableau; the pleasure of laughing and of crying; the pleasure of dreaming and of knowing; the pleasure of enjoying oneself and of suffering; the pleasure of desiring and of being protected from passions.... One can continue forever this little game of oppositions.
>
> (Ubersfeld 1982: 127)

Ubersfeld starts by designating some preliminary sources of theatrical pleasure. Audiences derive pleasure from those who accompany them to a performance (patrons rarely visit the theatre alone) and from the emission of 'barely perceptible signs of pleasure as well as loud laughter and secret tears – their contagiousness is necessary for everyone's pleasure' (Ubersfeld 1982: 128). As the 'game of oppositions' demonstrates, pleasure is multiform and, at the least, twofold: 'it is the pleasure of an absence being summoned up (the narrative, the fiction, elsewhere); and it is the pleasure of contemplating a stage reality experienced as concrete activity in which the spectator takes part' (Ubersfeld 1982: 128). Above all, the pleasure derives from activity, the involvement of the audience in the interpretation of the multiplicity of signs, both transparent and opaque:

> Theatrical pleasure, properly speaking, is the pleasure of the sign; it is the most semiotic of all pleasures. What is a sign, if not what replaces an object for someone under certain circumstances? Surrogate sign, a presence which stands for an absence: the sign for a god, the spool of thread for the mother, the stage for an absent 'reality.' Theatre as sign of a gap-being-filled. It would not be going too far to say that the act of filling the gap is the very source of theatre pleasure.
>
> (Ubersfeld 1982: 129)

Theatrical pleasure, then, emanates from the sign-clustering identified by semiotic research. The theatre audience shares with the spectator of an art work the inability to take in everything with a single look but, where the art work remains for subsequent looks, the theatrical performance is ephemeral. Pleasure results precisely from that ephemerality, from the necessity of making a selection of the elements offered.

Beyond the immediacy of the sign, Ubersfeld identifies pleasure in memory and, as Brecht purported, from understanding. Ubersfeld continues – and as this study has likewise stressed – 'theatrical pleasures are rarely passive; "doing" plays a larger role than "receiving"' (1982: 132). Like Jauss's model in *Aesthetic Experience and Literary Hermeneutics* (1982a), Ubersfeld locates receptive pleasure in identification with the hero. From Freud, she points to the pleasure in transgression (the voyeurism or *catharsis* of the audience) and, drawing on Sanskrit theatre, concludes: 'Theatrical pleasure... is the union of all affective elements plus the distancing we need to achieve peace.... But one must not forget that the theatre spectator is surrounded and pressed on by a sort of urgency, and that this pleasure is countered by its limits' (Ubersfeld 1982: 137). The limits of pleasure are marked by desire, 'desire as lack' (1982: 138). The spectator cannot arrest or touch the object of desire. Indeed, desire moves from object to object and should it stop and fix on a particular object, then the role of spectator is relinquished, the theatrical experience denied (1981: 342; 1982: 138). Pleasure is thus limited by the essential situation of

78

spectatorial dissatisfaction; not only because the spectator is not able to possess the object of desire but because, if he or she did, it would be something other than that which was desired (1981: 343; 1982: 138). The spectator cannot experience pleasure without experiencing its limits.

Desire, Josette Féral suggests, is at the centre of performance art and her endeavour is to identify the essential characteristics of this art form particularly as they mark the limits of theatre. Unlike conventional theatre, performance does not rely upon narrative and representation and, more importantly, it refuses meaning (Féral 1982: 171, 173):

> Performance does not aim at *a* meaning, but rather *makes* meaning insofar as it works right in those extremely blurred junctures out of which the subject eventually emerges. And performance conscripts this subject both as a constituted subject and as a social subject in order to dislocate and demystify it.
>
> Performance is the death of the subject.
>
> (Féral 1982: 173)

The lack of narrativity and failure of representation in performance frustrates the spectator, according to Féral, and furthermore the audience's competencies – on which theatre relies – are destroyed:

> Performance readjusts these competencies and redistributes them in a desystematized arrangement. We cannot avoid speaking of 'deconstruction' here. We are not, however, dealing with a 'linguistico-theoretical' gesture, but rather with a real gesture, a kind of deterritorialized gesturality. As such, performance poses a challenge to the theatre and to any reflection that theatre might make upon itself. Performance reorients such reflections by forcing them to open up and by compelling them to explore the margins of theatre.
>
> (Féral 1982: 179)

These studies by Ubersfeld and Féral herald a theatre research which takes the theoretical impetus of Freud, Lacan, Derrida and other post-structuralists to go beyond the dramatic text and beyond the text in performance. Bernard Dort suggests that the elements of text and performance are no longer in competition:

It is instead a contest which is being held before and for the benefit of us, the spectators. Theatricality, then, is not merely that *'density of signs'* that Roland Barthes spoke of. It is also the drifting of these signs, the impossibility of their union, and finally their confrontation before the spectator of this emancipated performance.

(Dort 1982: 67)

Yet pleasure, desire, confrontation, and the nature of viewing have not attracted the full attention of theatre theorists. On the other hand, the elements of viewing have been central for film theorists and, since Laura Mulvey's seminal article, 'Visual Pleasure and Narrative Cinema' (1975), a corpus of theory has emerged which is without doubt relevant to any study of audiences.

Particularly pertinent is the attention paid to the apparatus of traditional filmic pleasure which maintains an economically successful mainstream cinema. Certainly the cinema and theatre events have much in common. Both are public, generally take place in a building specifically designed for that purpose, and invariably their audiences watch in a darkened auditorium. Both audiences generally react as a group (John Ellis's term is co-voyeurs). Given my interest in theatrical practices which avoid a stage–auditorium 'barrier', it has been useful to look at the work of film theorists – and particularly feminist film theorists – on strategies which disrupt the homogeneity of the classic realist movie.

Despite the usefulness of such film theory and the obvious similarities between cinema and theatre, it is, of course, necessary to remember the finished nature of the cinema production. It is not modifiable in the same way as theatre. Where the theatre audience can (and does) always affect the nature of performance, this cannot take place in the cinema. Indeed, even when film-makers endeavour to take account of the experience for the audience, the distribution network appears reluctant to disrupt the normal production–reception hierarchy. The American handling of the Taviani brothers' *Kaos*, a film version of four short stories by Pirandello, is a case in point. Stephen Harvey writes:

The brothers worry that the 3-hour-plus running time of 'Kaos' might prove a bit much for movie audiences to endure. Therefore, the Tavianis made the heretical suggestions that in each country where 'Kaos' is released, the film's distributor should excise one story according to the perceived tastes of the local public. In an ironic switch, M-G-M/UA, which bought 'Kaos' for the United States, was aghast at the prospect – how could they presume to tamper with the work of artists like the Tavianis?.

(Stephen Harvey 1986: 40)

Even more significantly, film action is always interpreted by the camera, and the spectator's view of the signifying system(s) guided in a way that cannot be guaranteed by on-stage, live performance.

With these limitations in mind, we can return to 'Visual Pleasure and Narrative Cinema', Mulvey's influential discussion of how the spectator's unconscious structures viewing. Here she categorized the pleasure of looking at mainstream films (the Hollywood product) from a theoretical stance typical of the *Screen* critic in the 1970s, influenced strongly by psychoanalysis and Marxism.[14] The spectator's unconscious (which, according to the Lacanian model, structures responses) is, she argues, formed by the dominant order. Mainstream film, 'as an advanced representation system' (Mulvey 1975: 7) within that dominant order, encodes the erotic into the language of that order. For this reason (the dominant order being, of course, *inter alia*, patriarchal), woman is presented in a passive role. The on-screen female functions as icon; she is an erotic object both for characters in the filmic narrative and for spectators in the cinema.

Mulvey suggests that mainstream cinema, as a result of the conventions in which it has developed, portrays:

a hermetically sealed world which unwinds magically, indifferent to the presence of the audience, producing for them a sense of separation and playing on their voyeuristic phantasy. Moreover, the extreme contrast between the darkness in the auditorium (which also isolates the spectators from one another) and the brilliance of the shifting patterns of light and shade on the screen helps to promote the illusion of voyeuristic separation. Although

81

the film is really being shown, is there to be seen, conditions of screening and narrative conventions give the spectator an illusion of looking in on a private world. Among other things, the position of the spectators in the cinema is blatantly one of repression of their exhibitionism and projection of the repressed desire on to the performer.

(Mulvey 1975: 9)

The pleasure of looking satisfies a primordial human wish, but that pleasure is split between active: male and passive: female (Mulvey 1975: 9, 11). The active/passive heterosexual division of labour maintained by the dominant order has, Mulvey argues, controlled the structure of narrative: a man in the movies makes things happen (1975: 12). The man controls fantasy and acts as the bearer of the spectator's look. The male film actor is not an erotic object like his female counterpart. Instead, he is a powerful ideal ego.

Drawing on Lacanian psychoanalytic theory, Mulvey suggests that woman, despite her objectification, presents a problem: 'She also connotes something that the look continually circles around but disavows: her lack of a penis, implying a threat of castration and hence unpleasure' (1975: 13). Furthermore, the presentation of woman as icon 'displayed for the gaze and enjoyment of men, the active controllers of the look, always threatens to evoke the anxiety it originally signified' (1975: 13). For the male, there are two possible escapes from this castration anxiety. He is preoccupied with 'the original trauma (investigating the woman, demystifying her mystery), counterbalanced by the devaluation, punishment or saving of the guilty object (an avenue typified by the concerns of the *film noir*)' (1975: 13), or he turns the threatening object into a fetish object. This latter case, Mulvey indicates, accounts for the cult of the female movie star.

As Colin MacCabe points out, in classic fictional cinema the spectator is in a position where the image is primary, where it guarantees the truth (1976: 11), and central to this is 'the look' that Mulvey describes. The look, the apparatus of traditional filmic pleasure, Mulvey concludes, can be broken into three different components. There is the look of the camera, the look of the spectator, and the look between the characters of the screen illusion. 'The conventions of narrative film', she writes, 'deny the first two and subordinate them to the third, the conscious aim being always to eliminate intrusive camera presence and prevent a distancing awareness in the audience' (1975: 17). By subordinating those looks which are materially present, mainstream cinema dispels the threat of castration and serves the need of the male ego:

> [T]he camera's look is disavowed in order to create a convincing world in which the spectator's surrogate can perform with verisimilitude. Simultaneously, the look of the audience is denied an intrinsic force: as soon as fetish-istic representation of the female image threatens to break the spell of illusion, and the erotic image on the screen appears directly (without mediation) to the spectator, the fact of fetishisation, concealing as it does castration fear, freezes the look, fixates the spectator and prevents him from achieving any distance from the image in front of him.
>
> (Mulvey 1975: 18)

Mulvey's concentration on the male spectator, very much in evidence in that last quotation, generated a wealth of critical interest in his gender opposite. As part of an emerging corpus of feminist film criticism, the role of the female spectator has been an important focus, particularly measured against what Kaja Silverman describes as the now axiomatic description of the female subject in dominant cinema as object rather than subject of the gaze (1984: 131). Mary Ann Doane starts with Freud's lecture, 'Femininity', where, as she puts it, 'Freud forcefully inscribes the absence of the female spectator of theory in his notorious statement, "... to those of you who are women this will not apply – you are yourselves the prob-lem...."'[15] Similarly, Doane suggests, woman is the subject of the cinema's images but these images are 'not *for* her. For she *is* the problem' (1982: 75). With the male seemingly inscribed in mainstream cinema as *the* audience, Annette Kuhn suggests the following conclusion:

> [S]ocio-biological gender and gendered subjectivity are not necessarily coterminous, so that the specificity of the 'masculine' becomes in some way culturally universalised. If this is indeed the case, it certainly speaks to the

hegemony of the masculine in culture that dominant cinema offers an address that, as a condition of being meaningful, must in effect de-feminise the female spectator.

(Kuhn 1982: 64)

B. Ruby Rich decides that cinematic codes have so structured the absence of the female spectator that only two choices remain for her: 'to identify either with Marilyn Monroe or with the man behind me hitting the back of my seat with his knees' (in Linda Williams 1984: 87). Doane develops these possible choices. Beyond the adoption of a masculine response, Doane agrees with Rich that identification is another possibility, although she splits this into 'the masochism of over-identification or the narcissism entailed in becoming one's own object of desire' (1982: 87). Her third alternative (reminiscent of feminist reader-response) is for the female spectator to read the image against the grain, to take her pleasure in a radical way. Based on Foucault's analysis of repressive structures, Doane's polemic for a theory of the woman's gaze concludes with a challenge to received definitions, the problematizing of what was so authoritatively set up by Freud: 'Femininity is produced very precisely as a position within a network of power relations. And the growing insistence upon the elaboration of a theory of female spectatorship is indicative of the crucial necessity of understanding that position in order to dislocate it' (1982: 87). Dolan's book, discussed in the introduction, is a welcome addition to the field, but more might well be undertaken.

Reading against the grain is an obvious strategy for the female spectator. As we saw in the analysis of feminist reader-response critics, it is a useful tool for re-reading canonized works in order to expose 'universally held' (in other words, patriarchal) assumptions. Gillian Swanson notes that readings occur at the intersection of the positions offered by the text and the spectator's own social/cultural identity, and that when this identity leads to a 'quite different point of entry than that "assumed" by the text... a double level of "mismatches" and competing discourses may be possible' (1986: 22). Swanson is surely right in drawing our attention to the determining factors of race and class, as well as gender, in creating readings in tension with those assumed by the text. This inevitable tension in the spectator's position is one that is not only crucial in issues of film reception, but is also clearly apposite in consideration of theatre audiences. It nevertheless remains underinvestigated, as Andrew Higson points out, 'There is little attempt to deal with the question of the relation between the productivity of the text and metapsychology of the spectator, and the way in which the spectator is positioned in the enunciative address of the text, and the critical discourses which circumscribe the meaning of the text' (1983: 85). A recent issue of *Screen* (autumn 1988), entitled 'The Last "Special Issue" on Race?', serves, according to the editors, 'as a rejoinder to critical discourses in which the subject of race and ethnicity is still placed on the margins conceptually' (Julien and Mercer 1988: 3). The spectator who falls outside the classifications of white, male, and middle-class apparently still struggles at the margins of spectator-oriented and other discourses.

While Mulvey's 1975 article has been particularly influential, it has been so through stimulating questions about her central active/passive split, and by extending the once rigid bipartition of the gaze by gender. Mulvey herself has gone beyond her original structure and, in 'Afterthoughts on "Visual Pleasure and Narrative Cinema"'... Inspired by "Duel in the Sun", tries to dislodge her own earlier isolation of the masculine role of spectatorship with a possible role for the female of oscillation between masculine and feminine identifications (in Stacey 1987: 52).[16] Nevertheless, despite this searching out of alternative strategies of viewing, theorists have generally agreed that the practices of mainstream cinema, the realist movies of Hollywood, create 'the homogenisation of different discourses by their relation to one dominant discourse – assured of its domination by the security and transparency of the image' (MacCabe 1976: 12).

'Visual Pleasure and Narrative Cinema' concluded with a plea for counter-cinema, for films that would both challenge and displace the control of dominant cinema practice. Mulvey and other film theorists have made films that attempt such an alternative, and their work is an important contribution to an oppositional cinema which adopts Brechtian theatre practice, in particular the techniques of disrupting the narrative flow and of discouraging character identification. Both Kuhn and

Teresa de Lauretis point out, however, that deconstructive or counter practice does not necessarily displace the hegemony of mainstream cinema. They suggest that breaking down or indicating the limits of the apparatus of the look is not enough (de Lauretis 1984: 75; Kuhn 1982: 168). Indeed, as de Lauretis illustrates in a discussion of Michael Snow's *Presents*, the challenge may simply offer the spectator the same perspective:

> [I]n this film, the nexus of look and identification is produced and broken in relation to 'cinema'.... Because the epistemological paradigm which guarantees the subject-object, man-woman dichotomy is still operative here, as it is in classical cinema, *Presents* addresses its disruption of look and identification to a masculine spectator-subject, whose division, like that of the Lacanian subject, takes place in the enunciation, in the sliding of the signifier, in the impossible effort to satisfy the demand, to 'touch' the image (woman), to hold the object of desire and to secure meaning. Spectator identification, here, is with *this* subject, with *this* division, with the masculine subject of enunciation, of the look; finally with the filmmaker.
>
> (de Lauretis 1984: 75–6)

More effective are films which work outside the epistemological paradigm de Lauretis describes and many examples of films which deny the closure so typical of mainstream cinema can be found in feminist film practice. It is, of course, not surprising that feminist cinema has rejected the active/passive look, the male-centred source of pleasure. Kuhn describes feminist texts as setting up 'radically "other" forms of pleasure' based on the Barthesian concept of *jouissance* available in reading (1982: 168) and as having 'an openness of address in combination with matters of expression in relation to which spectators may situate themselves as women and/or as feminists' (1982: 177).

In her discussion of desire in filmic narrative, de Lauretis notes that success comes from the economic results of audience pleasure (buying tickets, popcorn, and other movie by-products) but that 'for a film to work, to be effective, it *has* to please. All films must offer their spectators some kind of pleasure... be it a technical, artistic, critical interest, or the kind of pleasure that goes by the names of entertainment and escape; preferably both' (1984: 136). Theorists since Mulvey

86

have been concerned with the female spectator who buys her ticket, but there have, as well, been more general investigations of the terms of the cinema-going contract. One such study is Edward Branigan's 'The Spectator and Film Space: Two Theories' (1981).

Branigan defines narrative in film 'as a position of the viewer with respect to a production of space, and subjectivity as a production of space attributed to a character' (1981: 55). Through an analysis of the camera (as a enabling construct for the spectator to understand filmic space) and of diegesis, and by way of Chomsky's theory of linguistic competence, Branigan decides that it should be possible in contemporary film theory to establish a description of the reading competence required for a single class of film. His aim is to codify the judgements a spectator undertakes in order to make meaning of a film narration. Branigan examines a short sequence of Fellini's *I Vitelloni* and, in the same manner as my earlier analysis of the opening of *The Fire Raisers*, looks at the denotative and connotative possibilities of each frame and suggests the hypotheses an audience arrives at. The idea of reading competence has, of course, been widely explored in reader-response criticism, and Branigan's desire to codify is precisely the one now being rejected in semiotic theatre research as neither attainable nor particularly useful. His article does, however, indicate the on-going attempt at understanding those generative systems which enable audiences to receive (and generally make meaning of) cultural products.

Like Branigan, John Ellis is concerned with the cinema-going contract. In his analysis of cinema as cultural product, he deals both with the public nature of the event and the role accorded to those who attend. Ellis takes as the starting point for his discussion the two distinct mechanisms which characterize cinema marketing: they are 'the single film in its uniqueness and its similarity to other films; and the experience of cinema itself. Cinema and film are both sold at the same point, at the point of sale of an admission ticket' (1982: 25). Ellis argues – and I believe this equally valid in the case of theatre – that the spectator does not buy the film, but the possibility of watching a film; the spectator does not buy the cinema but 'the anticipated experience' (Ellis 1982: 26). In this sense, it is an unusual consumer product. There are no tangible goods (except the paper ticket, again only a promise of the experience to come). As in theatre, the spectator spends money in anticipation of receiving pleasure from the product he or she has contracted to receive and the conditions in which he or she is to receive it. Ellis comments further: 'If the anticipated pleasure is not experienced money is not usually returned except in the case of a mechanical fault in the projection: even then, a refund is difficult to come by' (1982: 26). In theatre this is exacerbated when the anticipated pleasure of a particular actor's performance is denied and an understudy performs.

Ellis goes on to distinguish the two performances which the spectator purchases with an admission ticket:

> Cinema is enjoyed whether the film is or not (hence no refund on a dissatisfying film), and often people 'go to the cinema' regardless of what film is showing, and sometimes even with little intention of watching the film at all. Cinema, in this sense, is the relative privacy and anonymity of a darkened public space in which various kinds of activities can take place.
>
> (Ellis 1982: 26)

The experience of cinema, Ellis argues, is these days a quintessentially urban one, 'that of the crowd with its sense of belonging and of loneliness' (1982: 26). At one time, community cinemas where most of the audience members knew each other created a different experience, but today the majority of cinemas provide that urban experience Ellis describes. Indeed, even the sense of belonging created, say, from the large crowd lining up for admission is fragmented by the departmentalizing of audiences into small auditoria within a cinema complex.

In looking at the role of the cinema spectator, Ellis proposed that '[t]he institution of the narrative entertainment film itself proposes a definite kind of spectator' (1982: 79). The Hollywood product specifies an audience which 'is curious or expectant about a particular enigma, and demands that this curiosity should be satisfied in a particular way' (Ellis 1982: 79). Narrative cinema, Ellis contends, confines itself to conservative, familiar ideological trends in society in order to appeal to the widest possible audience. This search for the mass audience is, of course, often necessary simply to reclaim the vast sums expended on shooting the Hollywood 'blockbuster', but the implications of this conservatism were clearly apparent in the discussions of Mulvey and others.

Ellis, like the other *Screen* critics, describes the fundamental satisfaction of cinematic narration as voyeurism. In mainstream cinema, the spectator makes sense of the narrative from a position of separation and mastery: 'The film is offered to the spectator, but the spectator does not have anything to offer to the film apart from the desire to see and hear. Hence the spectator's position is one of power, specificially the power to understand events rather than to change them' (Ellis 1982: 81). This position of mastery and knowledge is, however, 'an extended game with the spectator, offering the promise of such a position, but withholding fulfilment of that promise until the end of the film' (Ellis 1982: 84). Like Branigan, Ellis sees the spectator's reading of the film as a constant juggling of hypotheses, of apparent knowledge, and loss of that knowledge. This process leaves the spectator in a state of anxiety, but an anxiety, however, which is 'provoked in safety, because its resolution is guaranteed by the institution of cinema itself, which is not in the habit of presenting incomplete films' (1982: 85). Anxiety arises out of the contradictory desires fostered by the mechanics of dominant cinema: the desire for the film to continue and the desire for narrative closure. When a film fails to please, Ellis suggests the reason that it has not provided 'the necessary play with phantasies, and final closing accomplishment of a position of mastery and knowledge. The anxiety produced in the expectation of its satisfaction is not dissipated; it returns as a kind of aggression' (1982: 87).

Central to the voyeuristic activity of the individual spectator is his/her membership of the audience at large. Ellis comments on how audiences will tend to relate to a film as individuals when the film narration is intelligible to the consensus. When that intelligibility is denied, the individual will resort to his/her group in one of two ways: questions will be asked in conversations between spectators after the conclusion of the film, or the film will be refused and the audience as a group will mock and criticize as the film plays (Ellis 1982: 87). Ellis also notes:

The presence of the crowd in the cinema is vital to the operation of the regime of cinematic representation. It enables a voyeuristic activity to take place that is necessary to produce the individual spectator as the point of intelligibility of the film. Perhaps it is to ensure the presence of co-voyeurs that people seek company to go to the cinema. The audience of an entertainment film is very seldom composed of isolated individuals, but rather of couples, groups of friends and sometimes even family groups. Many people feel a profound sense of shame at watching a film alone, not principally during the projection,... [but at those] moments when the house lights are up: it is possible to be seen clearly by other members of the audience, and to see them clearly. It is no longer a crowd, but a gathering of individuals, mutually suspicious rather than mutually affirming.

(Ellis 1982: 88)

Ellis's study of the apparatus of mainstream cinema is made largely in comparison to broadcast television. It is not, however, the intention of this study to deal with investigations of the role of the television audience for a number of reasons. Television, above all, lacks the sense of public event that attaches to both theatre and cinema. It denies the audience the sense of contact with the performers that is integral to any theatrical performance and, moreover, it denies the spectator-to-spectator communication (in both its positive and negative aspects) within the larger framework of audience as community.

This excursion into film theory serves to broaden the examination of the concepts of spectatorial pleasure and desire introduced in recent theatre research in the work of Ubersfeld and Féral. Both theatre and film theorists are clearly relying on psychoanalytic (and specifically Lacanian) models through which to explore the audience's experiences. Féral turns to the actor's body in performance theatre as the film theorists turn to the practices of counter-cinema as examples that refuse the usual, ideologically implicated, sources of pleasure. In Swanson and elsewhere we are reminded that the addressees of any cultural product are often gender and race specific, and that points of entry into reception are thus limited in this way.

How far this determines the audience for a particular theatrical product is the subject of discussion in the next chapter.

This collection of theories of reading and viewing brings together some disparate ideas on the constitutive elements of this process, and they form together, I think, a useful background against which we can place the specific conditions of theatre. The following discussion of the cultural phenomenon of the theatre audience obviously draws upon this broad range of approaches to reception but, I hope, goes beyond the confining status of addressee to suggest a more productive relationship, one of co-creation.

3

THE AUDIENCE AND THEATRE

CULTURE AND THE IDEA OF THE THEATRICAL EVENT

Despite the widespread influence of Brecht on contemporary theatre practice, and despite the extensive debate on the ideological gaze of the cinema audience, we lack any detailed picture of the theatre audience and, in particular, their role(s) in the production-reception relationship. The extensive criticism of reader-response theorists has not achieved a codification of reading practice, but it has made us more aware of the complexity of a process once considered 'natural'. Similarly the recent energies of theatre semiotics have not resulted in a codification of the elements of theatrical practice, but have established the multiplicity of signifying systems involved and the audience's role of decoding these systems in combination and simultaneously. Neither theories of reading nor theatre semiotics, however, go far beyond the issues facing an apparently individual subjectivity. Neither takes much notice of reception as a politically implicated act. Indeed, the relationship between production and reception, positioned within and against cultural values, remains largely uninvestigated. Yet all art forms rely on those cultural values for their existence and, among them, theatre is an obviously social phenomenon. It is an event which relies on the physical presence of an audience to confirm its cultural status.

The difficulty of examining readers through social coordinates was evident in Jacques Leenhardt's sociological research, but, as a public event, theatre demands that its audiences be examined in this way. And it is perhaps because of this difficulty that theatre audiences have been more or less

92

neglected. Typical of the generalizations used to characterize the theatre audience is Daniel Dayan and Elihu Katz's description of their apparently limited role:

What there is to see is very clearly exhibited: spectacle implies a distinction between the roles of performers and audience. Performers are set apart and audiences asked to respond cognitively and emotionally in predefined categories of approval, disapproval, arousal or passivity. Audience interaction with the performance may enhance it, but it is not meant nor allowed to become part of its definition.

(Dayan and Katz 1985: 16–17)

Dayan and Katz's analysis is an accurate, if skeletal, model of the immediate reception process for a certain type of theatre, but theatre is not monolithic. These critics do not take account, for example, of the shifting role of the audience in many forms of theatre. As we have seen, non-traditional forms of theatre practice have involved audiences in all stages of production, and have sought (rather than allowed) a central role for the spectator. More than this, such definitions of the audience's limited role skate past the ideological and social mediation of the cultural institution. The audience, by its physical presence as a group, is bound to the institution which produces theatre and, while Dayan and Katz suggest a generic audience for spectacle, the situation is really more complex.

Perhaps the limited approach of Dayan and Katz is not particularly surprising given the restricted focus of most empirical studies of theatre audiences. These, for the most part, have determined the social composition of traditional audiences to provide the cultural institutions with profiles of the 'typical' viewer. Two studies are mentioned here to indicate, in general terms, the methodology involved and the implications of data received. A study, published in 1966, by William J. Baumol and William G. Bowen surveyed audiences in the United States and Britain. Their data were collected from surveys inserted into programmes at 160 performances, yielding over 30,000 usable replies. Baumol and Bowen's research established two fundamental characteristics of the arts audience. It noted a 'remarkable consistency of the composition of audiences from art form to art form, from city to city and from one performance to another' (Baumol and Bowen 1973: 469) as well as identifying that the audience came from a very narrow segment of the national population: 'In the main, it consists of persons who are extraordinarily well educated, whose incomes are very high, who are predominantly in the professions, and who are in their late youth or early middle age' (1973: 469).

More recently (1979), C. D. Throsby and G. A. Withers have published *The Economics of the Performing Arts*. Their discussion of the economic issues facing this industry contains a survey of the 'empirical characteristics of those who provided market support for the performing arts' (1979: 95). Based on primarily Australian and American audience research, although also using available data from Canada, New Zealand, and Britain, they found, like Baumol and Bowen, that the proportion of the population exposed to performance was substantially higher for middle-aged, high income, high education, professional, managerial and white-collar groups (Throsby and Withers 1979: 96). Their conclusion was that 'when attending a concert or play in New York, London or Sydney you are likely to be sitting among a group of people whose financial status, education and occupation are strikingly similar' (1979:100–1).

Throsby and Withers' research of American audiences showed that while a higher income facilitates greater participation in leisure pursuits such as the arts (1979: 103), the predominant determining factor was level of education. This is further substantiated by the high percentage of teachers found in the audiences of the Baumol and Bowen surveys. This suggests then that the assumptions of the academic institutions might well play a significant part in determining the cultural product available (in mainstream theatre at least), as well as the horizon(s) of expectations brought to bear by those choosing to attend. A national idea of culture is certainly an important, and probably overriding, factor.

Andrzej Wirth, in an article comparing German, Polish, and American audiences, suggests that American audiences are very different to the European visitor who has been 'raised in the atmosphere of an institutionalized state theater' (1985: 8). In Germany, those theatres which receive state support are in the majority, and Wirth notes that '[t]he dominant tendency of the German theater culture still remains the rationalistic fixation on the message' (1985: 15). State support works not only in terms of economic support for the performing arts, but also in terms of their validation in a state-controlled education system. In Britain, as Baumol and Bowen's research showed, as well as in Germany, this leads to a more broadly based audience, trained in a particular cultural tradition, and also to a certain homogeneity of product. While state support might make cultural products available to more people, the range available for consumption will be limited by the state's conception of what constitutes (suitable) art. Shevstova has drawn the interesting comparison of US $20,000 scraped together by the San Francisco Mime Troupe (in amounts of $5 and $10, and without support from the major liberal funding organizations) so that they could attend an International Theatre Festival in Managua with Aust.$2,000,000 for twenty-seven Australian performances of the Peter Brook/CICT *Mahabharata* in specially equipped quarries (Shevstova 1989: 27). In countries where control is particularly tightly exercised, an audience homogeneity may be assumed and desired, even when this is not necessarily true. Wirth writes of Poland: 'Generous state support constitutes also a form of control, and the theater in Poland has developed refined forms of "slave talk" (*Sklaven-sprache*), to articulate the view of the intended audience of the national literature' (1985: 12).[1] Wirth's conclusions suggest a counterpart to my own about reader-response theory. The issues which emerged as central to reader-response criticism had an obvious and inextricable link to the institutions that produced them. Similarly mainstream art is produced and consumed by people with well above-average education – both are then products of the same institutional matrix.

Generally, then, empirical research has been of limited value beyond establishing the particular cultural construction of mainstream audiences. This research evidently confirms Dolan's view that the mainstream theatre addresses an audience which is white, male, middle class, and hetereosexual. The use of empirical research by cultural institutions assures, it seems, the maintenance of the existing relationship between mainstream production and the small percentage of the population who attend. Schechner, for example, describes the Guthrie Theater's use of a computerized audience analysis to determine whose patronage to solicit and how. He comments: 'Every theatre wants to pinpoint that "2 per cent" of the population who will pay to go to the theatre. The inescapable result is a middle-class audience' (1969: 34). Those broad research studies (Baumol and Bowen, Throsby and Withers) merely confirm that 'inescapable result'. This inevitable relationship between production and reception is the subject of the next section in this chapter.

Beyond the studies already cited, there has been some empirical research on a smaller scale, used to help existing theatre institutions (like the Guthrie) stay in the 'black' by locating potential subscribers or to test readings of specific plays.[2] A more interesting and useful approach surely is to survey outside, as well as inside, the major institutions. Analyses of audiences who attend other venues, from community theatres to outdoor performance events, might provide a more accurate picture of who experiences contemporary theatre, something much more broadly based than a survey of mainstream institutions would suggest. Two researchers who have attempted this, Frank Coppieters and Anne-Marie Gourdon, provide interesting results from this exploration of culture and the theatrical event.

Coppieters has endeavoured to find empirical methods which would be appropriate for theatre of all types and which would be suitable for examining the nature of audiences' reactions. He has developed the ethnogenic method of Rom Harré.[3] Ethnogenic research is based on the premise that the group is more than a number of individuals, but is instead 'a supra-individual, having a distinctive range of properties' (Coppieters 1981: 36). For this reason, such research is qualitative, rather than quantitative, preferring detailed investigation of typical members of the group and of typical social events. Performances of The People Show (fringe theatre from London) staged at his own university (Antwerp, Belgium) were the basis for Coppieters's study. To establish a framework, he analysed articles from recent issues of the *Drama Review*, a journal which regularly surveyed non-traditional theatre. From these articles, Coppieters drew up an analysis of the performance in terms of social event: 'The event was divided into episodes, e.g., "gathering", "dispersing", and further subdivided into "haptodes", the fine structures of the set of interpenetrating "episodes", within which the playing of the piece before the audience is contained' (1981: 37). His general findings are hardly surprising: audiences attending non-traditional theatre take more of a risk!

In May 1976 Coppieters set up his project based on two performances of The People Show. His data consisted of approximately 1,000 pages of interview transcripts with the main (university) audience; written impressions of, and interviews with, two school classes (chosen to provide group differentiation); and collected newspaper reviews. He found audience members made 'categorical' remarks, describing the show in terms of its difference from what was usually available for consumption at local theatres. Also commonly expressed was embarrassment. Usually this was accounted for in terms of frame breaking as there was no defined stage auditorium barrier. Those attending the second performance (which took place in daylight) were disturbed by the gaze-patterns of the actors and other members of the audience. Some felt uncomfortable because their visibility implied a role in the play's action (Coppieters 1981: 40-1). In fact, audiences generally felt frustration because they were denied the usual channels to making meaning. This started at the point of 'gathering' where the usual clues to type of play or performance were unavailable, and members of the audiences often felt disadvantaged from the outset (Coppieters 1981: 43-4).

Coppieters formed four general conclusions about aspects of audience perception:

(i) One's attitude toward/perception of/relationship with the rest of the public is an important factor in one's theatrical experience.

(ii) Perceptual processes in the theatre are, among other things, a form of social interaction.

(iii) Inanimate objects can become personified and/or receive such strongly symbolic loadings that any anxiety about their fate becomes a crux in people's emotional experience.

(iv) 'Environmental' theater goes against people experiencing homogeneous group reactions.

(Coppieters 1981: 47)

While Coppieters's research is particularly interesting because it looks at non-traditional theatre and its problematic form for those traditionally-researched audiences, Anne-Marie Gourdon's *Théâtre, Public, Perception* is a fascinating comparative study which combines a sociological breakdown of audiences with an analysis of perception. Gourdon concentrates on three performances, representative of the varied trends in French theatre: Girandoux's *Ondine* at the Comédie-Française, *Les Anges meurtriers* directed by Joan Littlewood at the Théâtre National Populaire, and *1793* by Théâtre du Soleil staged at Vincennes. Her detailed questionnaires look at all aspects of the audiences' perception of performances and point to expectations shaped by the place of performance, history of the institution or company or director, and stage environment as well as by the plays themselves. Those who have tickets for the Comédie-Française expect a conservative production with conservative values; those who attend performances by Théâtre du Soleil do not (Gourdon 1982: 197).

Gourdon finds, like the other empirical researchers, a similarity in social composition of theatre audiences: young, middle/upper class, well-educated, and so on. *But* her analyses of the audiences' perceptions of the theatrical experiences show significant differences in ideology, in appreciation, in taste, and in the importance accorded to 'entertainment' (Gourdon 1982: 197–8). The detailed analysis of specific aspects of perception reveal divergent approaches and expectations in the process of engaging with theatrical production. Coppieters's research on The People Show and Gourdon's on *1793* both suggest a different type of experience for audiences outside traditional theatrical institutions, but this research needs to be extended to those groups who perform in local (and especially rural) communities and for special interest groups – in other words, for audiences which do not reflect that homogeneity in social composition found elsewhere. Nevertheless, Coppieters's and Gourdon's work encourages us to see complex connections between actual theatre audiences and social systems, between the notion of a theatre-going public and contemporary culture.

As Janet Wolff points out, contemporary societies give recognition to the discourses of art and of aesthetics (1981: 141), and certainly theatre can never be divorced from the culture which produces it and which it, in turn, serves. To this end, Wolff describes the relationship between culture and artistic production, the artist and his materials:

> The forms of artistic production available to the artist play an active part in constructing the work of art. In this sense, the ideas and values of the artist, themselves socially formed, are mediated by literary and cultural conventions of style, language, genre and aesthetic vocabulary. Just as the artist works with the technical materials of artistic production, so he or she also works with the available materials of aesthetic convention. This means that in reading cultural products, we need to understand their logic of construction and the particular aesthetic codes involved in their formation.
>
> (Wolff 1981: 65)

If we refocus Wolff's analysis to take account of the audience, it is evident that they, like the artist, have ideas and values which are socially formed and which are similarly mediated. As the artist works within the technical means available and within the scope of aesthetic convention, so audiences read according to the scope and means of culturally and aesthetically constituted interpretive processes. The ideological under-pinning of the accepted codes of cultural production and reception has been foregrounded at least since Brecht's critique of naturalist theatre practice. We have been encouraged to see the cultural markers of any artistic product.

In order to identify and understand the cultural markers which designate and endorse the existence of theatre in a particular society, it is helpful to look at some general investigations of culture. Raymond Williams establishes that 'the social organization of culture, as a realized signifying system, is embedded in a whole range of activities, relations and institutions, of which only some are manifestly "cultural" (1981: 209). Certainly we should not talk of theatre as an art form in isolation from cultural practice generally and, while the sociology of culture remains a controversial discipline,[4] it is surely necessary that drama theorists maintain an interest in, and a dialogue with, that particular research. Western industrial societies, for example, assign a particular role for leisure and this supports an economically important entertainment industry. In this way, there is a predetermined need to seek out and maintain audiences for the arts. Gourdon notes that while most of those interviewed said they went to the theatre because it was an art form which particularly interested them, that interest is not culturally innocent. The love of art occupies a central place in bourgeois society and thus interest in the theatre demonstrates both taste and merit (Gourdon 1982: 31). If we consider theatre's role in any given cultural system, and then the audience's relationship both to the generally held concept of theatre and to specific theatre products, we are more likely to obtain a fuller comprehension of the production/ reception relationship.

Peter Stallybrass and Allon White have discussed the inter-relationship and dependency between high and low culture, and have noted that 'because the higher discourses are normally associated with the most powerful socio-economic groups existing at the centre of cultural power, it is they which generally gain the authority to designate what is to be taken as high and low in society' (1986: 4). These 'higher discourses' have, in many ways, restricted our understanding of theatre by limiting the codes which are used to recognize and interpret the theatrical event. Pavis's discussion of the critical reception of Brook's *Measure for Measure* in Paris exemplifies the wide-spread recourse to a particular discourse of criticism. Theatre critics from the major newspapers may no longer wield immense power – the ability to close a show overnight – but they still act as representatives of mainstream cultural ideology and their shared assumptions of what constitutes theatre reflect their status. Gourdon's subjects for research mark the limits (at least at the time of publication of *Théâtre, Public, Perception* in 1982) for academic study of theatre. But, as Suleiman pointed out in her criticism of Jauss's narrow definition of a horizon of expectation, there is always a diversity of publics. Indeed, even within the community of theatre critics, there is such a diversity. Critics writing for specialist or oppositional journals may well hold assumptions and expectations quite different from those identified by Pavis for the Parisian reviewers. Each public will clearly have a different horizon of expectations, and these can coexist among different publics in any given society. It should not, therefore, be the case that the assumptions of the middle-class mainstream audience

100

(typified in the discourse of Pavis's theatre critics and the focus of empirical research) are held as an uncontested norm. We might recall Leenhardt's investigation of readers and his conclusion that predominant unifying cultural systems are utilized 'according to the place of the individual in the systems of hierarchization' (1980: 223). Within cultural boundaries, there are obviously different viewing publics.

While challenges to reader-response criticism have assured that such differences be brought into play when analysing the contribution of the theatre audience, it would seem then that both an audience's reaction to a text (or performance) and the text (performance) itself are bound within cultural limits. Yet, as diachronic analysis makes apparent, those limits are continually tested and invariably broken. Culture cannot be held as a fixed entity, a set of constant rules, but instead it must be seen as in a position of inevitable flux. Similarly, methods of production and reception are redefined, and we need a better understanding of the changes which take place. Of particular interest is how theatre and theatre audiences create as well as accommodate such changes. Thus it is useful to examine some of the challenges to those received assumptions we saw in the theatre critics' analyses of *Measure for Measure*. The testing, breaking and/or rejecting of the theatre products that these critics recognize indicates the diversity of performance practices that today constitute theatre and, in this way, underscores the necessity of a more creative approach to dramatic criticism.

We might start with the fascination of the West in this century with theatre from alien cultures. Both Brecht and Artaud looked to the East for models with which to challenge the hegemony of Western theatrical practice, and the use of ritual in non-Western theatre has had an enormous impact on Western experimental theatre practice. Such ritualistic performances developed outside the boundaries of Western culture nevertheless present an evident attraction for theatre audiences of that culture. Roland Barthes wrote: 'I am fascinated by the Bunraku, the otherness of peoples interests me and only because these puppets come from elsewhere does my curiosity remain aroused' and commented on the performance of ritual songs and dances of the Hopi: 'Can we Westerners really consume a fragment of civilization totally isolated from its context?' (1985b: 120–1). The interest in this theatre is precisely its otherness, its seeming inability to be understood by conventional receptive processes. Eugenio Barba remarks that audiences behave 'as if there was a favoured element in the theatrical performance particularly suited to establishing the meaning of the play (the words, the adventures of the protagonist, etc)' (1985: 77). Western audiences have traditionally depended on the word and this, according to Barba, 'explains why a "normal" theatre audience member . . . often believes that he doesn't fully understand performances based on the simultaneous weaving together of actions, and why he finds himself in difficulty when faced with the logic of many oriental theatres' (1985: 77). Audiences cannot understand non-Western theatre by the same processes as they would apply to a performance of a Shakespeare play, but in its Western contextualizing (presentation in a building designated as a theatre space, the spatial boundaries of audience/stage, conventions of lighting, and so on), it is recognizable as theatre. This in itself testifies to the importance of the institution in the audience's recognition and understanding of theatre, and further reinforces the importance of kinetic-visual elements of performance. Together these implications point to a need to redress the imbalance of interest in the dramatic text.

Indeed, when Western theatre companies attempt to assimilate, or even present, these performances of an alien culture – in other words, to give them Western cultural signifiers – they inevitably create a different product. This might provide a more recognizable type of theatre for the Western audience, but it will accrue meanings which would be unavailable and incomprehensible to the audience of the originating culture. Victor Turner talks about the challenges of converting ethnographic data about the rituals of Ndembu village life into theatre with Richard Schechner's TPG. Central to any portrayal of the rituals of Ndembu culture was an understanding of the matrilineal social context. To convey this, the actors 'began a rehearsal with a ballet, in which women created a kind of frame with their bodies, positioning themselves to form a circle, in which the subsequent male political action could take place. Their idea was to show that action went on within a matrilineal sociocultural space' (Turner 1982: 97). Turner comments: 'Somehow this device didn't work – there was a covert contemporary political tinge in it which denatured the

Ndembu sociocultural process. The feminist mode of staging ethnography assumed and enacted modern ideological notions in a situation in which those ideas are simply irrelevant' (1982: 97). More than the Turner/Schechner collaborations, the experimental theatre of Peter Brook has demonstrated many of the problems with cross-cultural productions.[5] It is particularly interesting that the more recent theatre work of Grotowski, his Theatre of Sources and Objective Drama, has sought the collaboration of anthropologists, sociologists, behaviourists, and others to 'objectify' ritual practices, and that his workshops at Irvine are to involve the training of the 'visitor-participants' alongside the actors (Fowler 1985: 177–8).

Audiences are at best 'fascinated' with performances that do not fall into their cultural experience, performances that resist or deny the usual channels of decoding. Yet it is not an easy task, as semiotic research has shown, to locate a set pattern of responses even for theatre which represents a recognizable cultural product, the play produced by a mainstream organization. Even the mainstream cultural artefact presents a complexity of codes and possible responses which militate against the establishment of fixed rules and conventions for even a single generative system. A description of the receptive competence necessary appears similarly problematic. For example, at the centre of Western theatre culture are the plays of Shakespeare yet neither the production nor reception conditions for these plays are predictable.

Hamlet is surely one of the most frequently produced of Shakespeare's plays, but how useful would it be to question potential audiences on what they expect from the play? Today's productions rarely take up received interpretations of the play. We do not, in other words, get many productions which take as their impetus academic views on *Hamlet*, or even Hamlet. In contemporary theatre, there are few guarantees that a performance available for reception would bear much relation to institutionally received cultural readings of the play or would be intelligible on that basis. Baņuta Rubess writes of 'Hamlet, a new Canadian play' after a 1986 production by Vancouver's Tamahnous Theatre where

the audience is allowed to roam about the three floors of [a] house at will, flitting in and out of scenes, everyone creates and re-creates the play for themselves. . . . The beginnning of the production, the Players' scene, and the end are the only sections shared by the entire audience. Tired of Hamlet's complaints? Fine. Check up on Gertrude.

(Rubess 1986: 131)

Unconventional use of space and re-ordering is not, of course, innovatory but it does challenge accepted notions of high culture. London's Acme Acting took that challenge one step further. They were prepared to bring performances of *Hamlet* (or other 'classics' such as *The Birthday Party* or *A Streetcar Named Desire*) to the comfort of your own home. But perhaps one of the most provocative challenges to our cultural reception of Shakespeare, precisely because it was made within the foremost Shakespearean institution, was Michael Bogdanov's rewritten prologue to his production of Beaumont's *Knight of the Burning Pestle* for the Royal Shakespeare Company. The citizen and his wife, George and Nell, emerged from the audience as contemporary (1981), if caricatured, middle-class suburbans who had paid 'good money' to see some culture from the Royal Shakespeare Company who turned out not to be doing Shakespeare but some unknown called Beaumont. Their assault on the 'actors', both verbal and physical, facilitated for the modern audience an understanding of the romance genre Beaumont was satirizing. But, more importantly and beyond this, Bogdanov let his citizens vocalize the impatience (if not anger) of the 'average' taxpayer who has for the last twenty-five years been financially supporting a Royal Shakespeare Company which was seemingly as likely to perform contemporary 'rubbish' as Shakespeare.[6] Even when the Bard was staged, there was no Elizabethan costume or regard for poetry, but – as George and Nell complained – actors dressed in leather and chains!

Ndembu rituals and Shakespeare's plays might be seen to represent the cultural limits for theatre but, over the last thirty years, acceptance of what constitutes theatre, or at least performance, has, of course, been considerably stretched. Cultural markers have again and again been repositioned. Not only has the innovative, if controversial, work of Peter Brook and later directors at the RSC transgressed received assumptions about Shakespeare, but more generally there has been a determined attack on the expectations and tolerance of the mainstream, middle-class theatre audience. As Stallybrass and White note, however:

> It would be wrong to associate the exhilarating sense of freedom which transgression affords with any necessary or automatic political progressiveness. Often it is a powerful ritual or symbolic practice whereby the dominant squanders its symbolic capital so as to get in touch with the fields of desire which it denied itself as the price paid for its political power.
>
> (Stallybrass and White 1986: 201)

We have seen how the plays of Pinter and Beckett initially tested the tolerance and expectations of audiences, but became accepted as modern classics as those audiences became familiar with the necessary receptive strategies. An even more concerted attack than the plays of Pinter and Beckett can be seen in a work such as John Cage's 4'33". This relies, apart from the presence of a pianist poised to play, on the audience's noise and movement for the 4 minute and 33 second duration to create the work of art – an obviously demanding (and productive) role for the audience. As well as stretching musical boundaries, Cage is clearly questioning the concepts (although not the politics) of theatre and performance. The effect of such works, however, as Marco De Marinis points out in a comment about avant-garde performance in general, is to create and then rely on 'a select band of "supercompetent" theatregoers' (1987: 104). Not all challenges to the mainstream are, of course, accepted. Brecht suggested that innovations which require a repositioning of cultural markers will only be accepted if they rejuvenate rather than undermine existing society.

Perhaps for the reason Brecht suggested, there has, for many workers in marginalized theatre, been neither the opportunity nor the desire to participate in the mainstream. Not all writers and performers have been content to challenge from within the mainstream cultural definition and location of theatre. In the political and/or performance aims of alternative theatres, the idea of theatre is generally repositioned and invariably expanded. Some practitioners have started in the mainstream but have left to pursue alternative projects.

The careers of Dario Fo and Franca Rame are indicative of this process of refusing the implications of mainstream participation. In 1968 they abandoned the traditional Italian theatre and sought instead alternative playing spaces and, significantly, alternative audiences. They worked in tents, workers' clubs, occupied factories, and festivals. Fo says, 'When we reached the top and had this huge audience, we decided it was impossible to go on that way. We realized the middle-class audience was coming to see us and leaving the theater relieved, feeling proud, saying, "I feel democratic." We had become the Alka-Seltzer of the Italian bourgeoisie' (cited in Rosenberg 1986: 4). In the move to non-traditional spaces, Fo declares, '[t]he very first political act was to demonstrate to the people that they have a culture, a language of their own' (cited in Rosenberg 1986: 4). Fo and Rame's relinquishing of mainstream success in favour of broadening the concept of theatre, indeed of culture, to include a broader social group has been an important part of a widespread dissatisfaction with the available channels of production. Since 1968, the proliferation of emergent forms of drama (and especially political drama) have, without doubt, radically altered received concepts of theatre.

Such theatre, in its seeking out of non-traditional spaces and audiences, has brought about the devolution of performance from urban centres to a much broader geographic representation. Even in established theatre centres such as London and New York City, those emergent forms of theatre have led to a fragmentation (Broadway, Off-Broadway, Off-Off-Broadway) and to the attraction of different theatre publics. Schechner notes the explosive growth between 1960 and 1982 in Off- and Off-Off Broadway shows 'from 19 to 132 during an average week' (1982: 66) There appears to be only limited crossover between audiences of the mainstream and audiences of other theatre products. Where mainstream theatres cater for their target middle-class audience who are willing to pay those admission prices necessary to support big productions, many low-budget alternatives have had to target their product just as carefully. We saw in the theatre of Piscator a very specific tailoring to the Subscribers' Club (made up of union workers, communist youth party members, etc.) which brought about an almost complete correlation of social, political, and cultural codes. Such theatre then relies as much as the mainstream on meeting and exploiting the cultural formation of its audience; only the target sector differs. The same close correlation between production and reception ideologies has been evident in the emergence of gay, ethnic, and feminist theatre, although many of these groups – in an ironic inversion of Fo and Rame's history – have had to face difficult decisions about broadening their appeal to more traditional audiences in order to maintain or increase funding.

What these examples unquestionably establish is, as Gourdon's research also suggested, that theatre audiences bring to any performance a horizon of cultural and ideological expectations. That horizon of expectation is never fixed and is always tested by, among other things, the range of theatre available, the play, and the particular production. R. G. Davis, in his article 'Seven Anarchists I Have Known: American Approaches to Dario Fo', discusses the failure of *Accidental Death of an Anarchist* in North American production. He comments:

> So far, most US productions of *Anarchist* have tried to downplay or ignore the politics. Producers, directors, and players have aimed for a slapstick hit. Their thinking seems to be that the more the play is de-politicized, the better will be its reception from the public and the critics. The rub is that when you ignore the political content of *Anarchist* you swamp both the politics *and* the comedy.
>
> (Davis 1986: 318)

It is not that Fo's play cannot be performed for mainstream audiences; both *Anarchist* and *Can't Pay, Won't Pay* enjoyed long runs in London's West End. It is, as Davis's analysis makes clear, that the politics are central both to production and reception. Gavin Richards, playing the central role in the London production, incorporated satirical attacks on the British government within the original setting of Italian political corruption and, as Davis points out, 'English audiences assumed that Richards meant what he said and that the satirical condemnation of official government behaviour presented by the play was indeed its content. They got the political point of view on two levels' (1986: 315). Those audiences were encouraged to take a Brechtian critical stance, but, as the long run probably in itself substantiates, the play was not perceived as a threatening attack on parliamentary democracy. In North America, the depoliticizing at the production stage destroyed the play. As *Anarchist* is structured politically and relies on involving the political sense of audiences, it is hardly surprising that North American audiences were merely confused. Any expectations of a Marxist play were thwarted and thus the pleasure of endorsement, speculation, or rejection denied.

The horizon(s) of expectations brought by an audience to the theatre are bound to interact with every aspect of the theatrical event, and, for this reason, it is useful to examine the idea of the event and its general implications for the act of reception. Raymond Williams described the importance of occasion in the social perception of art. It is, with place, he suggests, the most common signal of art (1981: 131), and this claim is substantiated by a dramatic example:

> There is . . . the interesting case of the experimental company which 'staged' 'dramatic situations,' such as a fierce marital row, in restaurants, while appearing to be ordinary customers. Here the total absence of signals led to every kind of confusion, but its point was a testing of the function of such signals: did the normal 'framing' of such situations, which at the restaurant table might follow word by word and action by action the scene of a play, inhibit or qualify the response of 'others'/'an audience'?
> (Raymond Williams 1981: 133)

This too is the basis of Tube Theatre, where a comedic actor poses as a commuter on the London Underground: one audience consists of the groups of twelve or more who can book to watch the performance, the other consists of those travelling on the subway system for less entertaining purposes.

Both Williams's example and the premise of Tube Theatre indicate the frame that is usually in place for the audience's recognition of the theatrical event. Moreover it is apparent that the occasion for which an audience prepares is linked to its availability. An audience's idea of the event will vary according to their contact with theatre and other art forms, as well as according to their position in the socio-cultural system. In urban situations where a range of cultural products (including a mainstream and alternatives to it) is available in greater or lesser quantities, audiences will likely attach less importance to the event. Audiences might consist of avid theatre-goers, those who attend regularly (perhaps a Friday night ritual), the subscription holder, the infrequent or special occasion attendee, the visitor for whom this is a rare or 'only' opportunity, and so on. The investment in the idea of event returns even for the most avid theatre-goer, however, under certain conditions. First-night or gala performances, especially on Broadway, offer a distinct experience to their audience. The appearance of actors or directors with 'star' recognition can also enhance the idea of event. The name of Laurence Olivier brought a particular prestige to any production. The recent productions of Eugene O'Neill's *A Long Day's Journey Into Night* with Jonathan Miller directing Jack Lemmon or of *The Merchant of Venice* with Dustin Hoffman in the lead role were virtually assured box-office success. Audiences are prepared to pay for (and indeed then expect) a special kind of theatrical event when icons of the profession are involved. A similar enhancement results from the unique opportunity to see a foreign company. Non-Western theatre has, as we saw, had generally exotic appeal. Performance by Eastern bloc companies has also, paradoxically, provided a commodity particularly desirable through its scarcity. Visits by the Berliner Ensemble to Paris in 1954, to London in 1956, and to North America (Toronto) for the first time in 1986, generated both intellectual response and the sense that these performances were a 'must' for anyone interested in theatre.

In the major urban centres, the attraction of tourists to mainstream theatre has become increasingly important. Compared to the person who encounters theatre as part of a day-to-day cultural experience, the tourist likely sees the theatrical event as much more glamorous. Conversely, however, he or she may not attach as much value to its importance. Many of the best-known theatres in London and New York City rely heavily on ticket sales to visitors. Some productions, often those eschewed even by mainstream theatre-goers, rely entirely on the sporadic, usually tourist, attendee. The London production of Agatha Christie's *The Mousetrap* is probably the definitive example. Other shows have managed to appeal to both regular theatre-goers and the more occasional visitor, creating a waiting list and black market for tickets which both enhances the appeal and experience of the event. In this category, we can look to shows such as *Evita*, *Cats*, and *The Phantom of the Opera*, as well as the Royal Shakespeare Company's 'blockbusters', *Nicholas Nickleby* and *Les Misérables*.

Outside the larger urban centres, limited access to theatre will undoubtedly change an audience's sense of the theatrical event. In some instances, where there is generally no access to the theatre, potential audiences may have little conception of the theatrical event. This distance would inevitably create problems in reception and the event itself might be as difficult to decode as for the trained Western audience watching Oriental theatre. At best, it might become as fascinating. For the audiences of regional and community theatre, the idea of the theatrical event is clearly different from that available in the urban centre. It is neither as commonplace nor as glamorous. Again, however, no single concept pertains and the idea of event will vary on similar criteria.

In areas where there is little available theatre, the event may, of course, be seen as a comfortable ritual. John Ellis noted that 'cinema in smaller communities tends to perform a different function [from that in an urban centre] where most of the audience are acquainted with each other. Here the entertainment is related to particular characteristics of individuals or of the place itself. The film comes from outside, the cinema belongs to the particular place' (1982: 27). In theatre, the product may come from outside (a touring company) but it is just as likely to involve members of that community. Therefore, unlike its urban theatrical counterpart and more than its cinematic equivalent, the event of community theatre is able to act as social affirmation of a particular group of people. Many theatre groups working in less affluent urban or rural areas have sought precisely such an involvement at the community level.

The enormous growth over the last twenty years of theatre groups who work non-traditionally has emphasized in their particular practices the different signals attaching to the theatrical event. Above all, the event has been decentred both as occasion and place. Performances are no longer tied to traditional spaces with a fixed audience–stage relationship. The theatre groups have often looked to festivals in non-traditional theatre centres. Webb describes the importance of the Festival des Nuits de Bourgogne in the 1960s (1979–80: 209–10). Schechner describes the Gathering of August 1981 in St Peter, Minnesota as a 'movement that may spell the end of formalist isolation' (1982: 18). Robert Wallace describes Edmonton's fifth Fringe Theatre Event (1986) selling more than 130,000 tickets for 130 shows in nine days (1986: 117). Daniel Chumley writes of the importance for the San Francisco Mime Troupe of participation in an oppositional festival at Managua (1986) in light of prevailing international politics (1987: 291). Even more importantly, theatre has been introduced (or reintroduced) to regional cities and towns, and many companies have established a presence in rural communities where theatre was previously a little-known entity.

With these developments in theatre, the event is often relocated in non-traditional playing spaces, and it often takes place at non-traditional times (not necessarily evening performances with the occasional matinee). The 7:84 (Scotland) Theatre Company is typical of British oppositional groups who have played in major centres and festivals worldwide, but who have concentrated on creating theatre for remote rural communities and performing there on a regular basis. In North America, the Dakota Theatre Caravan has centred on the rural areas of South Dakota, the Roadside Theater on coal camps and farming communities in the Appalachians, and the Mulgrave Road Co-op on rural Nova Scotia.[7] Many other companies have worked directly with unions, often creating theatrical events in response to, and support of, strike action. In France, Ariane Mnouchkine has developed performances in rural areas 'to work on the clarity of their improvisations in front of peasants, a non-theatre-going group . . . . Through this practice the creators (author or acting company) learn from direct experience what is wanted by the audience rather than impose what they think the audience needs or enjoys' (Webb 1979–80: 213). (In this last example, of course, *the* audience is different in cultural and ideological formation.) In the Americas, El Teatro Campesino began as part of the United Farmworkers Strike against the grape growers of Delano, California. Since then, they have performed in Los Angeles, on Broadway, at the pyramids of Teotihuacan in Mexico, on American television in a PBS special with Linda Ronstadt and elsewhere.

All these different theatres create different kinds of events for the audience and, in their diversity, maintain occasion and place as signals for art which are heterogeneous and flexible. As Coppieters discovered in his research of The People Show, many of the audience's receptive processes are pre-activated by their anticipation of a particular kind of event. The nature of that anticipation is, we have seen, inevitably variable. Furthermore, the horizon of expectations drawn up by the idea of the forthcoming event may or may not prove useful in the decoding of the event itself. A crucial aspect of audience involvement, then, is the degree to which a performance is accessible through the codes audiences are accustomed to utilizing, the conventions they are used to recognizing, at a theatrical event. Intelligibility and/or success of a particular performance will undoubtedly be determined on this basis.

Before concluding this discussion of the theatrical event, I want to look briefly at the work of theatre anthropologists and of anthropologists/social psychologists interested in theatre as their research, often in tandem with non-traditional theatre practitioners, which has done much to expand our ideas on this topic. The International School of Theatre Anthropology run by Eugenio Barba at Holstebro in Denmark has been a significant centre for non-textual research. Susan Bassnett in reviewing the *Anatomia del Teatro. Un dizionario de antropologia teatrale*, a collection resulting from ISTA's 1981 summer school in Italy, comments that this work 'invite[s] us to transcend culturally determined expectations of theatre and . . . direct[s] us towards a reconsideration, from a trans-cultural perspective, of the nature of acting and of theatre itself' (1986: 189). While I would argue for the impossibility of transcending culturally determined expectations, such investigations inevitably contribute to the repositioning of cultural markers, to a broadening of our understanding of the theatrical process.

Anthropologists such as Victor Turner argue for the indispensability of the theatrical event. He writes: 'To look at itself a society must cut out a piece of itself for inspection. To do this it must set up a frame within which images and symbols of what has been sectioned off can be scrutinized, assessed, and, if need be, remodeled and rearranged' (1977: 35). Turner describes how 'public reflexivity takes the form of a *performance*' (1977: 33) where communication is achieved not merely through the code of language but through a

112

multivalence of others – gesture, dance, art, symbolic objects and so on. Social life, Turner notes, 'is characteristically "pregnant" with social dramas. It is as though each of us has a "peace" face and a "war" face, that we are programmed for cooperation, but prepared for conflict. The primordial and perennial agonistic mode is the social drama' (1982: 11). In the developed societies of the West, cultural systems such as theatre provide access to processes inaccessible in everyday life. Theatrical performances are, according to Turner, deliberately structured experiences 'which probe a community's weaknesses, call its leaders to account, desacralize its most cherished values and beliefs, portray its characteristic conflicts and suggest remedies for them, and generally take stock of its current situation in the known "world"' (1982: 11). Herbert Blau is surely right in identifying the 1960s as the time when Western society became particularly concerned with theatricalization in everyday life,[8] and this has had an effect on theatre practitioners and audiences alike. Blau writes:

> I tried to show . . . how thinking, in my own work, recycles itself between the illusions of theater and the realities of the world, the realities of the world and the illusions of theater, arriving at a kind of theater whose express subject is the *dis*appearance of theater; that is, the appearances from which theater is made and upon which it reflects are conceptually elaborated and in turn reflected upon until there is a denial, or refusal, by means of theater of the distressing and maybe crippling notion that in life there is nothing but theater.
>
> (Blau 1977: 62)

Experimental theatre in the USA (particularly Schechner's work with TPG), as well as the work of Barba, Brook, Grotowski, and many others, has explored the connections between social life and ritual, and the theatrical performance. The fascination with non-Western theatrical modes identified earlier is surely part of this same interest. Specifically for the audiences of this kind of theatre, but also more generally in light of the popularity of work such as Goffman's, audiences have become aware of the event of theatre as in some way important in socio-cultural processes. Schechner has noted how theatre has been developed to serve many other leisure attractions including discos, punk clubs, gay baths, sex theatres, theme parks, restored villages, wild animal parks, and zoos: 'I think audiences stream into these apparently different kinds of experiences because in all of them a person is absorbed into a "total space" where fantasies can be safely experienced and even, in some places, acted out'. (1982: 28–9).

Whatever the nature of the performance, it is clear that established cultural markers are important in pre-activating a certain anticipation, a horizon of expectations, in the audience drawn to any particular event. Multiple horizons of expectations are bound to exist within any culture and these are, always, open to renegotiation before, during, and after the theatrical performance. The relationship then between culture and the idea of the theatrical event is one that is necessarily flexible and inevitably rewritten on a daily basis.

SELECTION: THE RELATIONSHIP BETWEEN PRODUCTION AND RECEPTION

Against this background of theatre as a culturally-constructed product, signalled to its audiences by the idea of the event, we can explore the audience's experience of the event itself. But prior to examining the specific processes involved, it is pertinent to recall Manfred Naumann's statement that 'works produced always have forms of social appropriation already behind them; they have been selected for reception through social institutions, made available by the latter, and in most cases also have already been evaluated thereby' (1976: 119). The selection or creation of a dramatic work for public performance obviously makes that work available for selection by potential audiences. Theatre as a cultural commodity is probably best understood as the result of its conditions of production and reception. The two elements of production and reception cannot be separated, and a key area for further research is the relationship between the two for specific cultural environments, for specific types of theatre, and so on.

While the focus of this study is the audience's contribution to theatre, it is nevertheless of fundamental importance to underscore at least some of the intervening aspects of production which necessarily mediate an audience's experience. While some audiences are engaged in a productive capacity, generally they are seldom involved in the selection of specific works for performance. Thus, questions arise as to how easy it is to produce a script, where to stage that script, and for whom. Those in a position of economic (and thus cultural) power control what is available through mainstream channels. The hierarchy of production personnel can be complex (as was the case in the cited London production of *Streetcar* (see pp. 56–7)) and is usually restricted to a few powerful individuals or companies. While a Shakespeare play can be generally available for performance (anywhere from Stratford to your own home), certain types of performance – particularly experimental and/ or overtly political – may be only available in constituency areas or to particular demographic sectors.

Despite the determined testing of cultural limits in recent years, censorship, both overt and covert, also remains a decisive factor in the availability of theatrical performances. Censorship as an historical phenomenon evidences the control of those in social and economic power. The representatives of what Stally-brass and White define as the 'high discourses – literature, philosophy, statecraft, the languages of the Church and the University' (1986: 4) have again and again taken the decision as to what is appropriate for the public at large (even when that public simply equates with the educated middle class). This is well illustrated by recent events in British theatre. Until abolition of these powers in 1968, the Lord Chamberlain's Office exercised a fairly stringent system of censorship and, as Sinfield comments, '[a]s long as the makers and audiences of theatre were broadly at one with the dominant values in society, this caused little problem. . . . But the new movement perceived at once that censorship tended to privilege and legitimate traditional ideology and to suppress its own' (1984: 180). Plays such as Bond's *Saved* and *Early Morning* confronted the governance of the Lord Chamberlain and 'club' per-formances (such as those of the Royal Court's Theatre Upstairs) were used to circumvent his control.

But the abolition of this system of censorship has not meant that any play can be produced anywhere in Britain. The mainstream has accommodated playwrights whose works challenge the dominant ideology, but the cultural product is only acceptable if that challenge is contained within certain limits. The reactions to the presentation of Howard Brenton's

115

The Romans in Britain at London's National Theatre clearly show this. Ostensibly the outrage was caused by the portrayal of homosexual rape on stage. Thus we might recall Schechner's discussions of the sensitivity of theatre audiences to overt sexuality because of their awareness of the real presence of the actors (1969: 141), but whether the rape scenes were in fact the problem is highly contentious. Brenton's attack on the British presence in Northern Ireland was powerfully drawn and perhaps perceived by those in power as taking the challenge too far. The protests against Brenton's play did not succeed in preventing audiences from seeing it. Conversely they assured, through the status of notoriety, that tickets for all performances were immediately sold out. What the protests did achieve, however, was the focus of audiences on the play's overt sexuality and, in this way, defused the political potency of Brenton's script. The problems of *The Romans in Britain* are not, moreover, simply an isolated incident of difficulty with a political script in a liberal Western democracy. Other now infamous examples include Gatti's *La Passion du général Franco* which took over ten years to achieve performance and Fassbinder's *Garbage, The City and Death* which still has not had a public production.[9]

In less liberal climates, problems with availability of works for production are clearly exacerbated. The restrictions imposed on Poland's Theatre of the Eighth Day under martial law (loss of funding and property, 'official' disbandment, arrest) are indicative of attempts to curtail counter-government activity. The determination of the Theatre of the Eighth Day to persist (playing in churches, gyms, at open air venues and, when possible, outside Poland), on the other hand, exemplifies the political motivation of many marginalized companies to produce material despite their lack of access to (or, at worst, prohibition by) traditional cultural sponsors. In other situations, theatre directed at exploited or underprivileged groups (gays and lesbians, women, blacks and other racial groups, workers, those involved in strike action, the unemployed, the homeless) has necessarily developed outside the conventional routes of production, and it is perhaps in these areas that the correlation between production and reception has been most consciously developed. Even here, however, selection may well have been tempered by considerations of funding. Where groups are reliant on government grants, self-imposed censorship may well result. Recently I witnessed a women's group about to perform for an audience which included an assessor for the governmental agency which provided most of their funds. The question was whether or not to include a scene about a lesbian which would otherwise automatically be one of the many components of their show. Would this, they worried, have any affect on funding? Certainly Sir Horace Cutler, then leader of the now defunct Greater London Council, immediately waved the threat of a grant cut after seeing Brenton's *Romans*. The fears are not unrealistic.

Less visible and certainly less threatening than the exercising of either direct or indirect censorship is the inevitable process of evaluation that takes place in the selection of work for performance. Selection may be made on the basis of the success of other plays by the same author, company, director, actor, or genre. Again economic factors come into consideration. Economic factors often determine why particular products are available and constitute culture, and, more significantly, highlight once again the inextricable link between production and reception. Economic decisions at the level of production selection inevitably shape the audience's viewing of a particular work.

The relationship between those who produce and those who consume art is, however, not only tied to a state-supported performing arts industry, but is as prevalent when box-office economics are crucial to the existence of a particular theatre or company. Rosanne Martorella's research in the field of opera has demonstrated that the works produced are generally contingent upon the audience's prior knowledge and reception of those works. She has pointed out how companies which depend on subscribers simply cannot risk anything but the most popular works and furthermore, '[p]owerful board members who share similar tastes with the majority of the opera audience aggravate such a situation and have acted to constrain repertory selection and inhibit innovation further' (Martorella 1977: 356). Selection then must be made in response to the broad range of opera-goers and when a very high box-office return is economically crucial, repertories tend towards more conservative choices. Martorella offers the noteworthy example of New York City's Metropolitan Opera. For them, each percentage point of box-office capacity is worth around US$100,000 in terms of income. In the 1960s, attendance averaged 95 per cent. By 1975, attendance had dropped to 86 per cent thereby reducing box-office income by almost $1,000,000. Schechner, discussing the relationship between theatre and the major foundations which contribute financial support, suggests that the foundations have made certain that box-office returns control resident theatre through a policy of demanding at least the promise of a budget which avoids a deficit position. This sets up a controlling strategy, 'one which allies the foundations with the audience and then insures a special kind of audience' (Schechner 1969: 33).

One long-time affiliate of the Metropolitan, Francis Robinson, responded to Martorella's question of who controlled the development of artistic standards: 'The public. We put it as ABC. *Aida*, Bohème and *Carmen*' (Martorella 1977: 358). The increased reliance on subscription monies in the United States has led, it seems, to this extreme conservatism in repertory. While historically theatres have not relied as heavily as opera companies on pre-paid subscriptions,[10] Schechner has noted a relationship between audience and support from other sources. He remarks that when subscription and community funding reach certain levels (when they become large enough): 'foundation aid is easy to get . . . . Community support itself depends upon the subscription audience – a theatre must achieve a certain (though variable) level of "popularity" and "stability" before it becomes the darling of philanthropists and chambers of commerce' (1969: 34). In her report to the Ford Foundation on Hispanic theatre in the USA and Puerto Rico, Joanne Pottlitzer records that 72 per cent of the groups surveyed operated with annual budgets under US$100,000 and that only 4 per cent had in excess of $500,000 per annum. This she ties into lack of administrative expertise, notably in the areas of 'planning, fund raising, fiscal administration, and building and working with a board of directors' (Pottlitzer 1988: 61). For the small companies, these skills are apparently necessary evils but yet there are always the risks involved in loss of financial independence.

Martorella's study of opera reveals a standardization of repertory which strongly emphasizes the reciprocal relationship between production and reception. Schechner similarly posits a standardization and conservatism related to economic constrictions: 'The first aesthetic consequence . . . is a program of classic plays, the favorites being Shakespeare, Molière, Chekhov, Shaw, Miller and Williams. Little truly adventurous drama has been done by resident theatres – even within the scope of the writers they have chosen' (1969: 35). Schechner gloomily concludes that it is the well-known plays of the acknowledged greats which most please the targeted audience.

A further effect of repertory standardization is, according to Martorella, the emergence of particular production method-ologies: 'The way operas are produced has become most important in attracting audiences and in establishing aesthetic norms which prevail today. All energy seems to go toward incorporating new developments in lighting and stage-craft and developing an experience for the audience' (1977: 364). This consequence is not, I think, limited to opera companies relying on public subscription. The two major theatre institu-tions in London, the National Theatre and the Royal Shake-speare Company's Barbican venue, both recently constructed, have demonstrated an equally strong reliance on lighting and stage effects to heighten the theatrical experience for the audience. The intention in part seems to confirm the govern-ment's large financial contribution towards 'excellence' in theatre, and in part to justify the highly technical apparatus which that funding has provided for those stages. Whether in fact this increased reliance on technical apparatus has made the plays any more attractive to, or more enjoyable for, their audiences is, I suspect, a moot point. Beyond this, the influence of theatre size, technical ability, and level of funding has also clearly shaped the new drama commissioned for these institu-tions. Plays written specifically for these theatres by play-wrights such as Hare and Brenton have tended to be 'epic' structures with large casts and many scenes. Here again there is a direct relationship between funding and the type of work available for production and reception.

Martorella concludes that standardization of repertory has a long-term effect on what is available for reception: 'Given the time in which repertoire becomes firmly established and the complex institutional matrix to support it (including pub-lishers, the recording industry, educational institutions, mass media, unions etc.), repertoire is highly resistant to change' (1977: 364). In this way, whether control is exercised by the narrow social band who choose (and can afford) to attend mainstream cultural productions, or by governments or corporations, the result is apparently the same. Both Martorella's study of opera and Naumann's reception theory surveyed earlier suggest that this standardization of production methods and repertory is inevitable. Schechner comments: 'The theatre follows the path of least resistance to its audience and even programs its campaigns to reinforce old patterns of theatre attendance' (1969: 35).

Another path of little resistance is the choice of play already evaluated as a 'hit' through previous box-office success, and it is thus transferred, reproduced in a different location, or revived. In these instances, the production company relies on a play's previous ability to secure audiences and looks to reactivate the successful correlation of production and reception frames. In 1989, Joel Gray is performing in a production of *Cabaret* touring in America; in this instance, the producers can rely not only on past success on Broadway and other stages, but on the enormous popularity of the movie and of Gray's performance to attract 'new' audiences into regional theatres. In another example, Steven Putzel has described how wider audiences have been attracted to Sam Shepard plays as a result of his acting performances in successful movies such as *The Right Stuff*. Curiosity brings them to see if he can write as well as act. Putzel's analysis suggests that the repercussions of this broader appeal can be seen in Shepard's plays. His works, Putzel argues, cater 'to the horizons of expectations of his larger, more affluent audiences, rather than constantly confuting expectation and forcing complicit interpretation from his audience' (1987: 158). Putzel's case is a persuasive one but, in any event, it is certainly true that Shepard's acting career has influenced his marketability as a playwright.

Intertextual reference is clearly also a factor in the process of evaluating possible selections. Some selections exploit other productions that audiences may be familiar with: Manuel Puig's *Kiss of the Spiderwoman* has become a popular stage play since William Hurt's Oscar for his role in the movie version; Howard Brenton's *The Genius* draws on the National Theatre production of his own translation of Brecht's *Life of Galileo*. Other writers have drawn on already canonized texts: Stoppard's

Rosencranz and Guildenstern Are Dead, Peter Eliot Weiss's *Haunted House Hamlet*, Heiner Muller's *Hamletmachine*, and Denise Stoklos's *Denise Stoklos Unearths Hamlet in Irati* are only a few of the texts that take Shakespeare's play as their starting point. Another strategy has been to work with received assumptions about a particular text or type of theatre: Howard Barker's *Women Beware Women* retains the first three and a half acts of Middleton's seventeenth-century tragedy and then provides the original characters with plot and language of his own composition. Other productions deliberately contradict authorial intentions which then permanently change an audience's interpretive strategies and which ask the audience to measure this production against other more conventional presentations: JoAnne Akalaitis's 1985 production of Beckett's *Endgame* challenged the playwright's strict control of his scripts. In each of these instances, the production company seeks to produce an internal horizon of expectations which will attract audiences through challenging their own already-formed expectations/assumptions about a particular play or theatrical style.

The processes of evaluation entailed in the above production selections indicate the inevitability of choices being made in light of others already made. Material selected for production is always evaluated as potentially successful in meeting criteria for that company or theatre. Those criteria, while necessarily a part of the production, may not be immediately available for an audience, but may shape the way an audience decodes a particular performance. Many oppositional theatre groups have grown out of the social sector whose interests they seek to represent and, for this reason, many have made the production criteria an overt and self-conscious part of their work. Many look to the input of their audiences to influence, if not create, both performance scripts and production methods.

The establishment of Teatro Campesino during the United Farmworkers Union's strike against the grape ranchers was an act of empowerment for the Chicano workers. Actors performed scenes to explore the problems of the workers, but were also involved as boycott organizers and pickets. As founder Luis Valdez makes clear, the availability of the play was contingent on how the political struggle was evolving: 'After about the first month, the boycott against Schenley

Industries started and my two best actors were sent away as boycott organizers. There was a lot of work to be done, and sometimes we were too tired after picketing to rehearse so there was a lull for a month' (in Bagby 1986: 133). There are many other examples of companies which may be less politically practical, but equally concerned with the involvement of audiences at the stage of production. Le Théâtre du Soleil has invited factory groups to rehearsal in order that they can *improve* the dramatic work before it goes into performance. Le Théâtre Parminou specializes in commissioned theatre (*théâtre commande*) which, as company members Odette Lavoie and Maureen Martineau point out, leads them to 'working more and more "with" popular movements rather than "for" them' (1988: 26). They stress that the audiences are 'an important actor in the way we create. The collective creation has allowed us to involve people outside the company and indirectly to integrate the audience at the birth of the production. It is this relationship with the audience which is the foundation of our dramaturgy' (1988: 27). Augusto Boal sought in his experiments with the People's Theater of Peru to train and transform the spectator into actor (1979: 126). Indeed, the creation of open production scripts – scenes where audiences make choices or are free to try out possible solutions – has become a common feature in non-traditional theatre.

Unlike the dramatic device of Pirandello's theatre where in *Each in his Own Way* audiences are apparently given the choice of two or three acts,[11] these productions are constructed precisely on the principle of audience co-creation both in the interests of democratization and problem-solving. In Monstrous Regiment's production of Dacia Mariani's play *Dialogo d'una prostituta col suo cliente*, the input of the audience was integral to the play. This, of course, led to variations in performance but also, in Monstrous Regiment's view, to a fragmented experience which more closely resembled women's experience of the world (Bassnett-McGuire 1984: 464). At the WOW Cafe in New York City, a theatre constituted to present anything written by, directed by, or in the interests of women, a policy was implemented whereby 'anyone who showed up to an open staff meeting automatically joined the staff' (Solomon 1986b: 309). This resulted in a policy of open-booking for the Cafe; anyone who wanted to put on a show which reflected the theatre's constitution could do so. Its present goal is to put on 'work from within its own community – a priority not as cliqueish as it may sound since anyone who hangs around is absorbed into that community . . . . [T]his new commitment generated creative work and pushed WOW women toward inventing and finishing new projects' (Solomon 1986b: 311).

These indications of the range of production objectives and ideologies at work in mainstream and other theatres present some understanding of the relationship between production and reception. Whatever takes place at the production stage is bound not only to mediate the work available to audiences, but also to determine – at least in part – the characteristics of the audiences which are likely to attend. Inevitably, and as was particularly evident in Martorella's discussion of opera repertories, economic decisions occupy a controlling position.

In that research it was evident how economic priorities in mainstream opera have led to a standardization of, and conservatism in, repertories and this, it can be assumed, extends generally to material selected for mainstream theatre production. Few risks are taken because the potential for fiscal loss is too great. With 'safe' production selections, theatres must rely on dazzling productions and/or the involvement of stars to sell seats. Paradoxically both approaches are expensive and overall costs inevitably rise. Stanley Kauffman attributes the lack of serious material on Broadway to 'rising expense, not decline in audience quality' (1985: 360). He continues:

> The cultivation of the average American is demonstrably higher than it was when the Broadway range was wider. Broadway has priced itself out of seriousness, out of limited appeal, even though those limitations are broader than they would have been forty years ago. Most of what happens on Broadway hopes to reach the biggest audience, not the best, and must hope so.
>
> (Kauffman 1985: 360)

Unlike mainstream cinema, theatre cannot necessarily rely on long runs to recoup costs. Actors and/or theatres may only be available for limited periods and, in any event, continue to cost money on a week-by-week basis. Transfer to another medium (television or video or film) generally requires a new production, and taking a production on tour is increasingly an almost prohibitively expensive option. Ultimately, in the face of such high economic costs, more and more mainstream theatres remain dark, thereby limiting the performances available for audiences. Perhaps the only safe venues are those which are heavily dependent on subsidy from corporation, foundation, or government and which offer productions that will not endanger that level of funding.

In Britain, the Arts Council, as the major distributor of government subsidy for the theatre and other arts, has had a decisive role. A large proportion of the costs for London's National Theatre is met through government subsidy yet the theatre has still run into problems with deficits. Seat sales have been consistently high and prices have risen steadily, but the enormous operating costs maintain economic pressure. Higher seat prices have assured the predominance of middle-class Londoners or tourists as the theatre audience, and have virtually obliterated risk-taking in the repertoires of the Olivier and Lyttleton Theatres. The third playing space, the Cottesloe Theatre, intended for new drama and more adventurous selections, has been dark for extended periods. Attendance figures confirm that there is an audience for the National, but it appears to be the economic restrictions on production which work to restrict both availability and selection.

The Arts Council has also played a crucial role in the establishment of non-traditional theatre in Britain, and its subsidy has led to the increased availability of theatre outside the London area. While the Arts Council can claim much responsibility for the emergence of a prolific, non-traditional (and generally oppositional) theatre in the 1960s and 1970s, funding for such companies has become less and less available (Arts Council money being re-concentrated on the major producers, the National Theatre, the Royal Opera House, the Royal Shakespeare Company, and so on). Arts Council money has also become less attractive to some groups because of the political compromise it might represent. Other sources of funding, such as local councils, have also become more problematic. Graham Murdock observes: 'The Greater Manchester Council . . . recently cut their grant to the North West Arts Association by the amount earmarked for the radical theatre group, North West Spanner, as a protest against their Marxist orientation' (1980: 162). In this situation, increased demands have been made on less conservative councils, trade unions, and other community organizations. In the successful campaign to disband the Greater London Council, much media attention was centred on the amount of ratepayers' money which went to support oppositional theatre. The attack (like the one on Brenton's *Romans*) was, however, usually made in terms of sexual, rather than political, orientation–why should *your* money be spent on theatre by and for gays when it might be better employed in more traditional social services?

Rather than decimate oppositional theatre, cutbacks in national and regional subsidy have led to a strengthening of ties on a community or constituency level. In other words, the theatre producers are brought into closer contact with the audiences they seek and, however frugal these sources of funding, this may in fact lead to a more sympathetic fostering of non-traditional theatres. Steve Gooch marks one success of political fringe theatre as the establishment of a new relationship with audiences: 'Based on a broadly common political understanding as well as common aesthetic expectations, the division between product and consumer was replaced by the bond of interest between practitioners and spectators' (1984: 56).

Whether traditional or non-traditional, much European theatre relies on subsidy and the attending audience thus sits in a seat inevitably at least part paid for by someone else. It is often the case, as with the National Theatre, that the price paid for the ticket represents only a small part of the actual cost. In this sense, then, the audience member is always buying another's ideology, which is not necessarily coincident with his/her own. Clearly the price of admission is an important ritual in the cultural event of theatre. The high price of a seat at a hit Broadway show is perhaps part of the attraction of attending that kind of theatrical event. When the high price is coupled with scarcity, this creates a heightened sense of the anticipation John Ellis identified as central to the ticket purchase. The theatrical experience the audience enjoys can in this way be shaped by the economic transaction that signals the availability of performance. At the other end of the scale, non-traditional groups have often relied simply on passing round the hat at the end of performance. As Jorge Huerta explains of Chicano teatros, they are 'certainly not adverse to economic independence, but they purposely remain apart from commodity theater in an effort to reach working-class Mechicano audiences' (1982: 215). Huerta also notes the affiliation of some teatros with universities so that audiences on the college circuit who can afford to pay will subsidize (the implicitly more important) Barrio performances.

Ultimately theatre is an economic commodity. Money is generally exchanged for a paper ticket which, as Ellis pointed out (in the experience of cinema), promises the audience two performances: one is the show itself and the other is the experience of being in a theatre. To both performances is attached the anticipation of pleasure. When money is not exchanged, there is instead the commitment of the audience to attend and equally (but perhaps differently) the aim of spectatorial pleasure. Although the specific pleasures of being in the theatre and of watching a dramatic action will be discussed in later sections, at this point it is relevant to identify the stimulation of that pleasure in the act of selection of a particular theatrical offering.

While Stanley Kauffman has argued that the high price of theatre tickets is not only an economic necessity but part of the theatre-going thrill (1985: 359–60), Peter Brook has attacked the institution of theatre critics for discouraging audiences from risk-taking in the purchase of show tickets. He further blames the critics for short-circuiting the excitement of the theatre event. Brook identifies the New York audience as potentially one of the best in the world and comments:

> It seldom goes to the theatre because the prices are too high. Certainly it can afford these prices, but it has been let down too often. It is not for nothing that New York is the place where the critics are the most powerful and the toughest in the world . . . . [T]he circle is closed; not only the artists, but also the audience, have to have their protection men – and most of the curious, intelligent, nonconforming individuals stay away.
>
> (Brook 1968: 23–4)

New York audiences are not the only victims. Brook goes on to describe his production of Arden's *Sergeant Musgrave's Dance* at the Athenée in Paris. The reviews had been terrible

SELECTION

and the company was playing to virtually empty houses. As a desperate measure, they announced three free performances:

> Such was the lure of complimentary tickets that they became like wild premières. Crowds fought to get in, the police had to draw iron grilles across the foyer, and the play itself went magnificently, as the actors, cheered by the warmth of the house, gave their best performance, which in turn earned them an ovation.
>
> (Brook 1968: 24)

This evidence suggests the power of economics to alter the production-reception contract. By changing the idea of the event, but not the production itself, Brook drew in enthusiastic audiences. They did not need to rely on critical opinion as a gauge of value for money but instead responded to an unusual opportunity and altered their expectations accordingly. Furthermore, the interactive relationship between stage world and audience is evidenced by Brook's comments on the quality of performances given at these free shows.

Attention is also drawn to the importance of geographic location in the process of selection, both for production and reception. A theatre district such as Broadway obviously carries its own attractions and Kauffman describes the crowd that is drawn there each night to the various theatres as being 'as close to a sense of community as the New York theatre comes at present. Dingier than it used to be, going to Broadway is still a unique experience because of Broadway excitement' (1985: 363). But is this really the case? Non-traditional theatres have established other theatre communities and one example, the East Village in New York, illustrates a theatre district certainly different from Broadway, but with its own excitement and its own particular appeal to certain theatre audiences.

In an article entitled 'An Evening in the East Village', *The Drama Review* (McNamara and Dolan 1986) documented eight performances taking place on Friday evening, 30 November 1984. Many of the reports comment on the difficulty of finding the various locations and, clearly unlike their Broadway relatives, these theatres make little or no attempt to advertise themselves as theatres. While Kauffman might think Broadway is dingier than it used to be, Uzi Parnes writes that 'the East Village beyond Avenue A brings to mind images of Berlin

127

after the war. Many of the buildings here are shells, abandoned or torched by their owners to collect the insurance' (1985: 6). Notwithstanding this daunting description, the cluster of theatres in this area has undoubtedly been successful in finding its audience. Jill Dolan's description of the pre-show atmosphere at the Club Chandalier demonstrates this well: 'The crowd is mostly women, many of whom are recognizable from the 8:30 show at the WOW Cafe. The spectators mingle freely; many seem to know each other and are comfortable in the space. Performers are difficult to distinguish from spectators' (McNamara and Dolan 1986: 316). It is unlikely that Broadway and East Village audiences would find much in common with their experiences of theatre, but both rely on a geographic framework within which to select their entertainment.

Geographic location is always important. A play must be produced in a location that attracts an audience. Audiences who never attend the mainstream theatres of urban centres, either by choice or by lack of access, may be regular theatregoers at community theatres, clubs, or even through their place of work. The teatros of Chicano theatre has been developed around the location of the audience, rather than the more conventional route of looking for audiences to attend a particular playing space. Le Théâtre Parminou established themselves on a principle of 'democratization of culture geographically by defining our company as one that tours, and by choosing to live in a region outside Montreal or Quebec City. We toured our "popular" productions everywhere, from the smallest and remotest villages to all the big and medium-sized towns in Quebec' (Lavoie and Martineau 1988: 25).

Related to this democratization through geography is the question of performance time. The traditional evening performance is in many ways a central aspect of the mainstream theatrical event. This, unlike the practice of groups such as El Teatro Campesino, emphasizes the work/leisure split and thus promotes a sense of passivity in audiences. It also allows and encourages the arrangement of pre- and post-theatre eating. This enhances the sense of occasion, the pleasurable experience of an evening's entertainment. It also contributes to the economic viability of a leisure industry. Non-traditional theatres have not necessarily pursued the same time scheme. More daytime performances have taken place, often in the outdoors (parks, streets, festivals) in the hope of involving those who do not, for whatever reason, seek evening entertainment outside of the home. In many venues of popular theatre (clubs, union halls, bars), while the evening show is preserved, it is reframed by eating and drinking *along with* the performance. Flyers for The Company of Sirens' production, *Mother Tongues*, being performed in Toronto, indicate a gathering time for snacks followed by a show time half an hour later. The incorporation of eating and drinking facilitates audience activity and community, often an objective of these productions. While this may detract from concentration, it also, groups would argue, works against a soporific passivity in response.

One further element which mediates the selection process should be examined here. This is the influence of marketing or advertising on the audience's relationship to a particular performance. Peter Uwe Hohendahl has described the development of literary commodities for mass consumption and the role in this of marketing:

> In consumer culture, in a logical extension of the capitalist system, the reception of art was drawn into the realm of marketing, with its system of controlled production and consumption . . . . The sophisticated adaptation of calculated and manufactured needs to mass production compromised the bourgeois concept of autonomous culture.
>
> (Hohendahl 1982: 74)

In discussions of reader-response criticism, Naumann's elaboration of the varied mediations between text and reader demonstrated some of the strategies for effective marketing of a book. Advertising, reviews, commentary, discussions or extracts (particularly those presented on television or radio), prizes, and popularization of the author clearly work equally well on the theatre-goer. Scholarship, the teacher, and the professional critic all further serve to market the theatre product. Bad reviews can still limit the run of a production. More significantly, they often determine a very specific set of expectations in the audience and thus determine how that audience will receive the play.

In Hohendahl's analysis of the reception of the best-seller, it is clear that the success of a particular title among its many competitors is dependent upon a powerful and effective marketing strategy rather than on the intrinsic attractions of the book itself. Hohendahl comments:

> Since large amounts of capital are at stake, which must be amortized rapidly, the reception of a novel cannot be left to the usual needs of the audience. The public must be conditioned, even though it has already been largely disoriented by a flood of advertising stimuli. This conditioning begins with such seemingly innocuous matters as the design of the jacket and its blurb. It includes an intensive and extensive advertising campaign in newspapers and magazines carefully chosen for their particular readership, and also involves a planned release of information to the mass media, so that even before the book appears, public interest is aroused by provocative statements.
>
> (Hohendahl 1982: 189)

While most theatrical productions neither need nor receive such techniques of mass marketing, this approach is nevertheless closely followed in the case of the 'blockbuster' production designed primarily for mainstream audiences. The transfer of *Starlight Express* to New York from London provides a good example. With vast pre-production costs in preparing the theatre, advance ticket sales had to be sought rather than relying on positive public response after the usual marketing channels of reviews and word-of-mouth. Clearly the success of the London production provided a starting point for the creation of audience anticipation, but the mass media were effectively used to increase public awareness of and interest in the show's opening. Filmed excerpts of the London stage show were similarly used to stimulate anticipation of a New York production of *The Phantom of the Opera*.

As in most of the categories of selection, non-traditional theatre practice adopts other methods of reaching audiences. Often there is the similar aim of reaching the largest possible audience but, with a minimal advertising budget and quite different ideological motivation, strategies are obviously very different. Kate Davy's account of getting to a performance at the WOW Cafe provides a useful illustration:

> To find the theatre it is helpful to know the address, since the storefront that houses it does not call attention to itself – there is no sign on the building indicating that it is a theatre, only some flyers and photographs taped to the inside of the picture window and the window of the door. Although a performance was scheduled for the coming weekend, there was no way to know about it short of walking by the theatre at 33 E. 11th Street to read the unadorned, handwritten poster in the window that announced it.
> The poster stated that a play entitled *The Heart of the Scorpion* by Alice M. Forrester would be playing at 8:00 p.m. The performance was neither advertised nor listed in the newspapers, and because the theatre has a pay telephone, there is no way to look up the phone number or get it from directory assistance. Clearly, word of mouth was the primary vehicle for attracting an audience to this particular performance, presumably an audience already familiar with the theatre.
>
> (McNamara and Dolan, 1986: 339)

Davy points to the two most common 'advertising' techniques: word of mouth and a habit of attending a particular theatre. These two forms of advertisement worked to disconcerting effect in one experience of 7:84 in Scotland. McGrath describes their tour of the Orkney Islands:

> Small audiences in Stromness and Kirkwall, the two main towns. On our third, and last night, in Orphir, a small village in between, suddenly hundreds. Apparently nobody in Orkney goes to anything until someone else has gone and reported on it. A curious sensation at the box-office, waiting for a whole island full of people who are all waiting for each other.
>
> (McGrath 1974: xxi)

Certainly rural theatre seems to thrive on word of mouth to bring in theatre audiences. Dakota Theater Caravan played in Reva (South Dakota), a place with a population of nine centred around a gas station/store. Their audience totalled 100 (Friedman 1985: 200). Flyers provide another important advertising device for the low-budget production. These are particularly important for touring companies, for those who perform in non-traditional spaces such as public parks, and for those who establish strong ties with a particular community area.

These are obviously simple approaches to advertising the theatrical event, but potentially as effective as more sophisticated and costly devices in drawing in a specific (often constituency) audience with particular attitudes towards the event to be presented. The audience at WOW, for example, is clearly a constituency one and predisposed to receive the feminist, and generally lesbian, orientations of the dramas. The playwrights, actresses, and even characters of the plays[12] become well-known to the audience, and knowledge of their presence in a forthcoming production becomes sufficient advertising.

The elements of selection discussed so far – availability, economics, geography, and marketing – clearly apply, albeit in different ways, both to those producing and to those attending theatre. To this can be added one non-production element: the theatre-goer's commitment to planning, a process which can affect receptive mood. Many possibilities exist. Theatre-going may be habitual and the spectator is willing to attend virtually anything with tickets available on any particular night or the decision to attend a performance might be spontaneous. In either of these cases, little time will be available to construct a horizon of expectations specific to the performance selected. Conversely, the holder of a subscription ticket or the theatre-goer who has booked tickets some time ahead will have had at least the opportunity to prepare for that particular production. Reviews may have been consulted, the text may have been read, or other experiences of theatre drawn upon to construct ideas about the forthcoming event. While, on the one hand, the purchase of a subscription or the early booking of tickets can build interest and anticipation, surely on the other the remoteness of the decision to attend from the actual experience of the event might well add an element of unresponsiveness.

The topics approached by means of culture, event, and selection provide a sense of the complexity that necessarily attaches to the audience of theatre. All these aspects provide a frame for the direct experience of attending a performance. While always culturally contingent, decisions at this level have generally been taken by individuals or small groups. It is at the next stage that the spectator becomes more aware of his/her role as part of a collective group, the audience.

ON THE THRESHOLD OF THEATRE

The specific encounter of the spectator with the theatrical event forms the nucleus of this study. Above all, the role of the theatre audience involves the spectator's interaction with performance in both social (audience member) and private (individual) capacities. But these roles do not begin as the curtain rises. Already it is evident that issues such as cultural background and selection play significant parts in constructing these roles and, indeed, in getting audiences into theatres. In the circumstance of the theatre visit, the spectator takes on his/her role(s) before the performance *per se* begins.

As planning (or the lack of it) plays a part in shaping receptive mood, so the ease or difficulty of attendance has its effect. How did the spectator travel to the theatre? Did he or she already have tickets? The amount of leisure time generally available will affect the time committed to this particular activity? Or is the performance available in the workplace or at a union hall? Is the performance part of an extended leisure activity (a vacation, a night out, etc.), a celebration, a gathering of a local community, part of a university programme? Did travelling to the theatre involve a difficult journey or adverse weather conditions? All such elements of the gathering process are bound to influence the spectator's preparation for the theatrical event, and Schechner suggests that the process undertaken by the audience resembles the actors' preparation (1977: 122). Both, he argues, set in place the theatrical frame.

The milieu in which the theatre is located will also have a bearing on the audience's attendance. Stanley Kauffman's endorsement of the excitement of Broadway has already been described. The theatres of London's South Bank are designed to draw attention to their surrounding environment (the River

133

Thames, the Houses of Parliament, and so on) as a means of enhancing not only the experience of visiting the National Theatre, but also the sense of cultural activity. By contrast, the ABC streets of New York's East Village are, as Parnes described, part derelict, and threatening to those unfamiliar with that area. Certainly audiences who attend mainstream theatres, usually in central urban areas or attractive small town locations (the Stratfords of England and Ontario), largely enjoy a sense of visiting a district where culture is privileged and an import-ant part of established social activity. One of the concerns expressed in the choice of the Barbican for the building of a new London home for the Royal Shakespeare Company was that audiences would not be attracted to an area with no theatre-going tradition. Indeed, the Barbican was a district with a small resident population and where social activity ended in the early evening when business people left their offices and returned to their suburban residences. Despite these fears, audiences at the Barbican have in fact generated residual business. Restaurants already in the area have found evening customers, and new restaurant and other businesses have been established. In other words, a tradition of integrated social activity has quickly come into place in support of an internationally recognized cultural institution. Audiences out-side the mainstream, whether urban or rural, do not have the same experience of theatre attendance. But these audiences are often drawn from the local community, and thus they find the playing space an environment which is familiar and in that way comfortable.

The milieu which surrounds a theatre is always ideologically encoded and the presence of a theatre can be measured as typical or incongruous within it. That relationship further shapes a spectator's experience. Patronage is clearly an evalua-tive act and those who made the journey to Joan Littlewood's Theatre Workshop in the East End of London evaluated that theatre in the act of travelling. Not only were they travelling to an alternative theatre site, in itself unusual, but there was a sense of the theatre's merits in drawing crowds to a non-traditional theatre district. Many of Theatre Workshop's patrons would not otherwise have risked the venture into that part of London. Incongruity can, of course, make a particular political statement. Moreover this can apparently confuse the spectator's horizon of expectations: Nicola Perrin set up her show,

> [a]mong the downtown sin strip of Granville Street [Vancouver], amidst the triple-XXX film houses, video parlors and exotic dancing establishments, [and] the Hotel California, with a 15-metre nude blonde painted on the side of the building. . . . So, the sign outside the lobby that says Routines: A Domestic Peep Show, Shows Every Half Hour doesn't even catch your attention until you're five paces past it. A *domestic* peep show?
>
> (Lacey 1988: 15)

Perrin's 'site specific installation with performance art' involves her performance of housework against a taped background of women talking about cleaning. At 25 cents for twenty minutes – Perrin points out that the pornographic films usually run only three minutes for the same admission price – the performance has a somewhat confused reception: 'head-shaking is a frequent response . . . from the men who stray into the booth by mistake. [Perrin comments:] "Sometimes they walk out after a few minutes. Sometimes they stay, just out of politeness but they fidget a lot and look uncomfortable"' (Lacey 1988: 15). While the geographic location of the performance is central to Perrin's act of foregrounding women's experience, reactions are not all polite. The political implications of her performance are surely accentuated where the threat of violence is real, and the framing of the Granville Street district is clearly crucial to this particular work.

The site of performance is patently important. Along with occasion, Raymond Williams suggests place as the most common signal of art (1981: 131–2). Traditionally (although not always – Perrin's performance is an obvious example) the playing space has been contained in an area or building designated as theatre. That designation, as was evident in the example of otherwise unintelligible non-Western drama, acts to signal the event staged within as theatrical performance. Where the names of the actors playing are displayed outside in neon, this serves not only to lure a certain type of audience, but to promise a certain type of theatrical experience. In recent years, it has become increasingly common for multipurpose buildings (community centres, schools, union halls, bars, cafés, etc.) to serve as performance venues. Outdoor spaces (parks, historic sites, the street, etc.) have also become more popular. This has happened partly because these were the only spaces available to non-traditional theatre groups and partly, as Elam points out, 'in order to escape the tyranny of architectonic grandeur and its aesthetic and ideological implications' (1980: 63). This has the effect, Elam suggests, of looking back to earlier, non-institutional performances such as those of medieval theatre. Undoubtedly each particular variety of playing space provides the audience with specific expectations and interpretive possibilities. *Hamlet* performed to an audience sitting on the grass in a park cannot be the same experience as the *Hamlet* performed in a modern theatre technologically equipped for the presentation of plays.

The study of theatre buildings is not, of course, new. Historical developments in theatre architecture have been rigorously surveyed and researched. Theatre historians have, however, concentrated their studies on the shape and dimensions of the theatre and the relationship of building to plays produced. The audience has only been of limited interest in these studies. Their social composition and their numbers are used to explain architectural features, but generally research has not looked to the reciprocal effects of architecture on the audience and their reception of the plays. Peter Thomson has commented on the long time it has taken to interest architects in researching and documenting the English theatre (1975: 10), and their contribution would surely be decisive in a better understanding of how architecture works on the audience's interpretation of theatrical events.

The theatre building is a landmark as cultural institution. It is a physical representative of the art which dominant ideologies have both created and promoted. Yet, as Michael Hays observes in the introduction to his study of late nineteenth-century French and German theatre,

> [u]ntil recently, the social value and function of the buildings, the architectural forms which enclose the theater event, have remained largely unexplored territory. Critical investigation has instead focused attention on the smaller space of the stage or on the actor and the director. However rewarding such inquiries may be, they inevitably

tend to slight or even deny the existence of a larger area of action which contains these elements of the performance. This large theatrical space exists, however, and is first signaled by the willingness of actors and audience to converge in a specific place at a specific time. It is, in fact, the choice of location which first announces the conceptual as well as the spatial structure of the theater event, since the position, size, and shape of the place determine the physical and perceptual relationships between the participants as well as their number. Temporally, visually, and conceptually, the theater itself provides us with an initial glimpse of the way in which the lived experience of the performance is organized as a structural whole. And it is also this theater space which first allows us to propose a connection between the ordering principles of the theater event and those of society at large.

(Hays 1981: 3)

These physical and perceptual relationships are central to the audience's experience of a performance, and will always mediate readings of the fictional stage world. We might, however, start with a theatre's façade.

While some of the more recent designs for cultural institutions (such as the Pompidou Centre in Paris) have attempted democratization, architectural styles of theatres are generally recognizable as representing high culture. Some theatres which came into existence as centres for popular entertainment have been recuperated through time by high culture by virtue of their historic importance. Postmodern architects nevertheless insist that the 'tyranny of architectonic grandeur' which Elam identified as part of the cultural institution is by no means inevitable. Paolo Portoghesi demands that:

new building types must find a place that can interpret in institutional terms the new demand for culture and happiness, and the new needs of communication and recreation. Bourgeois society in ascent was able to give a stable form to its own needs through the creation of buildings like the theater, the public gallery, the museum and the library. Our present society . . . is still waiting for someone to creatively interpret these differences that mark the passage between an industrial civilization, homologated

137

on the model of mechanical production, and a post-industrial civilization, which tries to put man back at the center of his vision of the world.

(Portoghesi 1983: 77)

The last phase of theatre building, both in Europe and North America, was largely modernist in design and intention, and as such ideologically encoded to approve and welcome the bourgeois society which financed the institutions. It will be interesting to see what changes can be achieved by postmodern architects in creating institutions which are more available to the public at large.

In the meantime, non-traditional theatre has been produced in non-traditional, less institutional venues. In these instances, architecture may not play such an important role. The building may represent other than an institution of high culture and does not, then, overcode the performance in this way. Nevertheless the architectural elements of a community centre, a union hall, or of the factory gates (*outside* of which a performance is taking place), will impose ideologically on performances and the audience's perception of them. Where non-traditional theatre has been undertaken in traditional theatre buildings, efforts have been made to undercut the imposition of architectural features by whatever means possible. Gooch cites the insistence of Peter Cheeseman at the Victoria Theatre in Stoke on the creation of a friendly and familiar atmosphere around the foyer and box-office (1984: 16). As the exterior architectural elements frame the theatrical event, so theatre interiors continue that framing process. Cheeseman sought to counteract the institutional message of his theatre's exterior by a community atmosphere in the interior entrance area. Of course, the very existence of the foyer emphatically points to the social construction of theatre. The small groups of people who come to the theatrical event are deliberately assembled as a collective in a space which has, in its historical development, increasingly been designed to permit social display.

Hays observes that, unlike theatres from a century earlier where the stage took up a large proportion of total available space, from the beginning of the nineteenth century 'the rooms, the foyers and halls for the audience (often separated according to economic distinctions) began to take up more and more space and finally as much as the stage and house together. This is perhaps the most striking aspect of the new bourgeois theater of the period' (1981: 5). He cites Charles Garnier's proposals for the theatre (1871) which include foyers where the spectator is at leisure to study the characteristics of other members of the audience, to note dress and jewellery but, above all, to observe and sense being observed. This aspect of social display remains a primary function in even the more recently constructed theatres. While dress codes in English-speaking countries are undoubtedly more informal than those of French and German nineteenth-century theatres, the foyers of institutions such as the National Theatre and Lincoln Center are clearly designed with the purpose of promoting the pleasure of watching and being watched that Garnier salutes. Denys Lasdun, architect of the National Theatre, evokes classical precedents in his hopeful comments about the National's particular arrangement: 'The inter-connected foyers are not unlike the ancient hypostyle whose communal floors evoked a warm and lively participation by the members of its community' (1977: 29).

Foyers also serve practical purposes. They contain other facilities which are important in the creation of an integrated social occasion for the audience and which often provide additional revenue for the theatre. Cloakrooms, restaurants, and bars are the most usual services, but increasingly stores or counters selling theatre-related goods have been incor-porated. Clearly both mainstream institutions and smaller theatres welcome and need the extra money this can raise and, for the audience, it provides material evidence of both their support and cultural taste. The sense of cultural event can be boosted by a number of other foyer activities. In an endeavour to attract larger, and presumably appreciative, audiences, foyers become the site of additional cultural attrac-tions such as exhibitions and musical preludes. The foyer also functions as the site of receptions in celebration of first-night or gala performances, often an occasion when theatre personnel are available 'to meet the public'. In the mainstream institution, this can provide tangible evidence of the elitism the ticket price represents. In other theatres, the opportunity to mix practitioners and audience is more likely to foster a club-like atmosphere as well as acting as an effective tool to increase the audience's familiarity with the political and/or artistic aims of the company.

In the playing space itself, the area designated for the accommodation of the audience is obviously of central importance. As Hays suggested, it determines not only the physical and perceptual relationship of the audience to the stage, but the actual number of individuals who become the audience as group. While Grotowski has stated that it takes one spectator to make a performance (1968: 32), theatre productions generally seek a much larger audience. The percentage of seats occupied will inevitably affect reception both through its effect on the quality of actors' performances and through inter-spectator relations. The experience of the spectator in a packed auditorium is different from that of one in a half-empty theatre. When a theatre has very few spectators, the sense of audience as group can be destroyed. This fragmentation of the collective can have the side effect of psychological discomfort for the individual which inhibits or revises response.

To examine the influence patterns between seating area, audience, and stage, Elam draws upon the theory of proxemic relations established by anthropologist Edward Hall. This theory works to prove that use of space is governed by rules which generate a range of connotative cultural units. Hall divides proxemic relations into three main syntactic systems (fixed–feature, semi-fixed-feature, and informal space):

> Fixed-feature space involves, broadly, static architectural configurations. In the theatre it will relate chiefly to the playhouse itself and, in formal theatres (opera houses, proscenium-arch theatres, etc.) to the shapes and dimensions of stage and auditorium. Semi-fixed-feature space concerns such movable but non-dynamic objects as furniture, and so in theatrical terms involves the set, auxiliary factors like the lighting and, in informal theatrical spaces, stage and auditorium arrangements. The third proxemic mode, informal space, has as its units the ever-shifting relations of proximity and distance between individuals, thus applying, in the theatre, to actor–actor, actor–spectator and spectator–spectator interplay.
>
> (Elam 1980: 62–3)

As Elam notes, all three modes are usually simultaneously effective, but particular theatres will valorize one system over the remaining two. Theatre history provides examples of every kind of proxemic relationship ranging from the consciously structured (the proscenium-arch or its opposite, Gropius's Total Theatre) to the consciously flexible (medieval and much contemporary theatre).

Dominant theatre practice generally maintains the fixed-feature mode and, because of this, seating arrangements become important. They extend the social display initiated by the foyer. In the most extreme form of display, spectators were seated on the stage. Perhaps the nearest contemporary equivalent is the box. In these seats, sight of the stage is notoriously bad but the patrons accommodated are a focal point for the rest of the audience (the majority). With this exception, proximity to, and visibility of, the stage is usually proportionate to the price paid for the seat. The cheapest seats are farthest away, often with a restricted view, and distance their occupants not only from the stage action but from the rest of the paying audience. The social implications are self-evident. Theatres built in the boom of the 1960s and 1970s, while generally retaining a fixed stage–auditorium arrangement, were often designed to accommodate open seating policies and reflect, of course, the 'democratization' of those times.

Contemporary audiences in theatre buildings are, therefore, most used to fixed stage–auditorium relationships, and the predominance of this convention has led to its necessity for a comfortable theatrical experience. It will be recalled that Coppieters's research revealed a repeated reaction of embarrassment to The People Show precisely because of the lack of a fixed relationship. Barthes wrote: 'I do not like openings, or private screenings, or theatre premières. I need the anonymity of the commercial theatre, like that of any unknown group of museum-goers' (1985b: 120). The predominant architectural design of theatres – a foyer which encourages observing and observation in the small, familiar groups in which we attend the theatre, and an auditorium which assures anonymity (and thus reassurance) in the larger collective – has thus been received and translated by theatre audiences into psychological need. Elam notes that, while the spectator surrenders

141

his individual status upon entering the auditorium, he 'has his own well-marked private space, individual seat, and relative immunity from physical contact with his fellows (and even from seeing them). The result is to emphasize personal rather than social perception and response' (1980: 64–5). Such an effect is hardly surprising in light of the value accorded to the individual and his/her privacy in bourgeois culture. Neither is it surprising that oppositional theatre has determinedly sought to break up notions of space and to reinforce the social perception and response.

Elements of semi-fixed-feature relations are also part of the audience's experience at this pre-performance level. The condition of the stage set at the point of the audience's entry can provide an important first stimulus for the audience's perception of the play. Where it is available for consumption, it acts as the initiator of the decoding process and this inevitability has been exploited by many playwrights and directors. The pre-performance set can be the device which brings an audience's horizon of expectations into conflict with the performance's internal horizon of expectations established by a playwright and/or director. Arthur Holmberg's review of JoAnne Akalaitis's production of Genet's *The Balcony* shows both a director's exploitation of pre-performance and the audience's necessary adjustment of expectations:

> Whereas Genet's play takes place nowhere and everywhere, Akalaitis locates the action in a Central American Republic in the grips of a revolutionary convulsion. As spectators trickle into the auditorium, peons salsa to the rhythms of Ruben Blades in a tumble-down, shell-shocked barrio that spills off the stage into the audience .
> . . . . [B]efore the play proper begins Akalaitis has given us a visual image of the revolutionary as carnival.
>   (Holmberg 1987: 43: my emphasis)

In *Six Characters in Search of an Author*, Pirandello uses the pre-performance set to launch his attack on audience assumptions: 'The spectators will find the curtain raised and the stage as it usually is during the day time. It will be half dark, and empty, so that from the beginning the public may have the impression of an impromptu performance' (1952: 211–12). In

Stoppard's *The Real Inspector Hound*, the pre-production set not only provides the metatheatrical attack of Pirandello's play, but complicates the challenge with the inclusion of a very familiar setting, the drawing-room:

> The first thing is that the audience appear to be confronted by their own reflection in a huge mirror. Impossible. However, back there in the gloom – not at the footlights – a bank of plush seats and pale smudges of faces. The total effect having been established, it can be progressively faded out as the play goes on, until the front row remains to remind us of the rest and then, finally, merely two seats in that row – one of which is now occupied by MOON. Between MOON and the auditorium is an acting area which represents, in as realistic an idiom as possible, the drawing-room of Muldoon Manor. French windows at one side. A telephone fairly well upstage (i.e. towards MOON). The BODY of a man lies sprawled face down on the floor in front of a large settee.
>
> (Stoppard 1968: 9)

In a play which remorselessly parodies the genre of the dramatic thriller, the presence of a dead body on the stage acts as an irresistible lure for the audience. They are drawn to speculate as to whether the body is real or not (an actor or a dummy) and to construct elements of plot to explain this opening frame. In other plays or performances, more simply, audiences might be faced with stagehands preparing the set for the opening moment. In this instance, the theatricality is emphasized and, like the more determined examples of Stoppard and Pirandello, the device attempts to prevent the establishment of perfect illusion. It may, of course, be the case that audiences accept the convention (and necessity) of stagehands and thus agree to ignore them.

Diametrically opposed to this practice is the set concealed behind the theatre curtain. In this case the audience is unable to begin the decoding process based on literal evidence of the set, but is nevertheless reminded by the curtain (as well as by its likely counterpart, the proscenium-arch) of the theatrical frame. The curtain can also function to provoke the audience into speculation about the kind of set that will be revealed for the play they are about to watch. In British theatre of the interwar years, much of the attraction and splendour of performance centred on the lavish and unique sets. In such examples, the curtain's role was to increase audience anticipation and to enhance the pleasure of the opening moment when the curtain rose to reveal a magnificent set design.

The light set of the auditorium is a less obvious, but nevertheless possible pre-production tool. An audience admitted (as it often is) into an auditorium where the lights are subdued is reminded of its purpose in being at the theatre. The subdued lights encourage a subdued atmosphere in the auditorium at large, and prepare the audience for interpretive activity. Conversely, a well-lit auditorium continues the element of social display encouraged by the theatre foyer. The moment when the lights are dimmed then becomes a significant instruction to the audience as well as a means to heighten anticipation quickly and effectively. At the Metropolitan Opera House in New York, the dimming is accompanied by a mechanical withdrawal to the ceiling of the chandeliers which dominate the auditorium, a grand gesture which aims to guarantee a quiet and prepared audience for the opening moments of the performance.

The informal proxemic mode can also be available prior to performance. In non-traditional theatres it is not unusual for the actors to fulfil non-performing roles such as collecting tickets, ushering, or even serving behind the bar. Actors may welcome the audience into their seats. This can be done as 'actor', then reminding the audience of the actor/character split inevitable in theatrical production, or as 'character', thereby activating performance and interpretation on point of entry rather than through a more formal opening scene. A production of The Canterbury Tales by the Young Vic Company (which has toured extensively) used this to particular effect. By greeting and talking with the audience members as they arrived, they prevented audiences in formal auditorium arrangements from establishing their personal and private spaces in individual seats. It also allowed the Company to 'read' the make-up of their audiences in different locations. The effect was to establish a collective atmosphere and to break the stage–auditorium barrier before it was actively in place. Other instances of informal proxemics include the already on-stage presence of the actors. This presence can provide a stimulus for decoding (as in the case of the body in *The Real Inspector Hound*) or act as a possible interpretive strategy (actors concluding warm-up exercises publicly might, for example, signal a Brechtian production style).

One further element of pre-production should be included. This is the theatre programme. While this may be a simple sheet of paper listing the names of those involved with a particular production about to be staged, it can also be an elaborate publication which provides the audience with several points of entry to the production. Programmes can provide a history of a particular play, or of the theatre company. They can provide photographs of the actors or – more significantly – of the production to be seen. They sometimes supply biographies of the personnel involved; this might foreground, or at least remind the audience, of the presence of a star name. Programmes can also carry director's notes which may well be intended to promote a particular interpretation. Edward Bond, of course, has become notorious for the provision of long prefaces (such as his discussion of violence for the programme of *Lear*) which are certainly polemical and which are intended to provide an interpretive framework for the plays. Bond would appear to consider the programme an effective device in establishing contact with his audiences, but it is always the case that programmes may not always be supplied, they may be left unread, or read and then ignored.

More common, of course, is the listing of *dramatis personae* and the naming of places and times. The quantity and type of information will obviously vary, but some examples demonstrate well the potential in interpretive processes. Not surprisingly, contemporary audiences for historically distant dramas with typically complex plots are conventionally given most 'help'. Consider the listing of *dramatis personae* for the 1975 Old Vic production of John Webster's *The White Devil*:

DRAMATIS PERSONAE

MONTICELSO, a Cardinal, later Pope PAUL IV

FRANCISCO de MEDICI, Duke of Florence: in the last Act, disguised as MULINASSAR, a Moor

The Duke of BRACCIANO, husband first of Isabella, and later of Vittoria

GIOVANNI, his son by Isabella

Count LODOVICO, in love with Isabella; later a conspirator in the pay of Francisco

CAMILLO, first husband of Vittoria; cousin to Monticelso

FLAMINEO, secretary to Bracciano; brother to Vittoria

MARCELLO, his younger brother; of Francisco's household

ARRAGON, a Cardinal

JULIO, a Doctor

ISABELLA, the first wife of Bracciano; sister to Francisco

VITTORIA COROMBONA, wife first of Camillo, and later of Bracciano

CORNELIA, mother to Vittoria, Marcello, and Flamineo

ZANCHE, a Moor; servant to Vittoria; in love first with Flamineo, and later with Francisco

MATRON of the House of Covertites

LAWYER

SERVANT

AMBASSADORS

LADIES IN WAITING

GUARD

Even the most cursory glance surely leads an audience to 'read' the size of the cast and the intrigue of the plot. More attentive readers might perhaps take some pre-production time to decode the complexities of relationships and to posit character and plot. By contrast, we might look to a programme for Peter Handke's *The Ride Across Lake Constance* (Hampstead Theatre Club at the Mayfair Theatre, London 1973). This simply states:

THE ACTORS ARE
Jenny Agutter
Faith Brook
Nigel Hawthorne
Nicky Henson
Alan Howard
Gayle Hunnicutt
Nicola Pagett

Here the *absence* of information might provoke audience activity – endeavours to construct clues from other programme information, recall of reviews read, other work by the playwright, and so on. The uncertainty constructed by the programme format is, of course, mirrored in the play's subtitle ('Are You Dreaming or Are You Speaking') and these 'facts' might well combine to prepare the audience for an unconventional – or, at least, an unsettling – experience.

Places and times can be given in a detail which suggests importance. The programme for the 1983 production of Edward Bond's *Summer* at the Manhattan Theatre Club provides a framework for audiences which might be used in establishing expectations. It might also serve as a map with which the audience follows the action in performance:

The present.
Eastern Europe.
The terrace of a cliff house facing the sea.

Scene 1. The terrace late Friday night.
Scene 2. The terrace Saturday morning.
Scene 3. The terrace Saturday afternoon.
Scene 4. The island Sunday afternoon.
Scene 5. The terrace Sunday evening.
Scene 6. The terrace early Monday morning.
Scene 7. [The Agreement] The terrace late Monday morning.

More typical, perhaps, is a skeletal outline of the production's format. In the programme for the 1984 production of Stoppard's *The Real Thing* at the Plymouth Theatre, New York, it simply states: 'Two years elapse between Acts I and II.' None of Stoppard's metatheatrical play is hinted at, or, more importantly perhaps, given away.

Certainly the amount of information and the signposts a programme presents act as significant stimuli to the audience's decoding activity prior to any presentation of a fictional on-stage world. Perhaps the most important signpost in the programme is the play's title. Audiences are probably familiar with the title through many of the elements discussed already – selection (from advertising or word-of-mouth), from display outside and inside the performance venue, and so on. It has been suggested that the title *No Sex Please, We're British* is the (only) reason for that play's remarkable box-office success.

All these elements of pre-production will be emphasized or naturalized according to the ideology of the production itself. Nevertheless, whether in the foreground or not, these elements do serve to prepare further the audience for the reality of the theatrical event. The physical arrangement of a theatre as well as the degree of contact between performers and spectators at this stage may well limit, or even determine, the interpretive strategies adopted by the collective audience.

PERFORMANCE

However important the cultural overcoding of production and reception, the concentration of the audience's 'work' takes place, obviously, at the time of performance. Karen Gaylord describes the role adopted by the spectator confronted with the actuality of the theatrical event:

[T]he spectator serves as a psychological participant and empathetic collaborator in the maintenance and 'truth' of the fictive world onstage, is 'taken out of himself' and becomes for the time part of an ad hoc collective consciousness, ready to find meaning and significance in the events taking place on stage.

Thus the theatrical occasion involves a double consciousness for all concerned. The performance takes place on at

148

least two levels of 'reality' simultaneously and within at least two frames. The outer frames always embraces both audience and performers. The inner frame demarcates the playing space.

(Gaylord 1983: 136)

The model this study will use is also of two frames. In this instance, however, the outer frame contains all those cultural elements which create and inform the theatrical event. The inner frame contains the dramatic production in a particular playing space. The audience's role is carried out within these two frames and, perhaps most importantly, at their points of intersection. It is the interactive relations between audience and stage, spectator and spectator which constitute production and reception, and which cause the inner and outer frames to converge for the creation of a particular experience.

The spectator comes to the theatre as a member of an already-constituted interpretive community and also brings a horizon of expectations shaped by the pre-performance elements discussed above – or, as Herbert Blau describes it: 'An audience without a history is not an audience' (1987: 34). This 'history' constructs the outer frame and is confirmed by the existence of commonly acknowledged theatrical conventions. At the centre of the inner frame is the combination and succession of visual and aural signs which the audience receives and interprets, some fixed but the majority in flux, and which, as we saw earlier, signify on a number of possible levels (for example, denotative/connotative). It is the combination of these signs which permits the audience to posit the existence of a particular fictional world on stage with its own dynamic and governing rules.

The signs can be considered in two groups: those that are part of the actor and his craft, and those external to the actor's performance. These external signs derive from the set, props, lighting, sound, and music. The actor's performance involves language, voice, movement, and physical appearance (including costume, make-up, and facial expression). Linking the two is the utilization of the external signs by the actors either singly or in interrelationships. The audience is likely at the outset of a performance to read the stage as macrocosm. All elements may be taken as of more or less equal importance

149

in establishing a hypothesis of the nature of the on-stage world. As the performance continues, elements such as set tend to be assumed by the audience unless they are in some way drawn back into the spectator's focus (as in the case of a set change). As the world, and the characters within that world, become known, the audience's concentration tends to move to the smaller details (facial expressions, gesture, costume changes, and so on).

Like the individual reader, the audience inevitably proceeds through the construction of hypotheses about the fictional world which are subsequently substantiated, revised, or negated. The horizon of expectations constructed in the period leading up to the opening frame of the performance is also subject to similar substantiation, revision, or negation. Unlike the reader, however, the spectator of theatre experiences the 'text' within specific time constraints which deny the chance to repeat readings (except by attending a second, *different* performance of the same production) and which restrict what Eco described as 'inferential walks' (1979: 32). Some inter-textuality might be deliberately summoned by elements of production, but the 'walks' afforded the theatre audience are necessarily limited. The spectator's mind is, of course, free to wander and be inattentive to what is *on* stage, and this is probably inevitable in the course of any performance. Indeed, the practice seems to be actively encouraged (and thus controlled?) by dramatists who insert *longueurs* between passages which compel close attention. Nevertheless, the only particular times available for reflection and review are in the breaks determined by the producers, not the receivers. The curtain may be dropped or the lights faded to indicate an act or scene division, a change in time or location. This represents usually only the briefest of pauses. Scene changes might provide more time and an intermission offers at least the possibility of ten to twenty minutes uninterrupted reflection, although this opportunity tends to be experienced socially. Thus, any evaluation might well be made in terms of the small social group attending the performance together, rather than in terms of the private experience of the reader. Occasionally the audience is asked to reflect on and review the action by means of an on-stage device. This might be achieved through a flashback, a scene in which many of the scenic elements mirror an earlier scene, or through a device such as chorus or narrator. In the latter instance, the review process is necessarily complicated by the demand on the audience to hypothesize about (and invariably judge the accuracy/usefulness of) the character(s) presenting the commentary.

The hypotheses which constitute an audience's immediate reading are inevitably influenced by, as well as measured against, the internal horizon of expectations of a performance. Where the text of the performance is known to some or all of the spectators, the *mise en scène* will likely be read against that knowledge. In that way, the audience can judge the presentation of the fictional world as more or less meeting their expectations, as unusual (Richard Eyre's production of *Hamlet* where a single actor played both the lead role *and* the ghost of Hamlet's father), or as aberrant (Peter Eliot Weiss's *Haunted House Hamlet* for Tamahnous in Vancouver). Where a written (rather than improvised) dramatic text is produced, that text – whether familiar to the audience or not – will inevitably hold inscribed points of entry, strategies for interpretation. Beyond this, a director's intervention will inevitably create another horizon of expectations internal to the performance.

In twentieth-century theatre the director has become, as Dort reminds us, the most powerful figure, not only in terms of specific productions, but in the control of theatres and cultural centres (1982: 62–3). Textual strategies may well bear the ideological overcoding of the director. A director's production plan will, like the dramatic text, contain receptive strategies. How far the audience accepts the proposed receptive strategies will generally depend on some shared socio-cultural background between text and audience, director and audience, production company and audience. Many contemporary playwrights who have continued to write naturalistically (most usually retaining the naturalist character) have nevertheless worked against audience empathy by other strategies of Brechtian distancing which encourage a different focalization. Toby Silverman Zinman describes how Sam Shepard 'had the walls of the set of *Fool for Love* wired for reverberation and four speakers installed under the seats so that every slam of the door physically involved the audience. Thus the spectator moves closer to participant, and passivity becomes exciting dis-ease' (1986: 424).

151

Overcoding will also result from other pre-production elements which are put into place by the production team rather than potential audiences. Marketing is one obvious example. If a play is publicized as serious drama, then the on-stage signs will tend to be interpreted in light of this and comic elements devalued in the receptive process. Another important source of overcoding is the playing space. The imposition of architectural elements has already been discussed and, indeed, the relationship of the audience to the architectural features can be exploited to establish who recognizes the performance as theatre. In the 23rd Street storefront, the New York home of Squat Theatre,[13] those who pay the US$4 admission are seated facing a curtain which opens to reveal the busy street in lower Manhattan. Schechner comments: 'The actions onstage . . . are balanced/contrasted by actions in the street; and the actors of Squat are counterpointed by passersby who react to what they see through the window. The playing area is a limen linking two worlds' (1982: 88). The spectators sitting on risers (who are doing so as a result of a financial exchange) and witnessing the drawing of the curtain have been given signals which establish the theatrical frame. For the person walking by, the action is merely bizarre.

The audience's understanding of the stage world is then subject to their perception of an extensive code system. Perception is, in fact, an aspect of the theatre audience's role which has attracted critical attention. Gourdon's *Théâtre, Public, Perception* (1982), through the types of questions asked of the various French audiences, explores the dependency of perception upon the nature of the performance seen, upon the construction of the *mise en scène*. Her assessments of the different strategies for perception of particular productions are appealing precisely because of their base in actual performances. More theoretical studies include the work of Marco De Marinis (particularly 'Toward a Cognitive Semiotic of Theatrical Emotions'(1985)) and of Ed Tan. Tan's search is for a 'theoretical framework . . . in order to neatly describe the cognitive processes taking place, so to speak, in the heads of spectators' (1982: 158). Like Gourdon, Tan tests hypotheses in terms of actual audiences, and his move towards a union of empirical research and performance-oriented theory should develop our knowledge of how audiences construct meaning(s).

The approach of analysing actual performances/audiences seems to me to be the most interesting and worthwhile, and one I will return to later in this chapter. Notwithstanding this preference, and the recognition that textual analysis can only represent part of a complex network presented to the audience in live performance, the opening sequences from two plays (Henrik Ibsen's *A Doll's House* and Caryl Churchill's *Cloud Nine*) have been selected to illustrate possible strategies of reading/constructing the on-stage world. The sections of text discussed are reprinted in the Appendix. Both these plays, of course, have interesting stage histories and such histories can usefully provide a basis for suggesting variations in an audience's perception of these plays.

The opening of Ibsen's play is signalled by the revelation of a detailed set. It is the typical room of the naturalist play, to be framed by a proscenium-arch, and filled with furniture and other trappings which serve both to reflect the bourgeois late-nineteenth-century audience for whom the play was intended and to create a sense of the homeliness of the Helmers' lifestyle. Stage directions indicate the stove is lit and this provides two connotative effects: on a simple level, it signals a cold day (suggesting, most likely, winter) and, beyond this, it indicates the presence of family life (it is a room in general use). Lighting might be expected to complement this homely atmosphere and create an overall effect of softness. The audience's initial experience of the play is one of enjoyment, a privileged look into a fixed and finished world.

The audience's absorption of the wealth of set and prop detail, however, is interrupted by sound. The doorbell is heard. Beyond its purpose of interruption, the bell indicates the presence of an outside world and heightens the audience's anticipation of meeting the first character(s). If the play is familiar, the primary effect will be of anticipation. Nora is about to be introduced: expectations for the character can be measured and a first judgement of the suitability of casting made. For the more sceptical audience, the reminder of an outside world might herald the possibility of threat, the promise of disruption of this seemingly secure environment. Later in the play, of course, it is the mailbox which functions in this role and the audience (like Nora) is directed to listen for its interruption of the otherwise festive action. In this opening scene, stage directions indicate a moment's wait until the door is opened. It is a reasonable hypothesis that such a comfortable household would rely on a maid to screen arrivals, and this moment's delay builds further the significance of the first entry.

When Nora comes into the room, the audience is confronted with many new signs. There is her costume, her props (parcels), her humming, and the backdrop (framed by the hall door) of the porter bearing a Christmas tree and a hamper, as well as a maid by the front door. The winter hypothesis is reformed to a more specific time, just before Christmas. The porter and maid in their costumes, their background positioning, and distance behind the new focal point of the scene, Nora, indicate her status as well as their own. Nora's humming – reinforced by costume, props, make-up, lighting, gesture, and movement – provides initial signals about her nature and her happiness. The obvious hypothesis of a woman who is content and secure in her home life (initiated by the opening stage picture) is one which, of course, undergoes considerable revision in the course of the play.

The first spoken section of the play comes, then, after quite detailed hypotheses have been drawn up by the audience from a wealth of non-verbal signs. As might be expected for an opening sequence, the sign-clusters start at their most dense (the whole stage set) and, as the opportunity for hypothesis has been presented, the focus is narrowed and immediate interest is drawn to fewer signs more locally concentrated. By the time Nora speaks, the audience has absorbed the stage picture, has posited its relation to the outside world, has assumed Nora's position within it, and thus can concentrate on the language spoken and the character's specific gestures and movement. Nora's opening lines provide supplementary information and indicate activity. It becomes clear that Nora is a mother. The initial hypothesis of winter, revised to some time pre-Christmas, is now established (by means of the audience's interpretation of Nora's instructions to the maid) as Christmas Eve. Activity is expressed through her instructions to the maid and her question to the porter. Clearly Nora is moving around and across stage which the audience can perceive as another sign of her control and contentment. For those with some knowledge of the text, however, the continual movement of Nora, accompanied by that initial humming, indicates perhaps her nervous energy, the first cracks in the surface picture of bourgeois respectability and security.

As readers of *A Doll's House*, we learn from a later conversation between Nora and Mrs Linde that Nora has spent less than half the money Torvald gave her for her wardrobe on her clothes so that she could apply the rest to her debt (Ibsen 1965: 162). In performance, her costume might well reflect the simplicity and cheapness Nora describes. Where some in the audience may well read Nora as a beautful woman complemented by beautiful clothes (thus echoing Torvald's reading of his wife), others might well read the costume sign quite differently. They might question why the woman of this comfortable home does not have a more expensive wardrobe. For the knowledgeable audience, this reading most likely prevails. Furthermore, it does not then take the form of a question, but provides evidence of the kind of sacrifices Nora has made.

This outline of the opening of *A Doll's House* indicates the intensity of activity required of an audience confronted with performance. While the outer frame (cultural background, audience and production horizons of expectations, social occasion) will always mediate and control receptive strategies available, an audience's conscious attention is to their perception of the physical presence of a fictional world. The production history of *A Doll's House* indicates the importance to audiences of both outer and inner frames. After the play's première at the Royal Theatre in Copenhagen in 1879, the critical reception emphasized, not surprisingly, the social and political challenge of the content. But its original use of theatrical conventions did not escape attention either. Erik Bøgh wrote in his review for *Folkets Avis*:

[I]t is beyond memory since a play so simple in its action and so everyday in its dress made such an impression of artistic mastery. . . . Not a single declamatory phrase, no high dramatics, no drop of blood, not even a tear; never for a moment was the dagger of tragedy raised. . . . Every needless line is cut, every exchange carries the action a step forward, there is not a superfluous effect in the whole play . . . the mere fact that the author succeeded with the help only of these five characters to keep our interest sustained throughout a whole evening is sufficient proof of Ibsen's technical mastery.

(Bøgh: cited in Meyer 1971: 455–6)

A Doll's House became internationally known and produced, however, as a result of its challenge to cultural conventions of what was accepted as suitable material for theatrical production. It was because of the perceived scandal of this challenge that the first performance of A Doll's House in London was ten years later than the Copenhagen première. But the experience for the audience was undoubtedly different. Firstly, the furore surrounding Ibsen's play was well-known and no longer new. London had also seen some five years earlier Henry Arthur Jones's adaptation, The Breaking of A Butterfly. And perhaps most importantly, the British première of A Doll's House was staged at the Novelty Theatre with Janet Achurch playing Nora. Achurch and her husband, Charles Charrington, were famous for their staging of new drama at the Novelty, and thus the audiences attracted to their theatre were likely sympathetic to, rather than enraged by, the material presented. With all the publicity surrounding the play, London audiences would certainly have been curious to see the play. Harley Granville Barker commented: 'The play was talked of and written about – mainly abusively, it is true – as no play had been for years. Charrington lost only £70. This was not bad for an epoch-making venture in the higher drama' (cited in Meyer 1985: 35–6).

Obviously, then, diachronic analysis shows changes in cultural limits and different horizons of expectations shaping the audience's interpretation of specific stage signs. More recently, with Ibsen's play now an established classic, two movie versions of the play were released in the same year (1978). In one, Nora was played by Claire Bloom, an established and highly-regarded stage actress; in the other, Nora was played by Jane Fonda, a movie star and political/feminist activist. These casting choices undoubtedly reflected quite different internal horizons of expectations which, in turn, established different external horizons of expectations. As in the case of familiarity with a particular dramatic text, familiarity with actors in other roles is also often a part of a horizon of expectation which has to be revised or confirmed. Except for those few interested in the possibility of comparison, the two movies of *A Doll's House* attracted quite different audiences, and offered experiences quite remote from that of the 1879 audiences in Copenhagen.

In both movies the naturalism is heightened as the technical apparatus of cinema provides the maximum possible surface realism. But the audience's experience of either movie or proscenium-arch stage version is likely little different. *A Doll's House* offers the kind of experience identified for audiences of the classic realist film. Nora is the object of their gaze. On stage or on film, she is the subject of the signs, and she is the problem. Mulvey accounts for an audience's separation, their voyeuristic role, by the opposition of the dark auditorium and brilliance of the on-screen light. It is an opposition which applies equally to the conventional staging of Ibsen's play.

It is this separation which Brechtian theatre seeks to avoid. Even in the conventional auditorium–stage (dark–light) arrangement, this theatre refuses the audience a neatly-packaged fixed 'reality'. Conventional processes of decoding are continually challenged and the narrative continually inter-rupted. The opening of Churchill's *Cloud Nine* is clearly quite unlike that of *A Doll's House* and, in this play, the audience's interpretation relies far more on reading signs in contradiction than in combination. The opening stage picture of *Cloud Nine* has none of the elaborate details that were revealed to audiences of *A Doll's House*. Only three scenic components are involved. In their paucity, they may well be assumed to be of particular significance and importance. The low bright sun (signified by light and/or scenery) in combination with the verandah signal the setting of Africa. The flagpole with Union Jack establishes the British colonization, British power, and the time period. Sun and flag combine for an added ironic suggestion of the fading of that British Empire on which the sun was supposed never to set. The scenic components are, however, outnumbered by the actors representing 'the family'.

Unlike the opening of *A Doll's House* where the audience was afforded the opportunity to consume the set detail and familiarize itself with the world of the play, the action of *Cloud Nine* begins immediately. All the on-stage characters join in song, a rally of 'sons of England' to the flag. This draws the audience's attention to the flag and its signification, and to the family group. Grouped as if in a family portrait – and not all 'sons' of England – they represent quite obviously the first challenge to audience assumptions and decoding processes. The audience can decode relationships through costume signs and discover a husband and wife with son, daughter, grandmother, manservant, and governess. But these straightforward readings are contradicted by the sex, race, and physicality of the actors. The wife is played by a man, the young son by a woman, the black servant by a white, and the daughter is not an actor but a dummy. The usual recourse to hypothesis is foregrounded and problematized.

The audience's problems in dealing with the opening sequence are made explicit when Clive, the central male figure, steps forward to address the audience directly. His stage position, between the family group and the audience, suggests that he will provide a bridge to understanding. This is compounded by his status (head of the household) which denotes authority not only over the other characters but in providing much needed information for the audience. His opening lines confirm that status and his relationship to the other characters, but their structure as a pair of rhyming couplets again acts to make audiences aware of their hypothesis building and to cast doubt on a straightforward informational reading. When Clive brings forward his wife (played by a man) and introduces her, the audience is faced with Clive's unreliability. He sees her as a 'natural' wife and does not share the audience's confusion. The cumulative effect of the on-stage signs of the opening sequence is to throw the audience off-balance. In the absence of understanding, they may well react with laughter. Such a reaction is, at this point, a defence mechanism which protects their privileged position as audience. By interpreting the on-stage signs as ridiculous, the audience is not threatened by its own inability to make meaning.

In the course of *Cloud Nine* Churchill uses these distancing techniques to question society's assumptions of certain relationships as 'natural'. Churchill exploits the audience's inability to construct conventional hypotheses to promote an examination of the issues beyond the images presented. Their interest is held not by the surface reality focused on and through specific characters (the technique of *A Doll's House*)

158

but by the necessity to read beyond that reality. The overt theatricality of Churchill's presentation works against a conventional reliance on plot and character and instead asks that audiences question their assumptions not only about theatre but about the more general operation of cultural values.

As in the case of *A Doll's House*, however, diachronic analysis of particular productions reveals a shifting audience response to the play based, as might be expected, on the cultural values and expectations carried by different productions and the different audiences which see them. The opening production was staged by Joint Stock Theatre Company at the Dartington College of Arts. The theatre company had commissioned and collaborated with Churchill to create this play and thus their contribution to the ideological internal horizon of expectations was self-consciously inscribed. The questions raised about sexual repression and its relationship to the economic oppression of capitalist cultures reflected their own views as well as Churchill's. They had worked with the playwright to find dramatic techniques which would be effective for them as actors in the portrayal of these issues. Dartington, as a popular venue for fringe political theatre, would likely guarantee an audience familiar with the work of Joint Stock; moreover, that audience would most likely be sympathetic to the left-wing politics of company, playwright, and play. Their decoding of the opening sequence, then, may not have been as problematic as my analysis suggests. Some familiarity with a Brechtian approach may well have made the audience content to suspend judgement or even immediately aware of the cross-gender dressing as a technique to foreground sexual stereotyping.

Cloud Nine was revived at the Royal Court Theatre in London during the following year (1980) where audiences were likely of a similar socio-cultural formation to those which attended at Dartington. They would not have had such a close and familiar relationship with Joint Stock, but they would likely generally share the political sympathies and the awareness of theatrical strategies in oppositional theatre. In 1981, *Cloud Nine* was staged at the Lucille Lortel Theatre in New York City. Unlike the two British productions, the American production was an undoubtedly risky venture. Churchill provided a revised version of the play-text, and the director selected (Tommy Tune) was in some ways an unusual one. Tune's reputation as a successful director of musical theatre probably helped, however, to get this play into New York production.

Nicolas Surovy (who played Harry/Martin in the New York production) has described how various actors would not audition after seeing the script (Dunning 1981: C4) and clearly the American cast did not have the initial confidence Joint Stock had through their past history with Churchill (their joint creation of *Light Shining in Buckinghamshire*, their history as a collective, and their familiarity with Brechtian techniques). The New York production was none the less a critical and audience success, although it is interesting to note Churchill's own comments on her central revision for American audiences: 'There is a lot that is attractive about the New York ending, and it provides more of an emotional climax, which is why we did it. But on the whole I prefer the play not to end with Betty's self-discovery but with her moving beyond that to a first attempt to make a new relationship with someone else' (1984: ix). This suggests that the adoption of a discourse of American feminism (self-discovery) realigned Churchill's drama to address a targeted audience in terms that would meet an American, rather than British, horizon of expectations.

These analyses of *A Doll's House* and *Cloud Nine* are intended to illustrate likely processes of reception for audiences familiar with different experiences of theatre. Beyond this, the audience's freedom to select quite different processes of reading, or even to ignore the play entirely must not be discounted. Similarly, members of an audience may resist focal points. Instead of accepting the sign-cluster which represents the centre of the action, concentration may be diverted to signs other than those foregrounded by the performance or may even move to read unintentional signs against them. With these caveats, it is nevertheless recognized that a *mise en scène* is inevitably structured so as to give emphasis to a sign or sign-cluster intended to locate audience focalization on that aspect of the drama. In some cases, this focalization is foregrounded by specific dramatic techniques. Beckett's instructions for *Play* provide a good example:

Front centre, touching one another, three identical grey urns about one yard high. From each a head protrudes, the neck held fast in the urn's mouth. The heads are those, from left to right as seen from auditorium, of w2, M, and w1.[*] They face undeviatingly front throughout the play. Faces so lost to age and aspect as to seem almost part of urns. But no masks.

Their speech is provoked by a spotlight projected on faces alone.

The transfer of light from one face to another is immediate. No blackout, i.e., return to almost complete darkness of opening, except where indicated.

The response to light is not quite immediate. At every solicitation a pause of about one second before utterance is achieved, except where a longer delay is indicated.

Faces impassive throughout. Voices toneless except where an expression is indicated.

Rapid tempo throughout.

The curtain rises on a stage in almost complete darkness. Urns just discernible. Five seconds.

Faint spots simultaneously on three faces. Three seconds. Voices faint, largely unintelligible.

(Beckett 1978: 45: * w1 = first woman, w2 = second woman, and M = man)

The stage world of Beckett's *Play* – three faces, three voices, three urns, and a spotlight – is already minimal. His instructions indicate an endeavour to control the production as if it were a musical score with the effect of rarely offering more than three on-stage signs (the facial expression, the voice, and the language) for the audience to read. The possibility of interest straying to non-foregrounded or unintentional signs is virtually removed, and the minimal fictive world is thus likely to result in a concentration of intense decoding activity around the few signs available. Audiences in this way are encouraged to decode blackouts and silence or the three voices and faces simultaneously displayed as moments of particular significance.

Textual analyses can provide interesting and useful explications of strategies available for audience interpretation. But however detailed, these analyses can only represent a small part of the interactive relations that constitute the nexus of the two receptive frames. It is the actuality, rather than the possibility, of an audience balancing stage and other worlds that fosters theatrical experimentation such as Grotowski's

Theatre of Sources and Objective Drama. It is also this flexibility which makes yet another production of *Hamlet* possible.

With a focus on the audience, three aspects of interactive relations are important. They are audience–stage interaction in the field of fiction, audience–actor interaction, and interaction in the audience (Passow 1981: 240). The first level of interaction has been considered above. The audience also interacts with the on-stage presence of actors and the contribution of feedback is acknowledged by all actors. It is well known that an appreciative, knowledgeable audience can foster a 'better' performance from the actors and that a restless audience can disrupt the on-stage action, creating mistakes, lack of pace, and poor individual performances. Indeed, when actors make improvised attempts to control a restless audience, the result can be an imbalance of the total production-effect.

Certainly theatrical performance encourages audiences to appreciate the actors' skill. Brecht stressed in his *Verfremdungseffekt* that the actor should *show* a character with the effect that the audience would appreciate the tools of acting used in this demonstration. Conversely Method actors are admired for their skill in *becoming* the characters they portray. Audience members might be attracted to the voice of a certain actor or to specific physical abilities. The acrobatics of Peter Brook's production of *A Midsummer Night's Dream* made new demands on the actors, but also on the audience to appreciate specific skills in bringing a script to performance. More particularly, certain actors acquire a public persona and this, as we saw, can affect an audience's horizon of expectations. With the presence of a 'star' on stage, the audience is inevitably aware of a double presence (for example, Dustin Hoffman/Shylock) and it is generally the case, to a greater or lesser degree, that the audience is reading the actors' performance alongside the work being performed. Karen Gaylord's attention to a convention of Broadway theatre audiences exemplifies this practice:

> [W]hen a Broadway audience follows the custom of applauding the first appearance of the star onstage, they are, as attendants, applauding the skilled performer qua performer. In the process they break the frame of the

specific dramatic event and, momentarily, 'bracket' the illusion of the constructed reality on the stage.

(Gaylord 1983: 137)

This double recognition is not, of course, unique to theatre. Cinema also makes its audience aware of the double presence of actor/character but, in this medium, the supremacy of the image (the control of the camera's eye) serves to reduce the effect of double reading. In a film, audiences may always be aware of the presence of Meryl Streep or Jane Fonda, but accept the other characters on a single level. With the physical presence of the actor in the theatre and the ever-present possibility of mistakes, forgotten lines, or even accidents, the actor is always less likely to be subsumed by the character portrayed.

The very real presence of the actor accounts, Schechner suggests, for the theatre audience's general resistance to on stage nudity. He writes that the 'hierarchy of tolerance seems related to both the degree and the kind of involvement expected of the reader and viewer' (1969: 139). Reading is the most private of pleasures. In the cinema, the product for consumption remains at a distance, but the spectator has an awareness of the rest of the audience. In the theatre, because of the actor/character presence, '[l]ittle overt sexuality is permitted onstage because the audience knows that what happens to the character also happens to the actor' (Schechner 1969: 141). Certainly much contemporary theatre exploits the proxemic relations between spectator and actor. Not all audiences can accept the frame-breaking this involves. The stage–auditorium barrier can provide the secure position which permits reception. Coppieters, it will be remembered, found that environmental theatre worked against a homogenized group reaction (1981: 47). Certain audiences, however, are attracted by the frame-breaking practice and actively seek a participative role in performance.

As in the Coppieters's example of environmental theatre and, indeed, in theatre practice generally, inter-audience relations also play an important role. Semiotic analysis has stressed that the communication between specators usually determines a 'homogeneity of response' (Elam 1980: 96) despite variations in horizons of expectations and/or cultural values brought to

163

the theatre by the individual spectator. In almost all cases laughter, derision, and applause is infectious. The audience, through homogeneity of reaction, receives confirmation of their decoding on an individual and private basis and is encouraged to suppress counter-readings in favour of the reception generally shared (Elam 1980: 96–7, Ubersfeld 1981: 306). For this reason perhaps, Jeanie Forte asserts that the 'challenge for feminist dramatic criticism is one of empowerment, for women writers, performers, and reader/spectators' (1989: 125). Here empowerment might result in the breakdown of that homogeneity of audience response. Material aspects of performance can also have that same effect. In Coppieters's analysis of audiences of The People Show, the lack of aesthetic as well as real distance prevented the establishment of a homogeneous response. As individual spectators felt threatened by the light playing conditions and the gazes of the actors, the audience remained fragmented and alienated. Feedback and distance at some level are therefore of paramount importance in the formation of the collective consciousness of the theatre audience.

Yet, as Jurij Lotman points out, the individual does not lose integrality in the act of combination into larger groups. He concludes that it is the richness of the conflict between psychological personality and the collective intelligence which ensures the exceptional flexibility and dynamism of culture (cited in Shukman 1981: 327). It is surely the case that while the theatre audience is a collective consciousness composed of the small groups in which spectators attend theatrical events, it is also a specific number of individuals. As the analyses of cinema audiences indicated, many of the pleasures of the event, although shared by the audience at large, are enjoyed privately and individually. The pleasures derived from anticipation of a theatrical event generally and a particular performance specifically are, for example, commonly shared but will vary according to the individual's circumstances and attitudes. The pleasure of looking is as primary to theatre as to cinema. It is also as problematic. While a look may be inscribed by the performance text, without the controlling eye of the camera the possibility of aberrant or against-the-grain reception by the individual or the collective is always more likely. Furthermore, individuals can always refuse the

164

collective contract by walking out of a production or, less dramatically, by falling asleep. Certainly the collective contract is a fragile structure, and this is undoubtedly emphasized in performances where the spoken word is problematized. Sometimes companies offer the audience a choice: recently in Toronto *If My Mother Could See Me Now/ Inay, Kung Alam Mo Lang!*, a play about Filipino domestic workers, was organized into separate Filipino and English performances. Not only was the play performed in two different languages, but apparently looked to two different audiences. Even within a single audience, there can obviously be different levels of language comprehension and my own experience of attending a performance of Grand Kabuki on tour in North America made this particularly evident. Performing in Calgary, the Grand Kabuki drew a large audience from the many Japanese-Canadians living in Southern Alberta. The performance was in classical Japanese but was also available in simultaneous translation into English through the rental of a headset. Yet the addressees were split into those who watched (no headset) who understood the Japanese dialogue, those who watched (no headset) who did not understand the Japanese dialogue, those who watched with headsets who understood (some) Japanese (and some of the conventions of Kabuki), and those who watched with headsets who had no understanding. Some of those who watched/listened to the English translation discussed the play in Japanese at the intermission. The different levels of audience competency as well as the further interpretive stage of translation led to moments where response was fragmented. At other times, the audience shared a collective reaction. While audience homogeneity would seem to be most likely, it is worth remembering the vulnerability of that united response. That audiences generally concur as to what is a good play and what is bad merely evidences aesthetic codes as culturally determined.

While the collective response is nevertheless generally homogeneous, the individual's response to performance undoubtedly constitutes the core of the spectator's pleasure. Theorists with quite diverse interests have begun to explore the possible roles of such individual reactions as identification, desire, and fantasy, and their continued research will add more to our understanding of the interpretive processes behind the publicly expressed reception. Metz's analysis of the filmic spectator's 'waking daydream' suggests a parallel, if different, role for the theatre spectator. Metz comments: 'the impression of reality can be studied not only by comparison with perception but also by relation to the various kinds of fictional perceptions, the chief of which, apart from the representational arts, are the dream and the phantasy' (1976: 101). For the audience faced with the cultural object, he argues:

> the impression of reality, the impression of the dream, and the impression of the daydream cease to be contradictory and mutually exclusive, as they are ordinarily, in order to enter into new relations wherein their usual distinctness, while not exactly annulled, admits an unprecedented configuration leaving room at once for straddling, alternating balance, partial overlapping, recalibration, and ongoing circulation among the three.
>
> (Metz 1976: 101–2)

Metz acknowledges that his analysis does not include all types of spectator. The scholar or critic will likely repress fantasizing and daydream in the interests of his professional status (Metz 1976: 99) and the interplay of reality, fantasy and daydream Metz describes applies to a single social group. Analyses of other social groups may find the Freudian models he employs less helpful 'since they were established, despite their pretension to universality, in an observational field with cultural limits' (Metz 1976: 100). While performance and reception clearly result from interaction between individual and group responses, the cultural limits of, say, China would make much of this study, like Metz's cinematic one, inappropriate and would demand other areas for detailed exploration.

In the Western theatre audience that this study assumes, however, it is the tension between the inner frame of the fictional stage world, the audience's moment by moment perception of that in the experience of a social group, and the outer frame of community (cultural construction and horizons of expectations) which determine the nature and satisfaction of the interpretive process. John McGrath's hopes for the best political theatre articulate this well:

> The theatre can never *cause* a social change. It can articulate the pressures towards one, help people to celebrate their strengths and maybe build their self-confidence. It can be a public emblem of inner, and outer, events, and occasionally a reminder, an elbow-jogger, a perspective-bringer. Above all, it can be the way people can find their voice, their solidarity and their collective determination.
>
> (McGrath 1974: xxvii)

A performance can activate a diversity of responses, but it is the audience which finally ascribes meaning and usefulness to any cultural product.

Throughout this text I have tried to draw attention to those theatres which produce works resistant to dominant cultural readings, and as a conclusion to this section on performance I want to look at two such productions which are, in different ways, perhaps landmark events. The first is Luis Valdez's *Zoot Suit*, premièred in Los Angeles in 1978. The second is Holly Hughes's *Dress Suits for Hire*, premièred in New York City in 1987. Both these plays have generated academic attention, and both have played to constituency and non-constituency audiences. Their reception histories point to questions of gender, race, ethnicity, and class that are often misrepresented in dominant critical discourse. In 'White Privilege and Looking Relations: Race and Gender in Feminist Film Theory', Jane Gaines suggests a necessary shift in dominant modes of filmic analysis: 'the Freudian–Lacanian scenario can eclipse the scenario of race–gender relations in Afro-American history. . . . The danger here is that when we use a psychoanalytic model to explain black family relations, we force an erroneous universalisation and inadvertently reaffirm white middle-class norms' (1988: 12–13). She further suggests that we need to rethink film theory 'along more materialist lines, considering, for instance, how some groups have historically had the licence to "look" openly while other groups have "looked" illicitly' (1988: 24–5). We might also consider what happens when theatre addressed to the non-traditional spectator (which, in other words, reframes the look with a different concept of subjectivity and different fields of representation) moves into

167

dominant cultural fields. The experiences of *Zoot Suit* and *Dress Suits for Hire* are undoubtedly suggestive.

The background to *Zoot Suit* lies in an earlier performance by El Teatro Campesino at the Mark Taper Forum in Los Angeles. The success of *La gran carpa de los rasquachis* (1974) in attracting a Mechicano audience to a mainstream, indeed prestigious, Los Angeles auditorium had encouraged the artistic director of the resident Center Theatre Group, Gordon Davidson, to develop more of this 'minority' theatre.[14] Looking to produce a Chicano play, Davidson turned to Luis Valdez who came up with the idea of a play about the zoot suiters of the 1940s. The play that followed (which had the financial backing of a Rockefeller Foundation grant) is based on the zoot suit riots of 1943 with a particular focus on the Sleepy Lagoon murder trial involving the wrongful conviction for murder of the members of a Chicano street gang. The play incorporates fact with invented material in the usual Teatro Campesino performance style. Central to the performance is the figure of El Pachuco, who acts in *Zoot Suit* as a narrator of the history and a manipulator of audience response.

Tickets for the Mark Taper Forum production went on sale in April 1978 and the response was well beyond Davidson's initial expectations as Jorge Huerta comments:

> Everyone involved in the production knew that there was great community interest in the play, but when it sold out its ten-day run in less than two days, the reality struck home: Chicanos wanted to see plays about themselves. Tickets to the performances became prized possessions as people clamored to see what *Zoot Suit* was all about. Even before opening night, the producers knew that they had struck a chord in the Chicano community that had only begun to vibrate.
>
> (Huerta 1982: 177)

Reviews of the production were laudatory, but pointed up the need for Valdez to tighten up the script. Audiences, however, adored the play. What is particularly interesting is the social composition of those enthusiastic audiences:

> [They] were divided between the subscribers – basically a white, theater-going public – and the Mechicanos – most

of whom had never been to the Forum or any other legitimate theater to see a play. Many of the non-Spanish-speaking members of the audience felt left out when others laughed at the jokes in Spanish or *calo*, but they joined the cheering crowds who jumped to their feet at the end of each performance.

(Huerta 1982: 177)

The divided audience evidently had different experiences of the production, although both sectors 'enjoyed' the show sufficiently to secure a standing ovation at the end of every performance. For the Chicano audience, here was a rewriting of history, one which foregrounded the interests of their cultural group and which read the injustices of the American justice system. In Huerta's words, Valdez's play, above all else, revealed: 'a period in our history that is generally neglected in the history books' (1982. 179). But how did the traditional (white, middle-class) audience receive the play? They had, to take up Gaines's description quoted earlier, as historical privilege the licence to 'look'. Was the reframing of history, the Chicano perspective, merely fetishized as object? Perminder Dhillon-Kashyap has written how the Asian film 'beguiles white mainstream audiences' (1988: 121–2) without apparently threatening that audience's cultural privilege. It seems likely that the traditional audience would be able to bracket the events as *history*, while for the Chicano audience the trial also acted as a powerful metaphor for the injustices of their everyday experience. Notwithstanding these questions, the play was an overwhelming success which prompted its re-appearance to open the Forum's regular subscription season as a six-week run in August 1978 (Huerta 1982: 178).

As with the April performances, these sold out virtually overnight. *Zoot Suit* came back on stage in a revised version which included a tighter plot, stronger casting, and a more spectacular form through the addition of songs and dances (Huerta 1982: 178–9). After this six-week run, the play moved to a larger auditorium in Hollywood (the Aquarius) and continued to pack houses (Huerta 1982: 181). Huerta concludes:

Zoot Suit proved that in Los Angeles . . . Mechicanos from

169

all walks of life were willing to pay to see professional theater dealing with their cultural, historical, and political experience. Audiences came to Los Angeles from all corners of southern California to see this play, people from East Los Angeles and Beverly Hills mingling together at this historic event. Any doubts about whether Chicanos would support theater of this kind were dispelled when the production lasted almost a full year. *Zoot Suit* became more than theatre; it was an *event* that was supported by both Mechicanos and the non-Hispanics.

(Huerta 1982: 219)

With the combined successes of the Los Angeles productions, the decision was taken to try and get a theatre in New York City. This was a particularly momentous decision as *Zoot Suit* would become the first Chicano play to be staged on Broadway. The experience of *Zoot Suit* in New York City was, however, very different. With much pre-opening publicity as that first Chicano play on Broadway, the original cast launched the play at the Winter Garden in March 1979. The opening night audience enjoyed the show but the critics did not. *Zoot Suit* was emphatically rejected. Huerta cites the adjectives of the New York critics: 'overblown and undernourished', 'a great deal of loose material draped over a spindly form', 'simplistic . . . poorly written and atrociously directed', and 'bloodless rhetoric' (1982: 182).

With bad reviews, the traditional Broadway audiences stayed away but the producers sought out non-traditional theatre-goers (Hispanics and blacks). This kept the show open for four weeks, rather longer than most heavily criticized shows, but the failure (at least in terms of comparison with the Los Angeles success) showed that the dominant cultural machine (in its critics' discourse and in the economics of staging) was on Broadway more powerful than the enthusiasm of 'minority' audiences. The appearance of a Chicano play on Broadway was nevertheless a milestone and Valdez made the point to a New York interviewer that: 'This is a cultural stand and America has got to come to grips with it. Because we're not going to go away' (cited in Huerta 1982: 183).

Pottlitzer notes the impact that *Zoot Suit* has had as a positive model of professionalism on other Chicano/Latino theatres, although she notes that Valdez was criticized by many Chicanos at that time for selling out El Teatro Campesino to dominant cultural interests (1988: 21). The reception history of *Zoot Suit* shows how conditional the acceptance of non-traditional theatre has been, and raises the issues of how and why the legitimation of 'professional' status is necessary. It is ironic, as Shank points out, that while Valdez was accused by Chicanos of commercializing the *acto*, *Zoot Suit*'s failure in New York was largely because it was perceived by those critics as agitprop (1985: 194). Ultimately the history of El Teatro Campesino is a history of empowerment for Chicano people. The audiences of the early plays for the striking grapeworkers through to the enthusiastic Los Angeles responses to *Zoot Suit* identify a theatre culture *for* and *of* Mechicanos. Shank sums up their successes well:

> Since 1965 when his [Valdez's] Teatro began, approximately eighty others have been formed. . . . For Chicanos who have seen El Teatro Campesino or read about its successful European tours or know how Peter Brook in 1973 came to spend a summer working with the Teatro or how the director of the company was appointed by the governor to the California Arts Council – surely these people now know that it is possible for a Chicano to become a professional theatre artist.
>
> (Shank 1985: 194–5)

It might well be added that these people now know that it is possible to see representations which reflect a reality other than that of the Anglo-American. Non-traditional theatre has brought this experience to many different social, racial, and ethnic groups. In Britain, works such as Tunde Ikoli's *Sink or Swim* (about black and white youth in Peckham, a London district which was the site of street rioting in the early 1980s) and Sulin Looi's *All Sewn Up* (about the lives of South-East Asian women as British immigrants) have addressed important community issues *and* considered the way these 'minorities' perceive themselves in the world. There is always, of course, the problem when theatre companies seek to broaden their audiences as to where possible shifts in reception might take these plays of empowerment.

Jill Dolan, writing in anticipation of the transfer of Holly Hughes's *Dress Suits for Hire* from the East Village to an off-Broadway stage, wonders whether radical theatre is necessarily neutralized as 'a commodity consumable in a more mainstream economy' (1988: 120). She continues:

> It will be interesting and important to trace the ramifications of this step up – or into – the mainstream theatre hierarchy. The performers and playwright will happily see their income jump, and the production will be available to a much more diverse audience. Selling a lesbian text to mainstream spectators seems incongruous, but in the best of all possible worlds those spectators will come away from the performance thinking differently about their sexuality and gender assumptions.
>
> Or maybe not. Perhaps the context will prevail, and . . . obscure the meaning of what they see.
>
> (Dolan 1988: 120)

While the questions Dolan raises are undoubtedly valid, categorizing *Dress Suits for Hire* as lesbian text marketed to a mainstream audience is perhaps oversimplifying the process. While Hughes's play is about two lesbians, the work was originally written for performance at P.S. 122, an East Village club which draws a non-traditional, but largely hetereosexual, audience. Hughes has made it clear that *Dress Suits* was written with this venue in mind and that it is different from her work with the WOW Cafe (where a largely lesbian audience could be assumed). Indeed, Kate Davy has discussed different receptions of *Dress Suits* in various venues including audiences at the University of Michigan (where a traditionally-arranged auditorium led to mainstream appropriation, a fetishizing of the image (1989: 164)) and at the University of Milwaukee (where a middle-class and working-class lesbian audience engaged specifically with the lesbian address of Hughes's text (1989: 166–7)).[15]

Nevertheless, like *Zoot Suit*'s first for Chicano theater, *Dress Suits for Hire* represented a bold move in taking Hughes's work out of its constituency (either in the case of its lesbian audiences at WOW or the avant-garde audiences at P.S. 122) and into a more mainstream venue, the Interart Theater. *Dress Suits for Hire* opened there in February 1988. Hughes's play

172

was undoubtedly successful in this venue, enjoying an extended run and, eventually, an Obie award for actress Peggy Shaw. It is worth considering how this play was accommodated when Valdez's *Zoot Suit* was not. Firstly, the fact that Hughes's 'first' comes ten years later is significant. Non-traditional theatres have increased both in number and exposure over the last decade. Beyond this, the review of Stephen Holden in the *New York Times* provides some clues to why Hughes's play was well received by both audiences *and* critics.

The most noticeable strategy of Holden's review is to link Hughes's writing to the work of Sam Shepard, probably America's most successful and valued contemporary playwright. The review opens: 'Like Sam Shepard, her most obvious influence, Ms. Hughes . . .' (1988: C21). Further references include describing the opening of *Dress Suits* as 'an enigmatic Shepardian stroke' and noting that 'Ms. Hughes's more poetic writing recalls Sam Shepard' (1988: C21). And what is wrong with Hughes's play? Holden suggests that it 'lacks the pacing, suspense and structure of *Fool for Love*, the Shepard play it most closely resembles'. Thus *Dress Suits* is readily accommodated into the best of traditions of contemporary (male) American playwrighting, although shown to be not quite up to those standards. Secondly, in Holden's analysis, *Dress Suits* is aligned with John Waters's movies and Charles Busch's *Vampire Lesbians of Sodom* (in this latter case confirming Dolan's fears) which transforms the lesbian address into a tradition of camp and depoliticized entertainment. This positioning of *Dress Suits for Hire* suggests how the play is quite easily turned into that 'commodity consumable' Dolan anticipated, and the ultimate 'praise' for Hughes emphasizes this fate. Holden writes:

> But in portraying female sexuality – and lesbian seduction in particular – as a carnivorous free-for-all, it scrapes away decades of encrusted decorum from a subject that is too often treated with a hushed sentimentality. And it heralds the arrival of a brash, promising comic playwright.
>
> (Holden 1988: C21)

Apart from its problem in conflating lesbian seduction and female sexuality, Holden's conclusion handles *Dress Suits for*

Hire by labelling the comedy as a predominant characteristic. Hughes is not a political playwright, but a comic one. And traditions in comedy historically permit the challenging of those limits of decorum. By contrast, *Zoot Suit* was categorized as predominantly political. The Chicano challenge to the dominant cultural reading of history was directly perceived. The central 'El Pachuco' character (of course, male) was perceived as powerful and threatening to a traditional audience (at least in as far as it was constituted for the opening night by theatre critics). The aggressive humour of El Pachuco was less easily subsumed by traditional modes of comic writing. That one play foregrounded a male who was Chicano and the other two females who were lesbian suggests where the challenges to power are more seriously perceived.

The history of these plays with their different audiences points not only to the widespread development of non-traditional theatre, but also to the ways dominant cultural markers can be tested in more mainstream productions of these oppositional products. It also testifies to the ability of traditional theatre to accommodate other representations. The different critical responses to these two productions begs a fuller study of 'oppositional' theatre on the mainstream stages of New York and other major urban centres in America and elsewhere.

Before looking to the implications of this study of audiences, however, one further aspect of the theatrical event remains. This is the contribution of what occurs after the performance *per se* since the audience's immediate as well as later reactions to performance play a significant role in the maintenance of the theatre sector.

POST-PERFORMANCE

As the very first theatrical performances hinged on their public post-performance reception – the plays of Greek theatre were judged and the 'best' awarded prizes – we are reminded that the audience's role does not end with the last action within the fictional stage world. The feedback of the audience through applause and the appearance of the actors as actors to receive their judgment represent an important theatrical convention.

174

In the maintenance of this convention, receptive decisions are made immediately. A performance is judged good or bad, satisfactory or unsatisfactory, by the collective group and applause is measured accordingly. This act confirms the audience's position as collective and confirms, both for audience and performers, their ability to make meaning of the production. Nevertheless the ritual of the curtain call is not simply a sign of conclusion. It does in itself require the decoding of the audience, and relies upon a complex network of conventions (hierarchial relationships of actors in taking curtain calls, number of curtain calls individually and as a cast, and so on). The curtain call may be offered as a coda to the entertainment already presented or a bridge into another form of the event.

The number of curtain calls will generally relate to the applause generated and a balance between the two will provide the most satisfactory conclusion. Where curtain calls are overdone, the audience can feel impatient and the pleasure of the theatrical event may be diminished by the virtual imprisonment of the audience in their seats. Where curtain calls are felt to be too few, the audience may feel that their role has not been fulfilled or that it has been undervalued by the performers. Again the pleasure of the theatrical event is precariously balanced.

Non-traditional theatre practice tends to stress the importance of the immediate post-production period. A common strategy is to invite discussion between the audience and cast. This can, of course, be shunned by the audience who feel such direct contact is an evasion of their guaranteed privacy. It also has a tendency towards didacticism. In an attempt to counteract this, many groups have contextualized both performance and discussion by a programme of festivity. 7:84 Scotland, for example, always include a *ceilidh* at the end of their performances in Scotland. As a traditional form of entertainment in the Gaelic culture, it serves to break down barriers between performers and audience as well as to celebrate the issues discussed/presented in the preceding performance (McGrath 1974: xiv–xix). El Teatro Campesino followed an *acto* (short dramatic performance) with songs, all of which took place within a three to four hour farm workers union meeting (Bagby 1986: 139). After-performance activity, how-

175

ever, is not always politically motivated. Much experimental theatre has been interested in the role of ritual and uses the post-production period to make a conscious break in the theatrical frame. Allan Kaprow's production of *Iphigenia Transformed* concluded with the marriage ceremony and a celebration for the entire audience, courtesy of four cases of beer delivered by Euripides's *dea ex machina* (cited in Schechner 1969: 158).

Even in more traditional performances, the act of leaving the theatre is always important. It may provide a welcome release and the end of interpretive activity. On the other hand, the buzz of an excited audience, slow to leave the theatre, continues the interpretive process and is likely to enhance the experience of that production in the individual's memory. As with pre-production, the after-performance time may well include other social events which serve, among other things, to increase the pleasure of the event.

In a publicly experienced cultural event, the opportunity to talk about the event afterwards is important socially. Theatre audiences, as has been noted, tend to consist of small groups of friends, family, and so on. Reception of a performance can be prolonged by group discussion of all aspects from general appreciation to specific questions to other group members about small details of the production. Beyond the ability to talk over the production either immediately or some time after the performance, audiences may follow up by reading the text (if available), by reading reviews, or (at a later time) seeing another production or even a subsequent movie adaptation. All these acts have the potential to reshape initial decoding of the production.

All these elements of post-production are potentially significant in the audience's experience of theatre and all promote, if not ensure, the continuance of a culture industry attracting audiences to the theatrical event. It is the reciprocal nature of production and reception which characterizes the formation and reformation of cultural markers for theatre.

CONCLUSION

The involvement of the audience in the theatrical event is undoubtedly complex. In all its stages, from pre-production to post-production and especially for the duration of the performance itself, the traditional role for the spectator, as individual and as member of the collective gathering, is as Webb establishes – reactive: 'In general he takes as understood that the actors express and that he receives (spatially underscored by the conventional theatre architecture: *scène/salle*, light/dark, moving/sitting). The spectator agrees to give himself up to the performance' (1979–80: 206–7). With this social contract put into place, usually by the exchange of money for a ticket which promises a seat in which to watch an action unfold, the spectator accepts a passive role and awaits the action which is to be interpreted. Many non-traditional theatre events, however, retain the general terms of that contract only to question them. Activity which falls within the theatrical frame employed by the production company will be received by the spectators as dramatic action. The activity 'performed' for an onlooker who has not entered into the same contract will be read quite differently. It is an opposition which creates the experiment of Squat Theatre's show, *Pig*.

At this event the audience is seated behind the 23rd Street storefront with a view both of interior playing space and of the street outside: For much of the performance the street is a backdrop offering some gags:

> passersby doing double takes as they see something bizarre going on behind the window: like a goat eating vegetable scraps as a family sits at table, or a little girl parading

177

around in falsies; and the audience laughs at passersby, like Candid Camera live. . . . Often a few knowing persons, having seen *Pig* from inside, return to watch it from the street. Thus there are three audiences: insiders, outsiders, insiders-who-are-outside. From the perspective of theatre the insiders are natural; from the perspective of street life the outsiders are natural. The insiders-who-are-outside are artificials posing as naturals (to other passersby) or they are double artificials (to insiders).

(Schechner 1982: 88–9).

As Schechner comments, the actions in *Pig* are not significant as drama, a story, or as social critique, but serve to indicate the durability of the social contract. The effectiveness of the theatrical frame and the willingness of the audience to accept events within it as dramatic illusion are convincingly displayed in two more of Schechner's examples from *Pig*:

A taxicab drives up outside the theatre. A man gets out and draws a gun. Across the street another man stops and draws a gun. Between them traffic flows. Actually a few drivers, seeing the situation, duck as they cruise between the two drawn gunners. Then inside the theatre a woman performer draws a gun and takes aim at the gunman who had arrived by taxi. She shoots, he falls, but the glass between them is not shattered. Again a system is discernible. Taxi = natural = belongs on 23rd Street. Gunmen in the street = ambivalent situation: we in the theatre know this is part of the performance (or at least hope so); those in the street, this is New York remember, take precautions but go on their way. The woman drawing a pistol inside certainly makes clear that this is part of the play and that all the gunmen are artificial. The blank shot that drops a person but doesn't shatter glass proves a point. . . .

At the end of the shoot-out . . . four police cars scream to a halt in front of the theatre. The performers are checked. They have a permit. But didn't the police know this? Do they arrive every night? Are they part of the script? I [Schechner] ask after the performance: No, they rarely arrive these days, but our permit is running out, they are

178

warning us. To spectators inside, the arrival of the police looks like a TV drama. It's not natural because we know this is a performance. Yet to passersby perhaps scared by drawn guns the arrival of the police is natural, and welcome. To the police themselves it is a little game: Let's get the theatre people tonight!

(Schechner 1982: 89, 90).

When the theatrical frame is extended to the far side of 23rd Street (the presence there of one of the gunmen) the audience stretches, as Schechner points out, the limits within which they will decode everything as fictional sign. The police arrive, a non-theatrical event, but they are interpreted as yet another action in the assembly of *Pig*.

Spectators are thus trained to be passive in their demonstrated behaviour during a theatrical performance, but to be active in their decoding of the sign systems made available. Performers rely on the active decoding, but passive behaviour of the audience so that they can unfold the planned on-stage activity. Theatre which concertedly challenges the traditionally reactive role of spectator does not restrict itself to the event itself. The early work of the French group, Le Grand Magic Circus, is indicative of such endeavours. They divided performance into three distinct aspects: pre-spectacle, the spectacle itself, and post-spectacle. Each was designed to work with the participation of the audience:

The first period prepares the audience and actors. Actors are seen before making up, as they make-up; they sell sandwiches, give out *sangria*; they perform turns (e.g. conjuring, acrobatics) for small groups as they arrive; perhaps they talk to them and make them up or sometimes dance with them. For their part the spectators may initiate play among themselvs. The atmosphere is relaxed; the spectator's presence is acknowledged; the actors are catalysts and do not block audience responses. The spectacle itself is an open structure, a series of entertaining *tableaux* loosely connected by a central storyteller. Consequently, the spectacle can be adapted, lengthened or shortened according to the demands of the situation. . . . The scenic space encourages this type of informality. The action flows through, around and above the spectators who are free to change places. Even if they unwittingly 'colonize' an area used for acting, they are not expelled but are given parts to play in the scene. It is clear that the spectacle continues the atmosphere of free exchange of the pre-spectacle.

At the end of the performance the company strikes up a fast Latin American rhythm; the audience is invited to dance. Gradually the actors withdraw from both the instruments and the dancing. What was the audience is left to create its own entertainment.

(Webb 1979–80: 211–12)

Where audiences are consulted and involved in the structuring of the theatrical event, and are encouraged (at least in the immediate post-production period) to translate their reading of that event into action, then their role no longer maintains the fixity that dominant cultural practice assumes. In this way, the production/reception process acts bi-directionally in broader cultural perspectives. Cultural systems, individual horizons of expectations, and accepted theatrical conventions all activate the decoding process for a specific production, but, in turn, the direct experience of that production feeds back to revise a spectator's expectations, to establish or challenge conventions, and, occasionally, to reform the boundaries of culture.

In this study, many theatrical forms have been cited and these indicate the strength and diversity of non-traditional theatres. Within mainstream theatre, the minimalist experiments of writers such as Beckett and Cage have been accepted and conventionalized. Some oppositional practice has been recuperated and defused. Brecht is now a canonical figure and the works of his successors produced at major cultural institutions, attracting an audience which Sinfield suggests is 'generally split between its wish for a radical posture and its actual privileged position' (1983b: 187). Yet the sheer volume of theatre outside the mainstream institutions gives testament to the challenging of cultural boundaries. No longer can audiences for theatrical events be identified by profiles of the typical ticket holder at an established institution. The audience is as likely to be found in a public park or a union hall or a community centre as at a conventional theatre space. Non-traditional theatre may be at its most intense in London, New York City, or Paris, but is equally to be found in the Orkney Islands, the Cevennes, or Reva (South Dakota). Armand Gatti has persuasively argued that 'in order to create theatre, it is necessary to leave it behind; and so the first thing to do is to find another place where the theatre can express itself' (1982: 71).

Those practices which share little with traditional theatre and which cannot be absorbed into institutional playing spaces have, for a long time, been ignored. The companies are hard to find because they do not play in the 'usual' spaces, their texts are not published, their concerns are seldom those of dominant critical practice, and significantly they are often uninterested in the traditional theatre-goer or dialogue with academia. But the expansion of non-traditional theatre into many different communities brings theatre to people who may never before have had the experience of the theatrical event and who therefore assign theatre a place in their cultural boundaries which is little restricted with traditional definitions and expectations. In an article on Italo-Australian theatre, Tony Mitchell has articulated such a shift:

> [T]he face of traditionally Anglo Celtic Australian theatre is being radically altered on a grass roots, community-based level. . . . These groups reflect the poly-cultural make-up of Australian society and express it through a committed, socially meaningful form of popular theatre which speaks to audiences who are not reached by the increasingly exclusive and expensive theatre circuit. As such, they constitute the most stimulating and egalitarian growth area in Australian theatre.
>
> (Mitchell 1987b: 41)

The revolution this has generated for the theatre audience is ably demonstrated by contrast to Hays's description of the debilitated condition of French and German theatre audiences immediately prior to the First World War:

> At the moment one entered the theatre, one was engulfed by the bureaucratic structure which the place and the event represented. This was a theater that had institu-

tionalized the executive function. The dynamic kinesthesis which can be evoked by *participation* in an event was overwhelmed by complacency through the knowledge that everything was under the control of someone else.

(Hays 1981: 116)

Now so much non-traditional theatre restores the participative energies of the theatre spectator. That spectator has become the subject of the drama. In his work for the People's Theater of Peru, Augusto Boal has evolved a poetics of the oppressed which liberates the theatre audiences from the restrictions of Aristotelean and Brechtian practice. Aristotelean theatre, according to Boal, imposed a fixed and knowable world upon the audience. The audience is held passive, delegating 'power to the characters to act and think in their place. In so doing the spectators purge themselves of their tragic flaw - that is, of something capable of changing society' (Boal 1979: 155). Brechtian theatre, Boal argues, is only marginally better. The audience is brought to consciousness, but the power to act remains with the characters. Boal concludes:

The *poetics of the oppressed* is essentially the poetics of liberation: the spectator no longer delegates power to the characters either to think or to act in his place. The spectator frees himself; he thinks and acts for himself! Theater is action!

Perhaps the theater is not revolutionary in itself; but have no doubts, it is a rehearsal of revolution!

(Boal 1979: 155)

Boal's challenge to dominant ideologies may be expressed in an emotional rhetoric reminiscent of the charged theatre of Piscator, but his practice shares with the work of many other marginalized practitioners the devolution of power into the hands of the worker audience. With so much theatre activity operating outside recognized cultural institutions, the boundaries of culture are undoubtedly challenged and the feedback of non-traditional audiences has changed, above all else, the product which we recognize as theatre. As Stallybrass and White conclude, '[o]nly a challenge to the hierarchy of *sites* of discourse, which usually comes from groups and classes "situated" by the dominant in low or marginal positions, carries the promise of politically transformative power' (1986: 201). In summing up the history of El Teatro Campesino, Shank makes a parallel point. The *actos* may have achieved no more than the Farmworkers Union would have anyway achieved, but the work of Luis Valdez's teatro has fostered eighty others and they have all articulated the concerns and the values of America's Chicano population (1985: 194–5).

Figure 1, like the research from which it is drawn, is not intended to provide a prescriptive model of the audience's role in theatre. It is instead intended to demarcate the systems which are necessarily involved and which will vary, at every stage, according to the status of event and audience.

Figure 1

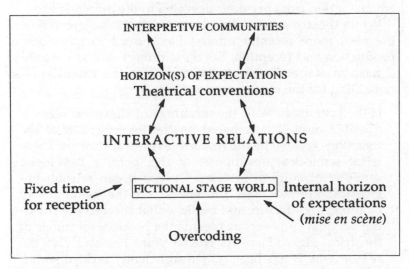

The model is a summary of the issues considered here and suggests in its relationships and in their bi-directional influence some important areas of future study. Certainly attention to the strategies of viewing demands re-readings of dramatic texts. Howard's reading of Shakespeare plays and Chaudhuri's consideration of *Equus* indicate what this might achieve. Nevertheless, with many of the works of non-traditional theatre unavailable as published texts and because there remains, in many areas, a limited access to theatrical events, the efforts of publications such as *The Drama Review* are to be applauded as they make available readings of dramatic productions. A pedagogy which looked to such readings as well as more orthodox dramatic texts might account more accurately for the forms which today constitute theatrical practice.

What has emerged from this study of the audience is the necessity to view the theatrical event beyond its immediate conditions and to foreground its social constitution. The description of an individual response to a particular production may not be possible or, indeed, even desirable. But, because of that individual's participation in a given culture and the importance of his/her culturally-constituted horizon of expectations, and selection of a particular *social* event, it is important to reposition the study of drama to reflect this. Recent developments have at least marked an encouraging emancipation from previous devotion to the dramatic text.

While theatre semioticians began with the segmentation of the text, more recently interest has moved to questions of production and reception. But these projects are as yet only in a nascent stage. Fischer-Lichte indicates the extensive task remaining for the theatre semiotician:

> [T]he investigation of the meanings of theatrical signs is possible only if it is based on the investigation of the meanings created by the respective cultural systems. Theatrical semiotics presupposes at this point a developed semiotic of cultural systems. Only if it can rely on linguistics, kinesics and proxemics, on the semiotics of clothing, architecture and music, will it succeed in providing adequate answers as regards the possible meanings of theatrical signs. Here its crucial point lies and also the reason why it has been only insufficiently tackled so far. Theatrical semiotics should therefore include in its further research – and to a greater extent – the findings of each individual branch of semiotics.
>
> (Fischer-Lichte 1982: 52)

It is perhaps the case that the concentration on the dramatic text has led theorists to align their discipline with the study of other printed fictional texts (the novel, the poem, etc.) where, in fact, the social nature of theatrical practice demands reference to at least the more social art forms (music, dance, film, architecture, etc.). The interactivity that necessarily takes place between spectators as well as between spectators and actors suggests that the inquiries into drama's correlation with the social sciences are potentially fruitful. The collaborations of Turner and Schechner have, for example, identified some of the cultural markers surrounding performance. Barba's International School of Theatre Anthropology will undoubtedly continue to produce research which will increase our understanding of the actor's performance. Shevstova's demands for a more developed sociology of theatre will further highlight the audience's contribution to the theatrical event.

Yet this study has its limitations too. What of theatre produced outside Western industrial societies? Anthropology-related theatre studies have indicated that the performances and rituals of non-Western societies have much to contribute to our general understanding of the theatre dynamic. It would be interesting to explore the modifications required to this model of the audience's role in order to accommodate different varieties of non-Western theatre. And, beyond this, how much of the model is applicable to the experiences of children's theatre? Further research might elucidate the essential conditions required of performance in order that *any* audience can construct meaning.

In some ways a more simple but equally important task is an increased knowledge of those non-traditional methodologies and performances which are being staged worldwide. Even in North America where publications about the media are prolific, there is a paucity of information available on the diverse and numerous productions being staged. The emergence of information concerning production/reception of theatre in North America, but outside New York City or university environments, seems at best haphazard. Clearly the study of non-traditional theatres on a worldwide basis is an enormous task. Yet when available work is compared, the existence of so much common ground encourages efforts towards a fuller knowledge of the companies in existence. In this study of audiences, theatre practitioners working in many different cultures have been cited and what has emerged from these different sources is a common determination to increase the spectator's activity to their mutual benefit. John McGrath in Scotland, Luis Valdez in the United States, Theatre-Action in France, Augusto Boal in

Peru and Brazil, Theatre of the Eighth Day in Poland, Terra Mia in Australia, Dario Fo and Franca Rame in Italy, and Le Théâtre Parminou in Canada represent only a few of the 'marginalized' who have established new audiences and who have achieved what Dort describes as 'the liberated performance'.

The aim of this study, therefore, is neither to prescribe a role for the theatre audience, nor simply to provide new strategies for interpreting the dramatic text. It is a testimony to the contemporary emancipation of the spectator. Further, it is hoped that this study of the audience's role serves to foreground the diversity of dramatic art and theatre practice in contemporary cultures. Theatre studies which concern themselves primarily and, occasionally, only with mainstream drama and its printed representatives describe theatre in the most limited sense.

APPENDIX

OPENING SECTION, IBSEN'S *A DOLL'S HOUSE*

A comfortable room furnished inexpensively, but with taste. In the back wall, there are two doors; that to the right leads out to a hall, the other, to the left, leads to Helmer's study. Between them stands a piano.

In the middle of the left-hand wall is a door, with a window on its nearer side. Near the window is a round table with armchairs and a small sofa.

In the wall on the right-hand side, rather to the back, is a door, and farther forward on this wall there is a tiled stove with a couple of easy chairs and a rocking-chair in front of it. Between the door and the stove stands a little table.

There are etchings on the walls, and there is a cabinet with china ornaments and other bric-a-brac, and a small bookcase with handsomely bound books. There is a carpet on the floor, and the stove is lit. It is a winter day.

[A bell rings in the hall outside, and a moment later the door is heard to open. NORA comes into the room, humming happily. She is in outdoor clothes, and is carrying an armful of parcels which she puts down on the table to the right. Through the hall door, which she has left open, can be seen a PORTER; he is holding a Christmas tree and a hamper, and he gives them to the MAID who has opened the front door.]

NORA: Hide the Christmas tree properly, Helena. The children mustn't see it till this evening, when it's been decorated.

(Ibsen 1965: 147)

OPENING SECTION, CHURCHILL'S
CLOUD NINE

Low bright sun. Verandah, Flagpole with Union Jack. The Family – CLIVE, BETTY, EDWARD, VICTORIA, MAUD, ELLEN, JOSHUA.

ALL: (sung)

Come gather, sons of England, come gather in your pride,
Now meet the world united, not face it side by side;
Ye who the earth's wide corners, from veldt to prairie roam,
From bush and jungle muster all who call old England 'home'.
Then gather round for England,
Rally to the flag,
From North and South and East and West
Come one and all for England!

CLIVE:

This is my family. Though far from home
We serve the Queen wherever we may roam.
I am a father to the natives here,
And father to my family so dear.
He presents BETTY. She is played by a man.
My wife is all I dreamt a wife should be,
And everything she is she owes to me.

(Churchill 1979: 3–4)

NOTES

CHAPTER 1   INTRODUCTION

1 Between Aristotle and the nineteenth-century theorists, there have, of course, been a number of other drama theorists who demonstrate a particular concern for the theatre audience and, particularly, the effects of drama on them. The most notable examples are Castelvetro, Lope de Vega, Diderot, and Lessing.

2 There are some interesting parallels to Marinetti's Variety Theatre in contemporary practice. Some of the East Village theatres operate as clubs – 8 B.C. ran over 600 performances in one year, financed entirely on bar takings. In Canada, the feminist theatre group Hysterical Women play clubs and bars because they feel the atmosphere (and audience) is more suited to their work.

3 Esslin's idea of drama teaching its audience the 'rules of social coexistence' was a common sixteenth-century theme. This idea is particularly developed in Scaliger's *Poetices*.

4 At the time of completing this manuscript, only the first part of Shevtsova's three-part account of the sociology of theatre is available. From her outline in this first instalment, the subsequent parts look likely to contribute to sociological analysis of audience formation and perception.

5 See Richard Fowler (1985) 'The Four Theatres of Jerzy Grotowski: An Introductory Assessment', *New Theatre Quarterly* 1.2: 173–8.

CHAPTER 2   THEORIES OF READING AND VIEWING

1 The influence of Piscator is acknowledged by Brecht. A discussion of their relationship can be found in Innes (1972: 189–200). The influence of Meyerhold is, however, more controversial. Innes suggests there is no direct link (1972: x) while Etkind suggests there is (1980: 84). In any event, Brecht's meetings with Tretiakov would have introduced him to the ideas of Russian formalists and futurists.

2 The *Verfremdungseffekt* remains controversial. For an idea of the differences in interpretation see *Screen* 15, special issue on Brecht (1974).
3 Etkind offers an interesting aside: while *ostranenie* translated for Brecht into *Verfremdung*, its re-translation was forbidden. In order to recover Brecht and not be accused of a return to formalism, the acceptable Russian translation of *Verfremdung* had to be a synonym of *ostranenie, ochuzhdenie*.
4 The idea of interpellation by ideology is, of course, from Althusser (see 1971: 172–83).
5 This relationship is expressed by Polan (1985: 96). For a detailed discussion of this, see Austin Quigley (1985) *The Modern Stage and Other Worlds*, London: Methuen.
6 A recent example is Ellen Schauber and Ellen Spolsky (1986) *The Bounds of Interpretation: Linguistic Theory and Literary Text*, Stanford: Stanford University Press.
7 Mailloux presents a useful critique of Holland's work in *Interpretive Conventions* (1982: 24–30).
8 Fish does not deal at any length with the act of framing. Erving Goffman's work, not surprisingly, has been particularly influential for other theorists; indeed, *Frame Analysis* is a recurring intertext. Goffman's ideas are taken up in the later discussion of Umberto Eco's work.
9 Their argument can be found in *Diacritics* 11. See Fish (1981) 'Why no one's afraid of Wolfgang Iser', *Diacritics* 11.1: 2–13, and Iser (1981) 'Talk like whales: A reply to Stanley Fish', *Diacritics* 11.3: 82–7.
10 Horizon, as Holub notes, was a familiar term for German theorists. He points out precedents in the work of Gadamer, Husserl, and Heidegger. 'Horizon of expectations' had been used by Popper, Mannheim, and Gombrich (see Holub 1984: 58ff.).
11 The survey of theories of reading offered here is not comprehensive. Generally the figures discussed posit theories that have, I feel, some application to theatre audiences. Important reader-response critics not included are Jonathan Culler and David Bleich (both of whom have written on the pedagogical implications of this theory) as well as Gerard Genette, Gerald Prince, and Tzvetan Todorov (who might be grouped as narratologists). The Suleiman and Crosman, and Tompkins anthologies provide quite full bibliographies of reader-response theory.
12 Pratt, considering Culler's notion of literary competence, writes wittily of the assumptions generally underlying reader-response criticism: '*we* apparently means certain literature professors (*not* Norman Holland) plus other educated people who think as they do' (1986: 42). Their neglect of the social and political aspects of reading suggests to Pratt 'less a reorientation of the discipline of literary studies than an elaborate shoring up of the dominant status quo, and of the interpretive authority of the academy' (1982: 42).

13 For further discussion of the breadth of Barthes's interests, see Annette Lavers (1982) *Roland Barthes: Structuralism and After*, London: Methuen; and Jonathan Culler's short survey (1983), *Roland Barthes*, New York: Oxford University Press.

14 The work of Christian Metz and Stephen Heath has been most influential. Articles in *Screen* volumes 14, 16, and 19 provide important examples of their work.

15 Sigmund Freud (1964) 'Femininity', in *The Standard Edition of the Complete Psychological Works of Sigmund Freud*, ed. James Strachey, London: Hogarth Press and The Institute of Psycho-Analysis, 113.

16 Other film theorists have turned their attention to the male counterpart. See Richard Dyer (1982) 'Don't Look Now – The Male Pin-Up', *Screen* 23.3–4: 61–73; and Steve Neale (1983) 'Masculinity as Spectacle', *Screen* 24.6: 2–17.

CHAPTER 3   THE AUDIENCE AND THEATRE

1 The demand for audience homogeneity in a country such as Poland is demonstrated in the treatment of Teatr Osmego Dnia (Theatre of the Eighth Day). Politically aligned with Solidarity, they had played to audiences of 600,000. Following Martial Law in 1982, they realized that they would be denied access to playing spaces because of their counter-government stance. They performed first in the streets and then, after losing funding and property in 1984 as well as being 'officially disbanded', they began to play in churches. Endeavours to take their plays outside of Poland were counteracted with only half the group being given passports. See Tony Howard's account of their twenty-two year history in ' "A Piece of Our Life" The Theatre of the Eighth Day', *New Theatre Quarterly*, 2.8 (1986): 291–305.

2 See Colin Duckworth (1972) *Angels of Darkness*, London: George Allen & Unwin, for analyses of questionnaires he gave audiences of Beckett's *Waiting for Godot* and *Endgame*.

3 Coppieters's bibliography cites a number of ethnogenic studies. See particularly Rom Harré (1974) 'Blueprint for a New Science', in N. Armistead (ed.) *Reconstructing Psychology*, Harmondsworth: Penguin.

4 Outlines of the various theoretical stances can be found in 'Representation and Cultural Production' by Michèle Barrett, Philip Corrigan, Annette Kuhn, and Janet Wolff (1979); and in Richard Johnson (1979) 'Histories of Culture/Theories of Ideology: Notes on an Impasse', both in Michèle Barrett *et al.* (eds) *Ideology and Cultural Production*,London: Croom Helm.

5 Brook converted ethnographic data about the Ik of Uganda for Western audiences and also travelled to Africa with eleven actors. A chronicle of his experiences there – which outline the problematics of performing for audiences experiencing extra-

cultural 'entertainment' – can be found in John Heilpern (1977) *Conference of the Birds*, London: Faber & Faber.

6 Peter Brook's period at The Royal Shakespeare Company established its reputation for controversy. His 'experimental' productions, such as Weiss's *Marat/Sade* and Artaud's *Jet of Blood*, created a furore which is detailed in Sinfield (1983b: 186–7).

7 Bruce McConachie and Daniel Friedman's book on theatre for working-class audiences in the United States collects useful data *and* analysis of these contemporary theatre groups.

8 Again, Erving Goffman has been influential. See his (1959) *The Presentation of Self in Everyday Life*, New York: Doubleday Anchor.

9 For the controversy around Gatti's play see Dorothy Knowles (1969) 'To be banned or not to be banned', *Drama* 93: 53–8. Also Webb (1979–80: 212). For the continuing controversy surrounding *Garbage, The City and Death*, see Denis Calandra's (1988) article, 'Politicised Theatre: The Case of Rainer Werner Fassbinder's *Garbage, The City & Death* (*Modern Drama* 31.3: 420–8).

10 A National Council of the Arts survey in the mid-1970s showed more than 50 per cent of total opera box-office sales were to subscription buyers, but less than 15 per cent of theatre ticket sales were accounted for in this way (cited in Martorella 1977: 360).

11 See Peter Davison (1982) *Contemporary Drama and the Popular Dramatic Tradition in England*, London: Macmillan, 136–7. *Each in his Own Way* appears to have two or three acts. The number played, according to Pirandello, depends on the attitude of the audience. It has, in fact, only two acts. Davison recounts an occasion when the audience made concerted efforts to demand a third act.

12 On 30 November 1984 the performance at the Club Chandalier was *Carmelita Tropicana Chats*. Tropicana's first guest was Tammy Whynot. Jill Dolan explains:

> The context for *Carmelita Tropicana Chats* is clearly a mix of invention and a kind of twisted reality that might not be easily distinguished by the uninitiated. Tammy Whynot . . . is a character Lois Weaver plays in Split Britches' *Upwardly Mobile Home* at the WOW Cafe. Weaver arrived at Club Chandalier in full costume and remained in character before and after the performance.
>
> (McNamara and Dolan 1986: 319)

This illustrates well these theatres' reliance on a constituency audience, and the effectiveness of word of mouth as an advertising network.

13 Squat Theatre originated in Budapest. They were banned there because their work was seen as obscene and politically open to misinterpretation. They now work in exile. Their name derives from their status in New York City as squatters (see Schechner 1982: 86).

NOTES

14 I am particularly indebted to Jorge Huerta's fine book on Chicano Theater for my discussion of *Zoot Suit*.
15 See *The Drama Review* 33.1 (spring 1989) for Davy's article, the text of Hughes's play, and an interview with Hughes.

BIBLIOGRAPHY

Adorno, Theodor W. (1984) *Aesthetic Theory*, London: Routledge & Kegan Paul.

Alter, Jean (1988) 'Decoding Mnouchkine's Shakespeare (A Grammar of Stage Signs)' in Michael Issacharoff and Robin F. Jones (eds) *Performing Texts*, Philadelphia: University of Pennsylvania Press, 75–85.

Althusser, Louis (1969) *For Marx*, trans. Ben Brewster, New York: Pantheon.

— (1971) *Lenin and Philosophy and Other Essays*, trans. Ben Brewster, New York and London: Monthly Review Press.

Arac, Jonathan (ed.) (1986) *Postmodernism and Politics*, Minneapolis: University of Minnesota Press.

Arden, John (1964) *The Waters of Babylon. Three Plays*, New York: Grove Press.

Aristotle (1894) *Theory of Poetry and Fine Art*, trans. S. H. Butcher, New York: Dover Publications, 1951.

Arnott, Peter D. (1959) *An Introduction to the Greek Theatre*, London and Basingstoke: Macmillan, 1978.

Artaud, Antonin (1964) *The Theatre and its Double*, trans. Victor Corti, London: John Calder, 1981.

Bagby, Beth (1986) 'El Teatro Campesino: Interviews with Luis Valdez' in Brooks McNamara and Jill Dolan (eds) *The Drama Review: Thirty Years of Commentary on the Avant-Garde*, Ann Arbor: UMI Research Press, 127–40.

Bain, David (1977) *Actors and Audience: A Study of Asides and Related Conventions in Greek Drama*, Oxford: Oxford University Press.

Barba, Eugenio (1985) 'The Nature of Dramaturgy: Describing

Actions at Work', *New Theatre Quarterly* 1.1 (February), 75–8.

— (1986) 'Theatre Anthropology', in Brooks McNamara and Jill Dolan (eds) *The Drama Review: Thirty Years of Commentary on the Avant-Garde*, Ann Arbor: UMI Research Press, 275–304.

Barrett, Michèle, Corrigan, Philip, Kuhn, Annette, and Wolff, Janet (eds) (1979) *Ideology and Cultural Production*, London: Croom Helm.

Barthes, Roland (1964) *On Racine*, trans. Richard Howard, New York: Hill and Wang.

— (1974) *S/Z*, trans. Richard Miller, New York: Hill & Wang.

— (1975) *The Pleasure of the Text*, trans. Richard Miller, New York: Hill and Wang.

— (1977) *Image Music Text*, trans. Stephen Heath, New York: Hill and Wang.

— (1979a) 'Barthes on Theatre', trans. Peter W. Mathers, *Theatre Quarterly* 9: 25–30.

— (1979b) 'Tasks of Brechtian Criticism', in Roland Barthes, 'Barthes on Theatre', *Theatre Quarterly* 9: 26–9.

— (1979c) 'Theatre and Signification', in Roland Barthes, 'Barthes on Theatre', *Theatre Quarterly* 9: 29–30.

— (1982) 'The Photographic Message' in *A Barthes Reader* ed. Susan Sontag, New York: Hill and Wang.

— (1983) *Mythologies*, trans. Annette Lavers, New York: Hill and Wang.

— (1985a) *The Grain of the Voice*, trans. Linda Coverdale, New York: Hill and Wang.

— (1985b) 'How to Spend a Week in Paris: 8–14 October 1979', in Marshall Blonsky (ed.) *In Signs*, Baltimore: Johns Hopkins, 118–21.

Bassnett, Susan (1986) 'Tasks of Theatre Anthropology', review of *Anatomia del Teatro. Un dizionario de antropologia teatrale*, ed. Nicola Savarese, *New Theatre Quarterly* 2.6 (May), 188–9.

Bassnett-McGuire, Susan E. (1984) 'Towards a Theory of Women's Theatre', in Herta Schmid and Aloysius Van Kesteren (eds) *Semiotic of Drama and Theatre*, Amsterdam: John Benjamin, 445–65.

Baumol, William J. and Bowen, William G. (1973) 'The Audience–some face-sheet data', in Elizabeth and Tom Burns (eds) *Sociology of Literature & Drama*, Harmondsworth: Penguin, 445–70.

Bazin, André (1967–71) *What is Cinema?*, trans. Hugh Gray, 2 vols, Berkeley and Los Angeles: University of California Press.

Beckerman, Bernard (1970) *Dynamics of Drama*, New York: Alfred A. Knopf.

Beckett, Samuel (1956) *Waiting for Godot*, London: Faber & Faber, 1965.

— (1978) *Cascando and other Short Dramatic Pieces*, New York: Grove Press.

Belsey, Catherine (1980) *Critical Practice*, London: Methuen.

Benamou, Michel and Caramello, Charles (eds) (1977) *Performance in Postmodern Culture*, Madison: Coda Press Inc.

Ben Chaim, Daphna (1984) *Distance in the Theatre: The Aesthetics of Audience Response*, Ann Arbor: UMI Research Press.

Benjamin, Walter (1973) *Understanding Brecht*, London: New Left Books.

Bentley, Eric (1964) *The Life of the Drama*, New York: Atheneum Press.

Berger, Carole (1978) 'Viewing as Action: Film and Reader Response Criticism', *Literature-Film Quarterly* 6.1 (winter), 144–51.

Blau, Herbert (1977) 'Letting Be Be Finale of Seem: The Future of an Illusion', in Michel Benamou and Charles Caramello (eds) *Performance in Postmodern Culture*, Madison: Coda Press Inc., 59–78.

— (1987) 'Odd, Anonymous Needs: The Audience in a Dramatized Society', *Performing Arts Journal* 10.1: 34–42.

Blonsky, Marshall (ed.) (1985) *In Signs*, Baltimore: Johns Hopkins University Press.

Boal, Augusto (1979) *Theatre of the Oppressed*, New York: Urizen Books.

Bogatyrev, Petr (1971) 'Les Signes du Théâtre', *Poétique* 8: 517–30.

Booth, Michael R. (1975) 'The Social and Literary Context', in Michael R. Booth *et al.* (eds) *The Revels History of Drama in English VI 1750–1880*. London: Methuen, 1–58.

Branigan, Edward (1981) 'The Spectator and Film Space: Two Theories', *Screen* 22.1: 55–78.

Braun, Edward (1977) *The Director and the Stage*, Milton Keynes: Open University Press.

Brecht, Bertolt (1977) *The Messingkauf Dialogues*, trans. John Willett, London: Methuen.

Brenton, Howard and Hare, David (1985) *Pravda*, London: Methuen.

Brook, Peter (1968) *The Empty Space*, Harmondsworth: Penguin, 1972.

Browne, Terry (1975) *Playwrights' Theatre*, London: Pitman.

Bruzy, Claude (1982) 'Les sémioses du théâtre', *Degrés* 31 (summer), e–e11.

Bullough, Edward (1912) ' "Phsychical Distance" as a Factor in Art and an Aesthetic Principle', *British Journal of Psychology* 5 (June), 87–118.

Burgess, David (1987) 'Brecht: 30 Years After', *Canadian Theatre Review* 50 (spring), 75–7.

Burns, Elizabeth (1972) *Theatricality*. London: Longman.

Burns, Elizabeth and Tom (eds) (1973) *Sociology of Literature & Drama*, Harmondsworth: Penguin.

Cain, William E (1981) 'Constraints and Politics in the Literary Theory of Stanley Fish', in Harry R. Garvin (ed.) *Theories of Reading, Looking and Listening*, Lewisburg: Bucknell University Press, 75–88.

Calandra, Denis (1986) 'Introduction', *Plays*, by Rainer Werner Fassbinder, New York: PAJ Publications.

— (1988) 'Politicised Theatre: The Case of Rainer Werner Fassbinder's *Garbage, The City & Death*' in *Modern Drama* 31.3: 420–8.

Carlson, Marvin (1984) *Theories of the Theatre*, Ithaca: Cornell University Press.

Chambers, Ross (1980) 'Le masque et le miroir. Vers une théorie relationnelle du théâtre', *Etudes littéraires*: 397–412.

Champagne, Leonora (1984) *French Theatre Experiment Since 1968*, Ann Arbor: UMI Research Press.

Chaudhuri, Una (1984) 'The Spectator in Drama/Drama in the Spectator', *Modern Drama* 27.3 (September), 281–98.

Chumley, Daniel (1987) 'Going South: the San Francisco Mime Troupe in Nicaragua', *New Theatre Quarterly* 3.12 (November) 291–302.

Churchill, Caryl (1979) *Cloud Nine*, New York: Methuen, 1984.

Coppieters, Frank (1981) 'Performance and Perception', *Poetics Today* 2.3: 35–48.

Coren, Michael (1984) *Theatre Royal: 100 Years of Stratford East*, London: Quartet Books.

Culler, Jonathan D. (1980) 'A Prologomena to a Theory of Reading', in Susan R. Suleiman and Inge Crosman (eds) *The Reader in the Text: Essays on Audience and Interpretation*, Princeton: Princeton University Press, 46–66.

— (1981) *In Pursuit of Signs*, Ithaca: Cornell University Press.

— (1983) *Roland Barthes*, New York: Oxford University Press.

Davis, R. G. (1986) 'Seven Anarchists I Have Known: American Approaches to Dario Fo', *New Theatre Quarterly* 2.8 (November), 313–19.

Davison, Peter (1982) *Contemporary Drama and the Popular Dramatic Tradition in England*, London and Basingstoke: Macmillan.

Davy, Kate (1987) 'Constructing the Spectator: Reception, Context, and Address in Lesbian Performance', *Performing Arts Journal* 10.2: 43–52.

— (1989) 'Reading Past the Hetereosexual Imperative: *Dress Suits for Hire*', *Drama Review* 33.1 (spring), 153–70.

Dayan, Daniel and Katz, Elihu (1985) 'Electronic Ceremonies: Television Performs a Royal Wedding', in Marshall Blonsky (ed.) *In Signs*, Baltimore: Johns Hopkins, 16–32.

Degrés (1982) 'Semiologie du Spectacle', *Degrés* 31 (summer).

de Lauretis, Teresa (1984) *Alice Doesn't: Feminism, Semiotics, Cinema*, Bloomington: Indiana University Press.

De Marinis, Marco (1982) *Semiotica del teatro. L'analisi testuale dello spettacolo*, Milano: Bompiani.

— (1985) 'Toward a Cognitive Semiotic of Theatrical Emotions', trans. Benjamin Thorn, *Versus* 41: 5–20.

— (1987) 'Dramaturgy of the Spectator', *The Drama Review* 31.2 (summer), 100–14.

Deutelbaum, Wendy (1981) 'Two Psychoanalytic Approaches to Reading Literature', in Harry Garvin (ed.) *Theories of Reading, Looking and Listening*, Lewisburg: Bucknell University Press, 89–101.

Dhillon-Kashyap, Perminder (1988) 'Locating the Asian Experience', *Screen* 29.4 (autumn), 120–6.

Diawara, Manthia (1988) 'Black Spectatorship: Problems of Identification and Resistance', *Screen* 29.4 (autumn), 66–76.

Dinu, Mihai (1984) 'The Algebra of Scenic Situations', in Herta Schmid and Aloysius Van Kesteren (eds) *Semiotics of Drama and Theatre*, Amsterdam: John Benjamin, 67–92.

Doane, Mary Ann (1982) 'Film and the Masquerade – Theorising the Female Spectator', *Screen* 23.3–4 (September-October), 74–87.

— (1984) 'The "Woman's Film": Possession and Address', in Mary Ann Doane, Patricia Mellencamp, and Linda Williams (eds) *Re-vision: Essays in Feminist Film Criticism*, Frederick, MD: University Publications of America, 67–82.

— (1988–9) 'Masquerade Reconsidered: Further Thoughts on the Female Spectator', *Discourse* 11.1 (fall/winter), 42–54.

— Mellencamp, Patricia, and Williams, Linda, (eds) (1984) *Re-vision: Essays in Feminist Film Criticism*, Frederick, MD: University Publications of America.

Dolan, Jill (1988) *The Feminist Spectator as Critic*, Ann Arbor: UMI Research Press.

Dort, Bernard (1982) 'The Liberated Performance', trans. Barbara Kerslake, *Modern Drama* 25.1 (March), 60–8.

Duckworth, Colin (1972) *Angels of Darkness*, London: George Allen & Unwin.

Dunning, Jennifer (1981) '*Cloud 9*, as Viewed by Those Floating on It', *New York Times* (6 November), C4.

Dyer, Richard (1982) 'Don't Look Now–The Male Pin-Up', *Screen* 23.3–4 (September–October), 61–73.

— (1988) 'White', *Screen* 29.4 (autumn), 44–64.

Eco, Umberto (1976) *A Theory of Semiotics*, Bloomington: Indiana University Press.

— (1977) 'Semiotics of Theatrical Performance', *The Drama Review* 21: 107–17.

— (1979) *The Role of the Reader: Explorations in the Semiotics of Texts*, Bloomington: Indiana University Press.

Eisenstein, Sergei (1949) *Film Form*, ed. and trans. Jay Leyda, New York: Harcourt, Brace & World.

Elam, Keir (1980) *The Semiotics of Theatre and Drama*, London: Methuen.

— (1988) 'Much Ado About Doing Things With Words (and Other Means): Some Problems in the Pragmatics of Theatre and Drama', in Michael Issacharoff and Robin E. Jones (eds)

Performing Texts, Philadelphia: University of Pennsylvania Press, 39–58.

Ellis, John (1982) *Visible Fictions*, London: Routledge & Kegan Paul.

Esslin, Martin (1961) *The Theatre of the Absurd*, Garden City, New York: Doubleday.

— (1976) *An Anatomy of Drama*, London: Abacus, 1978.

Etkind, Efim (1980) 'Brecht and the Soviet Theater', in Betty Nancy Weber and Hubert Heinen (eds) *Bertolt Brecht: Political Theory and Literary Practice*, Athens: University of Georgia Press: 81–7.

'An Evening in the East Village' (1986) in Brooks McNamara and Jill Dolan (eds) *Thirty Years of Commentary on the Avant-Garde*, Ann Arbor: UMI Research Press.

Féral, Josette (1982) 'Performance and Theatricality: The Subject Demystified', trans. Terèse Lyons, *Modern Drama* 25.1 (March), 170–81.

Fetscher, Iring (1980) 'Bertolt Brecht and Politics', in Betty Nancy Weber and Hubert Heinen (eds) *Bertolt Brecht: Political Theory and Literary Practice*, Athens: University of Georgia Press.

Fetterley, Judith (1978) *The Resisting Reader*, Bloomington: Indiana University Press.

Fischer-Lichte, Erika (1982) 'The Theatrical Code. An Approach to the Problem', in Ernest W. B. Hess-Lüttich (ed.) *Multimedial Communication 2: Theatre Semiotics*, Tubingen: Gunter Narr Verlag, 46–62.

Fish, Stanley (1980) *Is There A Text in this Class?*, Cambridge, Mass.: Harvard University Press.

— (1981) 'Why no one's afraid of Wolfgang Iser', *Diacritics* 11.1: 2–13.

Fo, Dario (1985) 'Some Aspects of Popular Theatre', *New Theatre Quarterly* 1.2 (May), 131–7.

Forsyth, Michael (1985) *Buildings for Music: The Architect, the Musician, and the Listener from the Seventeenth Century to the Present Day*, Cambridge, Mass.: MIT Press.

Forte, Jeanie (1989) 'Realism, Narrative, and Feminist Playwright – A Problem of Reception', *Modern Drama* 32.1 (March) 115–27.

Foucault, Michel (1978) *The History of Sexuality*, trans. Robert Hurley, New York: Pantheon Books.

Fowler, Richard (1985) 'The Four Theatres of Jerzy Grotowski: An Introductory Assessment', *New Theatre Quarterly* 1.2 173–8.

Freud, Sigmund (1953–74) *The Standard Edition of the Complete Psychological Works of Sigmund Freud*, ed. James Strachey, 24 vols, London: Hogarth Press and the Institute of Psycho-Analysis.

Friedman, Daniel (1985) 'Contemporary Theatre for Working-Class Audiences in the United States', in Bruce A. McConachie and Daniel Friedman (eds) *Theatre for Working-Class Audiences in the United States 1830–1930*, Westport, Ct: Greenwood Press, 197–246.

Frisch, Max (1962) *The Fire Raisers*, trans. Michael Bullock, London: Methuen, 1983.

Frye, Northrop (1957) *Anatomy of Criticism*, Princeton: Princeton University Press, 1973.

Fuegi, John (1987) *Bertolt Brecht: Chaos, According to Plan* Cambridge: Cambridge University Press.

— and Bahr, Gisela (1982) *Beyond Brecht*, Detroit: Wayne State University Press.

Gaines, Jane (1988) 'White Privilege and Looking Relations: Race and Gender in Feminist Film Theory', *Screen* 29.4 (autumn), 12–27.

Gardner, Carl (ed.) (1979) *Media, Politics and Culture: A Socialist View*, London: Macmillan.

Garvin, Harry R. (ed.) (1981) *Theories of Reading, Looking and Listening*, Lewisburg: Bucknell University Press.

Garvin, Paul L. (1964) *A Prague School Reader on Esthetics, Literary Structure, and Style*, Washington: Georgetown University Press.

Gatti, Armand (1982) 'Armand Gatti on Time, Place, and the Theatrical Event', trans. Nancy Oakes, *Modern Drama* 25.1 (March), 69–81.

Gaylord, Karen (1983) 'Theatrical Performances: Structure and Process, Tradition and Revolt', in Jack B. Kamerman and Rosanne Martorella (eds) *Performers & Performances: The Social Organization of Artistic Work*, New York: Praeger 135–50.

Girard, G., Ouellet, R., and Rigault, C. (1978) *L'univers du théâtre*, Paris: Presses Universitaires de France.

Gloversmith, Frank (ed.) (1984) *The Theory of Reading*, Brighton: Harvester Press.

Gooch, Steve (1984) *All Together Now: An Alternative View of Theatre and the Community*, London: Methuen.

Gourdon, Anne-Marie (1982) *Théâtre, Public, Perception*, Paris: Editions du Centre National de la Recherche Scientifique.

Greene, Gayle and Kahn, Coppelia (1985) *Making a Difference: Feminist Literary Criticism*, London and New York: Methuen.

Grotowski, Jerzy (1968) *Towards a Poor Theatre*, ed. Eugenio Barba, London: Methuen, 1980.

Hall, Edward T. (1966) *The Hidden Dimension*, New York: Doubleday.

Hall, Stuart, Hobson, Dorothy, Lowe, Andrew, and Willis, Paul (1980) *Culture, Media, Language*, London: Hutchinson.

Hare, David (1984) Interview, 'Making fun of Fleet Street', with Angela Wilkes, *Sunday Times* (16 December), 37.

Harvey, Stephen (1986) Review of *Kaos* by Taviani Brothers, *New York Times* (9 February), sec. 2: 40.

Harvey, Sylvia (1982) 'Whose Brecht? Memories for the Eighties', *Screen* 23: 45–69.

Hays, Michael (1981) *The Public and Performance: Essays in the History of French and German Theatre 1871–1900*, Ann Arbor: UMI Research Press.

Heath, Stephen (1974) 'Lessons from Brecht', *Screen* 15: 103–29.

Heilpern, John (1977) *Conference of the Birds*, London: Faber & Faber.

Hess-Lüttich, Ernest W. B. (ed.) (1982) *Multimedial Communication 2: Theatre Semiotics*, Tubingen: Gunter Narr Verlag.

Higson, Andrew (1983) 'Critical Theory and "British Cinema"', *Screen* 24.4-5 (July–October), 80–95.

Hinkle, Gerald H. (1979) *Art as Event: An Aesthetic for the Performing Arts*, Washington: University Press.

Hohendahl, Peter Uwe (1982) *The Institution of Criticism*, Ithaca: Cornell University Press.

Holden, Stephen (1988) 'Sexual Charades', review of *Dress Suits for Hire*, by Holly Hughes, Interart Theater, New York, *New York Times* (3 February), C21.

Holland, Norman N. (1968) *The Dynamics of Literary Response*, New York: Oxford University Press.

— (1973) *Poems in Persons: An Introduction to the Psychoanalysis of Literature*, New York: Norton.

— (1975a) *5 Readers Reading*, New Haven: Yale University Press.

— (1975b) 'Unity Identity Text Self', in Jane P. Tompkins (ed.) *Reader-Response Criticism*, Baltimore: Johns Hopkins University Press, 1980, 118–33.

Holledge, Julie (1981) *Innocent Flowers: Women in Edwardian Theatre*, London: Virago Press.

Holmberg, Arthur (1987) Review of *The Balcony* by Jean Genet, American Repertory Theatre, Cambridge, *Performing Arts Journal* 10.1: 43–6.

Holub, Robert (1984) *Reception Theory*, London: Methuen.

Horace (1977) *Satires and Epistles*, trans. Jacob Fuchs, New York: W. W. Norton.

Howard, Jean E. (1980) 'Shakespeare's Creation of a Fit Audience for *The Tempest*', *Shakespeare: Contemporary Critical Approaches, Bucknell Review* 25: 142–53.

— (1984) *Shakespeare's Art of Orchestration: Stage Technique and Audience Response*, Urbana and Chicago: University of Illinois Press.

Howard, Tony (1986) '"A Piece of Our Life": The Theatre of the Eighth Day', *New Theatre Quarterly* 2.8 (November), 291–305.

Huerta, Jorge A. (1982) *Chicano Theater: Themes and Forms*, Ypsilanti, Michigan: Bilingual Press.

Hughes, Holly (1989) 'Dress Suits for Hire', *Drama Review* 33.1 (spring), 132–52.

Huss, Roy (1986) *The Mindscapes of Art*, London: Associated University Presses.

Ibsen, Henrik (1965) *Plays: The League of Youth, A Doll's House, The Lady from the Sea*, trans. Peter Watts, Harmondsworth: Penguin.

Innes, C. D. (1972) *Piscator's Political Theatre*, Cambridge: Cambridge University Press.

Iser, Wolfgang (1974) *The Implied Reader: Patterns of Communication in Prose Fiction from Bunyan to Beckett*, Baltimore and London: Johns Hopkins University Press.

— (1978) *The Act of Reading: A Theory of Aesthetic Response*, Baltimore and London: Johns Hopkins University Press.

— (1981a) 'The Art of Failure: The Stifled Laugh in Beckett's Theater', in Harry R. Garvin (ed.) *Theories of Reading, Looking and Listening*, Lewisburg: Bucknell University Press, 139–89.
— (1981b) 'Talk like whales: A reply to Stanley Fish', *Diacritics* 11.3: 82–7.
Issacharoff, Michael and Jones, Robin F. (eds) (1988) *Performing Texts*, Philadelphia: University of Pennsylvania Press.
Itzin, Catherine (1980) *Stages in the Revolution: Political Theatre in Britain Since 1968*, London: Methuen.

Jameson, Fredric (1972) *The Prison-House of Language*, Princeton: Princeton University Press.
Jauss, Hans Robert (1979) 'Theses on the Transition from the Aesthetics of Literary Works to a Theory of Aesthetic Experience', in Mario J. Valdes and Owen J. Miller (eds) *Intepretation of Narrative*, Toronto: University of Toronto Press.
— (1982a) *Aesthetic Experience and Literary Hermeneutics*, trans. Michael Shaw, Minneapolis: University of Minnesota Press.
— (1982b) *Toward an Aesthetic of Reception*, trans. Timothy Bahti, Minneapolis: University of Minnesota Press.
Johnston, Claire (1979) 'British Film Culture', in Carl Gardner (ed.) *Media, Politics and Culture: A Socialist View*, London: Macmillan, 81–7.
Julien, Isaac and Mercer, Kobena (1988) 'Introduction: De Margin and De Centre', *Screen* 29.4 (autumn), 2–11.

Kamerman, Jack B. and Martorella, Rosanne (eds) (1983) *Performers & Performances: The Social Organization of Artistic Work*, New York: Praeger.
Kauffmann, Stanley (1985) 'Broadway and the Necessity for "Bad Theatre"', *New Theatre Quarterly* 1.4 (November), 359–63.
Kirby, Michael (1971) *Futurist Performance*, New York: E. P. Dutton.
Knowles, Dorothy (1969) 'To be banned or not to be banned', *Drama* 93 (summer), 53–8.
Kolodny, Annette (1985a) 'Dancing Through the Minefield: Some Observations on the Theory, Practice, and Politics of a Feminist Literary Criticism', in Elaine Showalter (ed.) *The*

New Feminist Criticism, New York: Pantheon Books, 144–67.
— (1985b) 'A Map for Rereading: Gender and the Interpretation of Literary Texts', in Elaine Showalter (ed.) *The New Feminist Criticism*, New York: Pantheon Books, 46–62.
Kowzan, Tadeusz (1975) *Littérature et Spectacle*, The Hague: Mouton.
— (1982) 'Signe zéro de la parole', *Degrés* 31 (summer), a–a16.
Kuhn, Annette (1982) *Women's Pictures: Feminism and Cinema*, London: Routledge & Kegan Paul.
— (1985) *The Power of the Image*, London: Routledge & Kegan Paul.

Lacan, Jacques (1982) *Ecrits: A Selection*, trans. Alan Sheridan, New York: Norton.
— (1985) 'Sign, Symbol, Imaginary', in Marshall Blonsky (ed.) *In Signs*, Baltimore: Johns Hopkins University Press, 203–9.
Lacey, Liam (1988) 'A Peep Show That Keeps It Clean', review of *Routines* by Nicola Perrin, *Globe and Mail* (29 August), A15.
Lasdun, Denys (1977) 'Humanising the Institution', in Colin Amery (ed.) *The National Theatre: 'The Architectural Review' Guide*, London: Architectural Press, 25–30.
Lavers, Annette (1982) *Roland Barthes: Structuralism and After*, London: Methuen.
Lavoie, Odette and Martineau, Maureen (1988) 'An Alternative Culture', trans. Lib Spry, *Canadian Theatre Review* 55 (summer), 25–9.
Leenhardt, Jacques (1980) 'Towards a Sociology of Reading', in Susan R. Suleiman and Inge Crosman (eds) *The Reader in the Text: Essays on Audience and Interpretation*, Princeton: Princeton University Press, 205–24.
Lemon, Lee T. and Reis, Marion J. (1965) *Russian Formalist Criticism: Four Essays*, Lincoln: University of Nebraska Press.
Lentricchia, Frank (1980) *After the New Criticism*, Chicago: University of Chicago Press.
Levine, Ira A.(1985) *Left-Wing Dramatic Theory in the American Theatre*, Ann Arbor: UMI Research Press.
Levine, Meredith (1987) 'Feminist Theatre-Toronto 1987', *Theatrum* 6 (spring), 5–10.

Lotman, Jurij (1977) *The Structure of the Artistic Text*, trans. Ronald Vroon, Ann Arbor: University of Michigan Press.

MacCabe, Colin (1976) 'Principles of Realism and Pleasure', *Screen* 17.3 (autumn), 7–27.

McConachie, Bruce A. and Friedman, Daniel (eds) (1985) *Theatre for Working-Class Audiences in the United States, 1830–1930*, Westport, Ct: Greenwood Press.

McGrath, John (1974)'The Year of the Cheviot', Introduction, *The Cheviot, the Stag, and the Black, Black Oil*, London: Methuen, 1981.

— (1981) *A Good Night Out*, London: Eyre Methuen.

McNamara, Brooks and Dolan, Jill (eds) (1986) *The Drama Review: Thirty Years of Commentary on the Avant-Garde*, Ann Arbor: UMI Research Press.

Mailloux, Steven (1982) *Interpretive Conventions: The Reader in the Study of American Fiction*, Ithaca: Cornell University Press.

Martorella, Rosanne (1977) 'The Relationship Between Box Office and Repertoire: a Case Study of Opera', *Sociological Quarterly* 18 (summer), 354–66.

Mayne, Judith (1984) 'The Woman at the Keyhole: Women's Cinema and Feminist Criticism', in Mary Ann Doane, Patricia Mellencamp, and Linda Williams (eds) *Re-vision: Essays in Feminist Film Criticism*, Frederick MD: University Publications of America, 49–66.

Metz, Christian (1976) 'The Fiction Film and Its Spectator: A Metapsychological Study', *New Literary History* 8.1: 75–105.

Meyer, Michael (1971) *Ibsen: A Biography*, Garden City, New York: Doubleday.

— (1985) *Ibsen on File*, London: Methuen.

Meyerhold, Vsevolod Emilevich (1969) *Meyerhold on Theatre*, ed. and trans. Edward Braun, New York: Hill and Wang.

Mitchell, Stanley (1974) 'From Shklovsky to Brecht', *Screen* 15.2: 74–80.

Mitchell, Tony (1987a) *File on Brenton*, London: Methuen.

— (1987b)'Italo-Australian Theatre: multi-cultural and neo colonialist Part 2', *Australasian Drama Studies* 11 (October), 37–46.

Moi, Toril (1985) *Sexual/Textual Politics*, London: Methuen.

Mukǎrovský, Jan (1977) *Structure, Sign, and Function*, eds and trans. John Burbank and Peter Steiner, New Haven: Yale University Press.

Mulvey, Laura (1975) 'Visual Pleasure and Narrative Cinema', *Screen* 16.3 (autumn), 6–18.

— (1981) 'Afterthoughts on "Visual Pleasure and Narrative Cinema"... Inspired by "Duel in the Sun"', *Framework* 15/16/17: 12–15.

Murdock, Graham (1980) 'Radical Drama, Radical Theatre', *Media, Culture and Society* 2.2: 151–68.

Naumann, Manfred (1976) 'Literary Production and Reception', *New Literary History* 8.1: 107–26.

Neale, Steve (1983) 'Masculinity as Spectacle', *Screen* 24.6 (November–December), 2–17.

O'Connor, John (1985) 'The Federal Theatre Project's Search for an Audience', in Bruce A. McConachie and Daniel Friedman (eds) *Theatre for Working-Class Audiences in the States 1830–1930*, Westport, Ct: Greenwood Press, 171–84.

Parnes, Uzi (1985) 'Pop Performance in East Village Clubs', *Drama Review* 29.1 (spring), 5–16.

Passow, Wilfried (1981) 'The Analysis of Theatrical Performance: The State of the Art', *Poetics Today* 2.3: 217–54.

Pasternak Slater, Ann (1982) *Shakespeare the Director*, Brighton: Harvester, Press.

Pavis, Patrice (1976) *Problèmes de semiologie théâtrale*, Québec: Les Presses de l'Université du Québec.

— (1980) *Dictionnaire du théâtre – Termes et concepts de l'analyse théâtrale*, Paris: Editions Sociales.

— (1982) *Languages of the Stage*, New York: Performing Arts Journal.

— (1985) 'La réception du texte dramatique et spectaculaire: les processus de fictionnalisation et d'idéologisation', *Versus* 41 (May–August), 69–94.

Peirce, Charles Sanders (1931–58) *Collected Papers*, Cambridge, Mass.: Harvard University Press.

Picard, Raymond (1965) *Nouvelle critique ou nouvelle imposture?*, Paris: Pauvert

Pirandello, Luigi (1922–3) *Naked Masks: Five Plays*, ed. Eric Bentley, New York: E. P. Dutton, 1952.

Polan, Dana B. (1985) *The Political Language of Film and the Avant-Garde*, Ann Arbor: UMI Research Press.

Portoghesi, Paolo (1983) *Postmodern*, New York: Rizzoli.

Pottlitzer, Joanne (1988) *Hispanic Theater in the United States and Puerto Rico: A Report to the Ford Foundation*, New York: Ford Foundation.

Poyatos, Fernando (1982) 'Nonverbal Communication in the Theatre: the Playwright/Actor/Spectator-Relationship', in Ernest W. B. Hess-Lüttich (ed.) *Multimedial Communication 2: Theatre Semiotics*, Tubingen: Gunter Narr Verlag, 75–94.

Pratt, Mary Louise (1986) 'Interpretive Strategies/Strategic Interpretations: On Anglo-American Reader-response Criticism', in Jonathan Arac (ed.) *Postmodernism and Politics*, Minneapolis: University of Minnesota Press, 26–54.

Pribram, E. Deidre (ed.) (1988) *Female Spectators: Looking at Film and Television*, London: Verso.

Putzel, Steven (1987) 'Expectation, Confutation, Revelation: Audience Complicity in the Plays of Sam Shepard', *Modern Drama* 30.2 (June), 147–60.

Quigley, Austin E. (1985) *The Modern Stage and Other Worlds*, New York: Methuen.

Rawlence, Chris (1979) 'Political theatre and the Working Class', in Carl Gardner (ed.) *Media, Politics and Culture: A Socialist View*, London: Macmillan, 61–70.

Rosenberg, Scott (1986) 'Dario Fo, Italy's Political Clown, Pays A Visit', *New York Times* (25 May), sec. 2: 4.

Rothenberg, Jerome (1977) 'New Models, New Visions: Some Notes Toward A Poetics of Performance', in Michael Benamou and Charles Caramello (eds) *Performance in Postmodern Culture*, Madison: Coda Press Inc., 11–18.

Rubess, Baņuta (1986) 'Vancouver: Hamlet, A New Canadian Play' *Canadian Theatre Review* 49 (winter), 131–5.

Schechner, Richard (1969) *Public Domain*, Indianapolis and New York: Bobbs-Merrill.

— (1977) *Essays on Performance Theory 1970–1976*, New York: Drama Book Specialists.

— (1982) *The End of Humanism*, New York: Performing Arts Journal.

— and Schuman, Mady (1976) *Ritual, Play, and Performance: Readings in the Social Sciences/Theater*, New York: Seabury Press.

Schmid, Herta and Van Kesteren, Aloysius (eds) (1984) *Semiotics of Drama and Theatre*, Amsterdam: John Benjamin.

Shank, Theodore (1969) *The Art of Dramatic Art*, Belmont: Dickerson Publishing Co.

— (1979) 'Political Theater, Actors and Audiences: Some Principles and Techniques', *Yale Theater Review* 10.2 (spring), 94–103.

— (1985) 'El Teatro Campesino: The Farmworkers' Theatre', in Bruce A. McConachie and Daniel Friedman (eds) *Theatre for Working-Class Audiences in the United States, 1830–1930*, Westport, Ct: Greenwood Press, 185–96.

Shevtsova, Maria (1989) 'The Sociology of the Theatre, Part One: Problems and Perspectives', *New Theatre Quarterly* 5.17 (February), 23–35.

Shklovsky, Victor (1965) 'Art as Technique', Lee T. Lemon and Marion J. Reis (eds), *Russian Formalist Criticism: Four Essays*, Lincoln: University of Nebraska Press, 3–24.

Showalter, Elaine (1985a) 'Feminist Criticism in the Wilderness', in Elaine Showalter (ed.) *The New Feminist Criticism*, New York: Pantheon Books, 243–70.

— (ed.) (1985b) *The New Feminist Criticism*, New York: Pantheon Books.

— (1985c) 'Towards a Feminist Poetics', in Elaine Showalter (ed.) *The New Feminist Criticism*, New York: Pantheon Books, 125–43.

Shukman, Ann (1981) 'The Dialectics of Change: Culture, Codes, and the Individual', in Peter V. Zima (ed.) *Semiotics and Dialectics: Ideology and the Text*, Amsterdam: John Benjamin, 311–30.

Sidnell, Michael J. (1984) *Dances of Death: The Group Theatre of London in the Thirties*, London: Faber & Faber.

Silverman, Kaja (1984) 'Dis-Embodying the Female Voice', in Mary Ann Doane, Patricia Mellencamp, and Linda Williams (eds) *Re-vision: Essays in Feminist Film Criticism*, Frederick, MD: University Publications of America, 131–49.

Silverman Zinman, Toby (1986) 'Sam Shepard and Super Realism', *Modern Drama* 29.3 (September), 423–30.

Sinfield, Alan (ed.) (1983a) *Society and Literature 1945–1970*, London: Methuen, 173–97.
— (1983b) 'The theatre and its audiences', in *Society and Literature 1945–1970*, London: Methuen.
Slatoff, Walter J. (1970) *With Respect to Readers*, Ithaca: Cornell University Press.
Solomon, Alisa (1986a) Participant at Roundtable: 'The Critic and Political Theatre', Thirty Years After Brecht International Conference, Toronto (25 October).
— (1986b) 'The WOW Cafe', in Brooks McNamara and Jill Dolan (eds) *The Drama Review: Thirty Years of Commentary on the Avant-Garde*, Ann Arbor: UMI Research Press, 305–14.
Stacey, Jackie (1987) 'Desperately Seeking Difference', *Screen* 28.1 (winter), 48–61.
Stallybrass, Peter and White, Allon (1986) *The Politics and Poetics of Transgression*, Ithaca: Cornell University Press.
Stoppard, Tom (1968) *The Real Inspector Hound*, London: Faber & Faber.
Stourac, Richard and McCreery, Kathleen (1986) *Theatre as a Weapon: Workers' Theatre in the Soviet Union, Germany and Britain, 1917–1934*, London: Routledge & Kegan Paul.
Styan, J. L. (1960) *Elements of Drama*, Cambridge: Cambridge University Press.
— (1975) *Drama, Stage and Audience*, Cambridge: Cambridge University Press.
Suleiman, Susan R. and Crosman, Inge (eds) (1980) *The Reader in the Text: Essays on Audience and Intepretation*, Princeton: Princeton University Press.
Swanson, Gillian (1986) 'Rethinking Representation', *Screen* 27.5 (September–October), 16–28.

Tan, Ed (1982) 'Cognitive Processes in Reception', in Ernest W. B. Hess-Lüttich (ed.) *Multimedial Communication 2: Theatre Semiotics*, Tubingen: Gunter Narr Verlag, 156–203.
Thomsen, Christian W. (ed.) (1985) *Studien zur Ästhetik des Gegenwartstheaters*, Heidelberg: Carl Winter Universitatsverlag.
Thomson, Peter (1975) 'The Study of Drama', in Stanley Wells (ed.) *English Drama*, Oxford: Oxford University Press.
Throsby, C. D. and Withers, G. A. (1979) *The Economics of the Performing Arts*, London: Edward Arnold.

The Times (1958) Review of *The Birthday Party*, by Harold Pinter, *The Times* (20 May), 3.

The Times (1964) Review of *The Birthday Party*, by Harold Pinter, *The Times* (18 June), 18.

Tindemans, Carlos (1982) 'Coherence. Putting "pieces" together.' *Degrés* 31 (summer), i–i16.

Tompkins, Jane P. (ed.) (1980) *Reader-Response Criticism*, Baltimore: Johns Hopkins University Press.

Turner, Victor (1977) 'Frame, Flow and Reflection: Ritual and Drama as Public Liminality', in Michel Benamou and Charles Caramello (eds) *Performance in Postmodern Culture*, Madison: Coda Press Inc., 19–32.

— (1982) *From Ritual to Theatre*, New York: Performing Arts Journal.

Ubersfeld, Anne (1977) *Lire le Théâtre*, Paris: Editions Sociales.

— (1981) *L'Ecole du Spectateur: Lire le Théâtre 2*, Paris: Editions Sociales.

— (1982) 'The Pleasure of the Spectator', trans. Pierre Bouillaguet and Charles Jose, *Modern Drama* 25.1 (March), 127–39.

Valdes, Mario J. and Miller, Owen J. (eds) (1979) *Interpretation of Narrative*, Toronto: University of Toronto Press.

Versus (1985) 'Semiotica del la ricezione teatrale', *Versus* 41.

Walcot, Peter (1976) *Greek Drama in its Theatrical and Social Context*, Cardiff: University of Wales Press.

Wallace, Robert (1986) 'Edmonton: Fringe Binge', *Canadian Theatre Review* 49 (winter), 117–19.

Wandor, Michelene (1981) *Understudies: Theatre and Sexual Politics*, London: Methuen.

— (1986) *Carry On, Understudies: Theatre and Sexual Politics*, London: Routledge.

Webb, Richard C. (1979–80) 'The Spectator as Creator in Contemporary French Theatre', *Theatre Research International* 5.1 (winter), 205–18.

Weber, Betty Nancy and Heinen, Hubert (eds) (1980) *Bertolt Brecht: Political Theory and Literary Practice*, Athens: University of Georgia Press.

Willett, John (ed.) (1964) *Brecht on Theatre*, New York: Hill and Wang.

Williams, Clifford John (1970) *Theatres and Audience: A Background to Dramatic Texts*, London: Longman.

Williams, Linda (1984) 'When the Woman Looks', in Mary Ann Doane, Patricia Mellencamp, and Linda Williams (eds) *Re-vision: Essays in Feminist Film Criticism*, Frederick, MD: University Publications of America, 83–99.

Williams, Raymond (1981) *Culture*, London: Fontana.

Wimsatt, W. K., Jr (1954) *The Verbal Icon*, New York: Noonday Press, 1958.

Wirth, Andrzej (1985) 'The Real and the Intended Theater Audiences in Germany, Poland and the United States: A Comparative Study', Christian W. Thomsen (ed.) *Studien zur Ästhetik des Gegenwartstheaters*, Heidelberg: Carl Winter Universitätsverlag, 6–17.

Wolff, Janet (1981) *The Social Production of Art*, London: Macmillan.

— (1983) *Aesthetics and the Sociology of Art*, London: George Allen & Unwin.

INDEX

213

Wallace, Robert 111
Wandor, Michelene 61–2
Waters, John 173
Webb, Richard 15–16, 110–11, 177, 179–80
Webster, John: *The White Devil* 145–6
Weiss, Peter Eliot: *Haunted House Hamlet* 121, 151
White, Allon 100, 105, 114, 182
Willett, John 25
Williams, Linda 84
Williams, Raymond 99, 108, 135
Williams, Tennessee 119; *A Streetcar Named Desire* 56–7, 104, 115

Wimsatt Jr, W. K. 37
Wintergarden (New York City) 170
Wirth, Andrezej 94–5
Withers, G. A. 94, 96
Wolf, Fredrich 31
Wolff, Janet 32–3, 35, 55, 98–9
Women's Theatre Group 61
WOW Cafe 122–3, 128, 131, 132, 172–3

Young Vic Theatre Company 144

Zinman, Toby Silverman 151–2